More than two hundred years on, the Napoleonic Wars still fascinates, with fresh perspectives and new information continuing to develop our understanding of the era. Drawing on cutting-edge research presented at the British Commission for Military History's inaugural 'War and Peace in the Age of Napoleon' Conference, this volume presents a rich array of papers from both established and emerging experts of the period. Featuring the work of Edward Coss, Andrew Bamford, Jacqueline Reiter, Alistair Nichols, Vanya Bellinger, Gavin Lewis, Silvia Gregorio-Sainz, and Hailey Stewart, *The Sword and the Spirit* examines some of the people, personalities, and policies that shaped the conflict.

From assessments of Napoleon's mental state, to the actions of individuals such as Sir Home Popham and Carl von Clausewitz; from the siege of San Sebastian to the fields of Waterloo, this book considers the impacts that patronage, diplomacy, psychology, personal experiences, and the disobedience of established practices all had on the waging of war. In the process, it demonstrates the truth of Napoleon's remark that the sword will always be conquered by the spirit.

Zack White is a PhD Researcher at the University of Southampton specializing in the Napoleonic era. He is presenter of the podcast 'The Napoleonicist', and runs the online hub and forum www.thenapoleonicwars.net. He has previously written on subjects ranging from the relationship between the Duke of Wellington and his troops during the Peninsular War, to popular attitudes towards the same conflict and morale amongst British troops during the period. He is currently writing on crime and punishment in the British Army during the Napoleonic Wars. A former secondary school teacher, and inaugural Editor-in-Chief of the academic journal *Romance, Revolution & Reform*, White is also a Committee Member for the Waterloo Association.

The Sword and The Spirit

Proceedings of the first 'War and Peace in the Age of Napoleon' Conference

Edited by Zack White

Helion & Company

Helion & Company Limited
Unit 8 Amherst Business Centre
Budbrooke Road
Warwick
CV34 5WE
England
Tel. 01926 499619
Email: info@helion.co.uk
Website: www.helion.co.uk
Twitter: @helionbooks
Visit our blog at http://blog.helion.co.uk/

Published by Helion & Company 2021
Designed and typeset by Mach 3 Solutions Ltd (www.mach3solutions.co.uk)
Cover designed by Paul Hewitt, Battlefield Design (www.battlefield-design.co.uk)

Cover: Hanau, by Horace Vernet, Francisque-Martin-François and J. P. Quénot.
(Anne S.K. Brown Collection)

ISBN 978-1-914059-31-5

British Library Cataloguing-in-Publication Data.
A catalogue record for this book is available from the British Library.

Contents

Contributors' Biographies

Andrew Bamford obtained a doctorate from the University of Leeds in 2009. His thesis dealt with manpower management in the British Army 1808–1815 and a revised version was published in 2013 by the University of Oklahoma Press as *Sickness, Suffering, and the Sword*. Subsequent publications include a history of the British forces in the Netherlands 1813–1814 and a study of the 12th Light Dragoons during the Napoleonic Wars. Edited works include a primary source collection, an annotated memoir, and an essay collection dealing with aspects of the military response to the 1745 Jacobite Rising which includes a chapter co-written with his wife Lucy. He is currently preparing a short history of the Peninsular War for Routledge's 'Wars and Battles of the World' series. In 2015 Andrew was invited to set up the 'From Reason to Revolution 1721-1815' series for Helion & Co., and he remains series editor to this date. He is also a council member of the Society for Army Historical Research and has written several articles for its journal.

Vanya Eftimova Bellinger is an Assistant Professor of Strategy and Security Studies at Air University (U.S. Air Force). In 2015, she published her book, *Marie von Clausewitz: The Woman Behind the Making of On War* (Oxford University Press USA). Previously, Bellinger taught as a Visiting Professor at the U.S. Army War College (2016–2018). She is the winner of the 2016 *Society for Military History Moncado Prize* for her article 'The Other Clausewitz: Findings from the Newly Discovered Correspondence between Marie and Carl von Clausewitz,' *The Journal of Military History* 79 (April 2015). Currently, Bellinger is a doctoral student at King's College, London. She is a graduate of Norwich University's Master in Arts Program in Military History (Cum Laude, 2011). She received her BA in Journalism and Mass Communications from the Sofia University, Bulgaria.

Dr Ed Coss is emeritus professor of history at the U.S. Army Command and General Staff College. He is a Fellow of the Royal Historical Society and was named the Army's Civilian Educator of the Year in 2010. Coss is a member of the Society of Military History and the British Commission for Military History. He has written or contributed to five books, including *All for the King's Shilling: The British Soldier under Wellington, 1808–1814*, which won the literary prize from the International Napoleonic Society in 2011. He has presented at scores of conferences, worldwide, usually on topics related to the experience of men in battle. His current focus is the neurophysiology of fear and the mitigating effects of primary group cohesion on the physiological responses of individual soldiers in the combat environment. His latest project is annotating *Feld Grau, the WWI Autobiography of Johann Wehmann*, which he hopes to finish by late summer.

Dr Silvia Gregorio Sainz is a Lecturer in the English Department at the University of Oviedo (Spain). She holds a BA with an Award for Excellency and a PhD in English Studies, as well as an MA in Socio-Cultural Analysis and History and an MA in TEFL. Her research focuses on Anglo-Spanish relations in the first half of the nineteenth century, particularly during the Peninsular War and its aftermath. Recent publications include 'The Last Napoleonic Redoubt in Northern Spain: The British role' in *Romanticism, Reaction and Revolution* (Peter Lang, 2019); 'The Bishop of Santander in the 1808 British Press: an unusual tracking' (*Spagna Contemporanea*, 2014) and 'The siege and destruction of Castro Urdiales according to British sources: The role of the British allies in the defence of the Cantabrian town' (Gobierno de Cantabria, 2015). In 2019 she presented a paper entitled 'The hardships of peace: logistics and everyday life in Santander (1813–1814)' at the Seventh Wellington Congress.

Gavin Lewis graduated from the University of Birmingham in 2018 with a first-class honours degree in War Studies before completing an MA in the History of Warfare at King's College London. His research interests are in 18th and 19th century military cultures, martial masculinities and the history of emotions. He has recently been working on a research proposal which centres on the British army during the French Revolutionary and Napoleonic Wars, and hopes to turn this into a PhD project within the next few years.

Alistair Nichols had a 30-year career as a police officer during which he undertook a social science degree at Portsmouth University. With a longstanding interest in researching the history of foreign units in the British Army during the French Revolutionary and Napoleonic Wars he has written a number of articles and books. These include *Wellington's Mongrel Regiment: A History of the Chasseurs Britanniques Regiment* (2005), *Wellingtons' Switzers: The Watteville Regiment (1801–1816) a Swiss Regiment of the British Army in Egypt, in the Mediterranean, Spain and Canada* (2015) and *They Turned Out So Ill! The Independent Companies of Foreigners 1812–1814* (2018). He is co-author of *For God and King: A History of the Damas Legion 1793–1798: A Case Study of the Military Emigration during the French Revolution*, with Hughes de Bazouges, to be published by Helion in 2021.

Jacqueline Reiter received her PhD from the University of Cambridge in 2006 on the role of national defence in British political debate during the French Revolutionary and Napoleonic Wars. Her first book, *The Late Lord: the Life of John Pitt, 2nd Earl of Chatham* (Pen and Sword, 2017), illuminated the political and military career of Pitt the Younger's elder brother. Her articles have appeared in *History Today* and the *Journal of the Society for Army Historical Research* and she has blogged for the *History of Parliament*. She has co-written a chapter with John Bew on British war aims for the forthcoming *Cambridge History of the Napoleonic Wars* and is currently writing a book on Sir Home Riggs Popham for Helion.

Hailey A. Stewart is a doctoral candidate at the University of North Texas where she is also a Student Fellow with the Military History Center. Her dissertation focuses on the problem of Hanover in British politics from 1800 to 1806. More specifically, her research investigates George III's separate management of British and Hanoverian politics, the collision of British and Hanoverian policies in times of conflict, and the role hostilities played in positioning Hanover within the British Empire.

Introduction: Character, Morale, and Personal Endeavour in the Napoleonic Wars

Zack White

> Do you know what I admire most in the world? It is the inability of force to organise something. There are only two powers in the world, the sword and the spirit. I mean by the spirit the civil and religious institutions. In the long run, the sword is always beaten by the spirit.[1]

Although not intended as a comment on the power of an individual's character, this famous quote by Napoleon Bonaparte epitomises why many find the study of conflict so compelling. It is now more than half a century since E. P. Thompson's article in the *Times Literary Supplement* brought the notion of 'history from below' into more mainstream use.[2] Since then, the examination of the past through the exploration of the lives and experiences of 'ordinary' men and women, rather than from the perspective of national leaders, has increasingly become the norm. Napoleonic era researchers have embraced this as much as anyone, as their work over the past decade has demonstrated. High quality volumes continue to develop our understanding of the period's significant figures from the Duke of Wellington, to Napoleon Bonaparte, and Ali Pasha of Ioannina.[3] However, a plethora of titles have shifted focus towards endeavouring to understand the experiences and impact of those from the lower echelons of society, whether they be from specific units, slave plantations or prisoners of war.[4]

In the process, we have garnered a far more nuanced appreciation of the role that individuals from all walks of life played in shaping the course of the Napoleonic Wars. At

1 L. de Fontanes, *Oeuvre de M. de Fontane* (Paris: Libraire de l'université royale de France, 1859), p.xcii. Translation by the author.

2 E. P. Thompson, 'History from Below', *Times Literary Supplement* 65 (1966), pp.279–280.

3 See for example R. Muir, *Wellington: The Path to Victory* (Yale: Yale University Press, 2013); M. Broers, *Napoleon: Soldier of Destiny* (London: Faber & Faber, 2014); Quentin Russel and Eugenia Russel, *Ali Pasha: Lion of Ioannina* (Barnsley: Pen & Sword, 2018).

4 See for example R. Griffith, *Riflemen: The History of the 5th Battalion 60th (Royal American) Regiment, 1797–1818* (Warwick: Helion & Co., 2019); R. Bessel, N. Guyatt and J. Rendall (eds), *War, Empire and Slavery, 1770–1830* (Basingstoke: Palgrave Macmillan, 2010); C. Kennedy, *Narratives of the Revolutionary and Napoleonic Wars* (Basingstoke: Palgrave Macmillan, 2013).

the forefront of this development has been a growing understanding of what motivated the rank and file to fight during this period. Edward Coss's *All for the King's Shilling* set a benchmark for this discussion, making a compelling argument that camaraderie between soldiers, or primary group cohesion, was the key element in the success of the British army on campaign.[5] By contrast, Andrew Bamford's *Sickness, Suffering and the Sword* emphasised the role of the regimental system, and the impact that loyalty to the regiment could have on motivating men.[6] Both notions form part of a wider theoretical framework of soldier motivation outlined by Stephen Westbrook in 1980 , which consisted of remuneration, coercive and normative or symbolic methods.[7] As Coss highlights, primary group dynamics form part of the normative element of Westbook's model, as do Bamford's arguments relating to the regimental system. Coss's and Bamford's works served as a catalyst for further research into the topic, with Michael Hughes having shown the applicability of these notions to Napoleon's *Grande Armeé*, whilst Ilya Berkovich's *Motivation in War* has highlighted that these ideas can be traced back much further to the armies of the *Ancien Regime*.[8] In the process it has become clear that a very different interpretation of Napoleon's '*l'esprit*' to the one he intended was fundamental to the outcome of the Napoleonic Wars. Whilst it has long been appreciated that *l'esprit de corps* is a crucial element for the outcome of campaigns, it is nonetheless clear that the study of history from below has generated fresh understanding of the interpersonal dynamics at play in armies of this period.

This emphasis on the collective spirit of regiments, or even whole armies, is not to belittle the vital role played by individuals at key moments throughout the Napoleonic era. As Gareth Glover's voluminous *Waterloo Archive* has testified to, popular interest is as high as ever in the actions, experiences and recollections of individuals in combat. It is therefore clear that, when considering Napoleon's comment that 'the sword is always beaten by the spirit', a much wider interpretation of the notion of spirit than religious and civil institutions is essential.

By taking this wider construction of the notion of spirit, our understanding of the multitude of factors influencing conflict during this period is deepened further. War obviously does not occur within a vacuum, and the civilian-military dynamic played as crucial a role in the Napoleonic Wars as in other conflicts. Research into the period has benefitted substantially from the work of individuals such as Gavin Daly, Kevin Linch and Katherine Aalestad, highlighting how the interaction between the civilian and military worlds had a profound effect on both combatants and non-combatants.[9] The actions of soldiers had

5 E. Coss, *All for the King's Shilling: The British Soldier under Wellington, 1808–1814* (Norman: Oklahoma University Press, 2010).

6 A. Bamford, *Sickness, Suffering and the Sword: The British Regiment on Campaign, 1808–1815* (Norman: Oklahoma University Press, 2013).

7 S. Westbrook, 'The Potential for Military Disintegration', in *Combat Effectiveness: Cohesion, Stress, and the Volunteer Military*, ed. by S. Sarkesian (Beverly Hills: Sage Publications, 1980), pp.244–278, p.247.

8 M. Hughes, *Forging Napoleon's Grande Armeé: Motivation, Military Culture, and Masculinity in the French Army, 1800–1808* (New York: New York University Press, 2012), pp.14–15; I. Berkovich, *Motivation in War: The Experience of Common Soldiers in Old-Regime Europe* (Cambridge: Cambridge University Press, 2017), p.26.

9 G. Daly, *The British Soldier in the Peninsular War: Encounters with Spain and Portugal, 1808–1814* (Basingstoke: Palgrave Macmillan, 2013); K. Linch, *Britain and Wellington's Army: Recruitment,*

the potential to rouse resentment and hostility amongst local people, generating a spirit of resistance, whilst the recruitment of large proportions of the population meant that popular opinions amongst civilians could also held by the rank and file. Popular sentiments were also, arguably, contagious, with despondency from individuals in the army on campaign having the potential to cause a similar mood back home, and vice versa.[10] As the French discovered to their cost in the Iberian Peninsula, a failure to manage popular sentiment appropriately could have a catastrophic effect on the ability of an army to subjugate the populace and fight campaigns.

The spirit of resistance that emerged across Europe in response to the spread of the French Empire has also been well researched, allowing us to appreciate how diverse it was in terms of its origins, impact and how it was expressed. Johan Joor, for example, has corrected the perception that the Dutch people were passive in the face of French occupation, demonstrating the generally non-violent and Protestant-inspired nature of protest in the country.[11] Malcolm Crook has equally shown that the spirit of resistance was also alive and well in France, using his work on the plebiscites of Napoleon's reign to open a window into French popular opinion, revealing a more complex reality than the voting results suggest.[12]

The study of history from below has therefore provided us with a far more comprehensive appreciation of the multi-faceted way in which both the collective spirit and the spirit, or character, of individuals played a key role in the course of the Napoleonic Wars. Of course, not all of these examples indicate that the spirit was all-conquering. In the case of Napoleon's plebiscites for example, and notwithstanding that some results were doctored, there was a far larger body of opinion that supported Napoleon's actions.[13] Nonetheless, it is apparent that researchers are engaged in a complex discussion on a wider range of issues relating to this period, highlighting that study of the Napoleonic era continues to thrive.

It was within the context of this rich environment of recent research that the editor of this volume, alongside William Fletcher and Eamonn O'Keeffe, had the pleasure of organising the British Commission for Military History's *War and Peace in the Age of Napoleon Conference* at King's College London in September 2019. The high quality and breadth of the papers delivered at the event is a testament to the rigour which continues to underpin research into the Napoleonic era. Choosing papers to take forward for publication in this volume was therefore extremely challenging, though it is noticeable that all of those selected

---

Society and Tradition, 1807–15 (Basingstoke: Palgrave Macmillan, 2011), K. Aaslestad, 'Patriotism in Practice: War and Gender Roles in Republican Hamburg, 1750-1815', in K. Hagemann, G. Mettele and J. Rendall (eds.), *Gender, War and Politics: Transatlantic Perspectives, 1775-1830* (Basingstoke: Palgrave Macmillan, 2010), pp.227–246.

10 See for example Z. White, 'From Cintra to Salamanca: Shifting Popular Perceptions of the War in the Iberian Peninsula, 1808–1812', *British Journal for Military History*, 1:3 (June 2015), pp.60–79, p.78.

11 Johan Joor, 'A Very Rebellious Disposition': Dutch Experience and Popular Protests under the Napoleonic Regime (1806–1813)' in A. Forrest, K. Hagemann and J. Rendall (eds.), *Soldiers, Citizens and Civilians: Experiences, and Perceptions of the Revolutionary and Napoleonic Wars, 1790–1820,* (Basingstoke: Macmillan, 2009), pp.181–204.

12 M. Crook, 'Confidence from Below? Collaboration and Resistance in the Napoleonic Plebiscite', in in M. Rowe (ed.), *Collaboration and Resistance in Napoleonic Europe: State-formation in an Age of Upheaval, c. 1800–1815* (Basingstoke: Palgrave Macmillan, 2003), pp.19–36.

13 Crook, 'Confidence from Below? Collaboration and Resistance in the Napoleonic Plebiscite', p.21.

embrace the multi-faceted notion of how the 'spirit' of individuals played a vital role in the events of the period.

Edward Coss's chapter demonstrates the merits of adopting an interdisciplinary approach to the study of history. Working in collaboration with a team of psychologists, he has developed some careful, yet eye opening conclusions on Napoleon's mental state, with profound implications for our understanding of how his actions might be interpreted. In discovering that there is a significant possibility that Bonaparte was afflicted by Narcissistic Personality Disorder, Coss compels us to consider the impact of personality on public policy.

In the first of two chapters in this volume on Sir Home Popham, Jacqueline Reiter offers a further interesting case study of the impact that strong willed mavericks could have on conflict, whilst also highlighting the limitations that at times existed within the patronage system. In doing so, her work provides a useful counterpoint to the recent analysis of Rory Muir which highlighted the importance of individuals being vocal about their achievements in order to secure opportunities and promotions.[14] In the case of Popham however, Reiter shows that being vocal was actually a disadvantage, in part due to the fact that Sir Home was too forthcoming in proclaiming his achievements. Whether the spirit was all-conquering, was therefore partially dependent on how palatable that spirit, or rather personality, was to others.

If Popham could have had any inclination that a quarter of this book would be devoted to discussions of his life's work, it would no doubt have further inflated his already considerable ego. Nonetheless, Silvia Gregorio-Sainz's chapter offers a different and equally revealing perspective on the man, exploring the impact that Popham had in Spain, as part of a case study of the port of Santander in the summer of 1812. Her work shows how the individual and collective spirits intertwined as Popham sought to negotiate with Santander's officials in the face of a degree of local opposition and scepticism towards the British.

Gavin Lewis's chapter is more demonstrative of the impacts of the sword and the collective spirit, as he explores the sacking of San Sebastian. Lewis rigorously interrogates the origins of the oft-repeated remarks on how sackings of towns were habitual after they had been stormed, in the process showing that the scale of British troops' misbehaviour has been somewhat overstated. Whilst looting was widespread, in part due to social norms amongst the soldiers, the evidence of the worst atrocities is limited and confined to a small minority of troops. This in turn encourages us to reappraise the impact that expectations amongst the rank and file had on the conduct of soldiers on campaign.

There were, of course, times when the character of an individual could have a detrimental impact on the events they were involved in, and this point is ably demonstrated in Andrew Bamford's chapter. Focusing on the creation of Provisional Battalions by the Earl (later Duke) of Wellington in the latter stages of the Peninsular War, he shows that Wellington's stubbornness, and narrowminded fixation on his desire to retain veterans in his army had an adverse effect on the British Army's manpower crisis. By refusing to compromise with the Commander-in-Chief, the Duke of York, Wellington's character actually left him worse off for men, and the British Army less able to fulfil its commitments across the globe.

14 R. Muir, *Gentlemen of Uncertain Fortune: How Younger Sons Made Their Way in Jane Austen's England* (New Haven: Yale University Press, 2019), pp.57–58.

The impact that misrepresentations of an individual's or social group's character can have on popular perceptions of history form the basis of two chapters in this volume. In Alistair Nichols's case, he demonstrates the damage caused by the tendency of scholars to focus too narrowly on the issue of desertion amongst foreign troops in the British Army. His research seeks to act as a stepping-stone for further discussion about the true character of the foreign units, emphasising the more complex service record that they enjoyed, and highlighting the dependability of many units raised outside the British Isles.

Vanya Bellinger's chapter, meanwhile, seeks to rehabilitate the reputation of Carl von Clausewitz, who has often been subjected to unduly harsh criticism for his actions during the Waterloo campaign. Through a careful deconstruction of the Prussian campaign, she highlights how Clausewitz was not a flawed staff officer, but rather responded appropriately to the strategic challenges that the Prussians faced.

Equally interestingly, Hailey Stewart's chapter provides a welcome shift away from armed operations to highlight that the endeavours of individuals off the battlefield were just as important and revealing. She focuses on the diplomatic discussions between Britain and Prussia over Hanover in 1801, explaining how British envoy to Prussia Lord Carysfort sought to dissuade Prussia from occupying Hanover, whilst seeking to maintain Britain's interests in the region through diplomatic means, rather than through the use of force.

Ultimately, it must be concluded that Napoleon was right. The spirit does indeed beat the sword, though perhaps not in the manner that he suggested. The chapters in this volume demonstrate the profound impact that individual characters had on the period, for better or worse. It remains to be debated whether civil and religious institutions had a greater impact than the spirit which motivated troops, or that influenced the actions of people like the Emperor himself. Yet nowhere is the power of the spirit better demonstrated than by the fact that 200 years on from Napoleon's death, fascination in his achievements and the events which he played a crucial part in, remains unabated.

1

A Damning Diagnosis: Napoleon, Narcissism, Depression, Traumatic Brain Injury, and Post Traumatic Stress Disorder

Edward J. Coss

Victor Hugo, commenting on the artist Peter Paul Rubens, noted that 'A great man is born twice: the first time as a man, the second time as a genius.'[1] Perhaps he is born a third time when he is fully assessed and understood. This certainly applies to Napoleon Bonaparte. While he is perhaps the most written about military leader in history, the complex nature of his personality and his machinations to weave together the historical record in such a way as to protect and glorify his reputation leave him something of an enigma. Knowing Napoleon's psychological make-up, or as much as one can approximate after 200 years, is essential to unravelling his world view, decision-making processes, and motivations; only in this way might we create a coherent construct of Napoleon's way of seeing and dealing with the world. Even almost two centuries after his death, identifying the psychological forces that engendered Napoleon's behaviours still matters. Independent analyses by five professional psychologists of Napoleon's words, and those shared with his close subordinates who intimately observed him, reveal that he carried far more emotional baggage than has ever been explicitly recognised.[2]

The original focus of the analysis was on whether or not it appeared that Napoleon exhibited symptoms of Post Traumatic Stress Disorder (PTSD), as defined in the *Diagnostic and Statistical Manual for Mental Disorders-5* (DSM-5), the clinical tool of the American Psychological Association (APA).[3] Upon the advice of the team of psychologists, all former students of mine who expressed interest in this project, we expanded our intent to include

1 Patrice Gueniffey, *Bonaparte 1769–1802* (London: The Belknap Press, 2015) p.49.
2 The views expressed in this report are those of the author and do not necessarily reflect the official policy or position of the Department of the Army, the Department of Defense, or the U.S. Government.
3 American Psychological Association, *Diagnostic and Statistical Manual of Mental Disorders, Fifth Edition,* (Arlington: American Psychiatric Publishing, 2013) pp.271–280.

signs of possible Traumatic Brain Injury (TBI) due to Napoleon's close calls on the battlefield.[4] As the team members shared ongoing research, they unanimously suggested that we examine the historical record for any indications of Narcissistic Personality Disorder.[5] We looked for positive and questionable traits or incidents. We were not predisposed towards any specific findings; we had no idea, precisely, what we would find. We were armed only with hunches and a willingness to explore. We went where the evidence took us.

As it turns out, Napoleon does not meet the criteria for PTSD, which was surprising given his nearly 20 consecutive years at war. He does not exhibit behaviours that match those required for diagnosis according to the DSM-5, such as reoccurring nightmares, guilt, bouts of remorse, or harrowing recollections.[6] Nor were there enough observations to assess TBI, even though he was twice knocked unconscious, once for a significant period of several hours. There was no recognition during Napoleon's time that cognitive and emotional impairments might be related to blows to the head. Thus, no one expected Napoleon to display any symptoms; he was not closely watched and no links between the accidents and his decisions or moods were recorded.

Our most significant final assessment of the French emperor was that he seemed to exhibit nearly all of the diagnostic criteria for Narcissistic Personality Disorder. This is a matter of no small import, as the APA notes that persons with this disorder:

> Have a grandiose sense of self-importance ... are often preoccupied with fantasies of unlimited success, power, brilliance, beauty, or ideal love ... generally have a lack of empathy and have difficulty recognizing the desires, subjective experiences, and feelings of others ... Vulnerability in self-esteem makes individuals with narcissistic personality disorder very sensitive to 'injury' from criticism or defeat ... Though overweening ambition and confidence may lead to high achievement, performance may be disrupted because of intolerance of criticism or defeat.[7]

The sources appear to indicate that, due to this disorder, Napoleon was, perhaps, mentally burdened to such an extent that his high intelligence and ability to make rapid decisions were at least partially negated by the inherent limitations of this illness. These psychological symptoms would have affected Napoleon, every day, throughout his career. He was able to convince himself that no goal was unattainable, regardless of situational variables and dynamics, all the while winning, and frequently abandoning, people who aided or opposed him. He was capable of exhibiting great charisma and purposely cruel behaviour. He was an individual who was highly skilled at getting people to care about him and what he thought. The diagnosis of possible Narcissistic Personality Disorder brings into focus the thorny issues behind his compulsions and his need to rise above all others.

---

4 APA, *DSM-5*, pp.624–627.
5 APA, *DSM-5*, pp.669–672.
6 APA, *DSM-5*, pp.271–272. While we can never know this definitively, these symptoms do not appear in Napoleon's dictations or the recollections of those men who were with him over his career and his six years at St. Helena. Thus, we are fairly safe in the belief that the absence of these issues does, indeed, preclude him from a PTSD diagnosis.
7 APA, *DSM-5*, pp.670–671.

It must first be understood that there are fundamental limitations to this study. Obviously, none of the five assessing psychologists had Napoleon under their professional care. This is a key ethical component of the APA regarding the assessment of public individuals. This, just recently, became relevant after the publication in 2017 of *The Dangerous Case of Donald Trump: 37 Psychiatrists and Mental Health Experts Assess a President*.[8] In this work, the psychiatrists involved felt morally obligated to issue their pronouncements because of what they felt was the greater public good regarding the 'malignant normality' aspects and the precipitating dangers of Donald Trump's mental wellbeing, as well as their related obligations as 'witnessing professionals' to warn the public.[9] There was a backlash from the APA over their approach and violation of Section 7, informally known as the 'Goldwater Rule,' of the association's Principles of Medical Ethics: 'It is unethical for a psychiatrist to offer a professional opinion unless he or she has conducted an examination and has been granted proper authorization for such a statement.'[10] The name references an incident in the 1964 presidential election during which 1,200 psychiatrists made public their evaluation that Barry Goldwater was not fit for that office, using inflammatory language. In 1966 he sued them and was awarded $75,000 in punitive damages. Seven years later, the APA instituted Section 7, prohibiting mental health professionals from engaging in such conduct.[11] The enforcement of Section 7 in the Donald Trump case initiated a spirited public defence by Bandy Lee, the book's editor, who argued that the danger was real, that the authors had a moral obligation to offer their views, and that they should not be silenced.[12]

The APA's ethical guidelines, however, do provide a window of opportunity when it comes to evaluating individuals of the past. The standards state that:

8 Bandy Lee (ed.), *The Dangerous Case of Donald Trump: 37 Psychiatrists and Mental Health Experts Assess a President* (New York: Thomas Dunne Books, 2017). Lee is a forensic psychiatrist at the Yale School of Medicine and the president of the World Mental Health Coalition.

9 Lufton, 'Introduction', in *The Dangerous Case of Donald Trump*, p.xv-xix.

10 N.A. (No Author), 'American Psychiatric Association The Principles of Medical Ethics,' 2013 edition, Section 7, p.9. Also see 'APA Commentary on Ethics in Practice' (December 2015) p.12.

11 Jerome Kroll and Claire Pouncey, 'The Ethics of APA's Goldwater Rule,' *Journal of the American Academy of Psychiatry and the Law*, 44:2 (June 2016), pp.226–235. This article explores the realities and perceived limitations of the Goldwater Rule. In the foreword to *The Dangerous Case of Donald Trump*, Robert Lufton argues that the rule continues to cause unintended damage. He notes that it constrained mental health professionals from speaking out against CIA efforts to implement 'enhanced interrogation' techniques. He offers that 'this malignant normality was essentially supported by the American Psychological Association in its defense of the participation of psychologists in … techniques that spilled into torture.' Lee, editor, *The Dangerous Case of Donald Trump*, p.xiviii. The updated and expanded volume (2019) looks critically at the harmful effects of absolute adherence to the Goldwater rule, in spite of the APA's refusal to in any way alter the rule, even going so far as to state that the 'duty to warn' exception applied only to patients.

12 Bandy Lee, 'Mental Health Experts see Trump as Dangerous, but Our Professional Gatekeepers Protect Him,' Opinion Piece, *USA Today* 11 October 2019. She argues that 'during the Trump administration, the APA expanded the Goldwater Rule and used this guideline to openly denounce professionals who would speak up as 'unethical' and engaging in 'armchair psychiatry.' A former APA president even released a video message warning that speaking out might be 'political partisanship disguised as patriotism.' <https://www.usatoday.com/story/opinion/voices/2019/10/11/donald-trump-mentally-unfit-american-psychiatric-association-column/3917647002/>, accessed 15 May 2020.

> When, without any personal examination, the psychiatrist renders a clinical opinion about a historical figure, these limitations [as presented above] must be clearly acknowledged. Moreover, labelling public figures *cavalierly* with psychiatric conditions, based on limited or indirect clinical knowledge is not consistent with this approach and undermines public trust in the profession of psychiatry ... In some circumstances, such as academic scholarship about figures of historical importance, exploration of psychiatric issues (not diagnostic conclusions) may be reasonable provided that it has a sufficient evidence base and is subject to peer review and academic scrutiny based on relevant standards of scholarship.'[13]

This ethical challenge needs be acknowledged at the outset, so as to allay concerns that the methods used herein to examine the psychology of the historical figure of Napoleon were questionable, whimsical in nature, or that the psychologists and the author have in any way attempted to bypass mental health or historical standards in the commission of this work. We acknowledged, up front, that a consistent, integrated mental health picture of Napoleon could only emerge through a compressive and measured analysis. The psychologists involved in the following clinical assessment of Napoleon were scrupulous in their methods and cautionary evaluations. Any errors are mine, alone. This study is the result of a careful, intense, multi-disciplinary, two-year collaborative effort.[14]

There have been other attempts to analyse the psychological states of various historical leaders. The most valid have been studies of Adolph Hitler conducted by mental health professionals. There have been scores of such analyses, including two by Carl Jung in 1939 and 1942.[15] The most well known is probably Erich Fromm's *Anatomy of Human Destructiveness*, which concluded that Hitler had narcissist issues and a related destructive personality.[16] While there remains controversy over the exact nature of Hitler's psychological disorders and the variances in diagnoses, these studies have revealed much about Hitler's mental state. Even here, however, the blending of history and psychology was not without flaws, as the mental health professionals were often not conversant with historical methodologies and sometimes unintentionally polluted their examinations by using just a handful of biographies or surveys given to historians and assessing these highly select commentaries rather than the words of Hitler, or those of his contemporaries who recorded

13 'APA Commentary on Ethics in Practice,' p.12. Italics added by author.

14 The diagnoses were provided by psychologists (Majors) Patricia Razuri, Angela Shrader, Stacey Krauss, Shannon Ford, and (Lieutenant Colonel) Sam Preston, all current Army officers with years of clinical experience and former students of mine. (Their ranks were as of May 2020.) We shared compelling discussions of Napoleon and his mental state for months and even years before we collectively began this paper. I am fortunate to have talented professionals, such as these, willing to take on this enticing, but at times laborious, examination of Napoleon's mental health. These officers were, in a word, *fabulous*, to work with. The views expressed in this report are those of the authors and do not necessarily reflect the official policy or position of the Department of the Army, the Department of Defense, or the U.S. Government.

15 Frederick L. Coolidge, Felicia L. Davis, & Daniel L. Segal, 'Understanding Madmen: A DSM-IV Assessment of Adolf Hitler,' *Individual Differences Research*, 5:1 (2007), p.31; Carl Jung, 'Hitler on the Couch,' *Omnibus Magazine* (1942), pp.134–137.

16 Erich Fromm, *Anatomy of Human Destructiveness* (New York: Holt Paperback Books, 1988).

same, as the basis of their studies.[17] Fromm's work, for example, relied primarily on just one secondary source for all his historical insights into Hitler and his family; he also quotes Albert Speer, Hitler's Minister of Armaments and War Production, far more than he cites Hitler or his writings, an imperfect method at best.[18]

More recent works also fall into this trap. D. Jablow Hershman and Julian Lieb's *A Brotherhood of Tyrants* examines the psyches of Napoleon, Hitler, and Stalin.[19] While both the authors are psychiatrists, they seem to know little about history and the need for supporting material. The authors provide anecdotes but offer not a single historical or psychological citation in the entire book, thus reducing the book's credibility to nearly zero. Nassir Ghaemi's work, *A First-Rate Madness*, comes closer to merging both disciplines, yet still comes up short.[20] Ghaemi, a professor of psychiatry, looks at the mental states of William Tecumseh Sherman, Winston Churchill, and Mahatmas K. Gandhi, among others. The problem is that he relies on few to no primary sources, leaning on the words of others but not the individuals, directly. Moreover, in the Sherman chapter, only four citations (out of 54 in the chapter) are to works related to psychology. This was the pattern throughout the book, with other chapters having little in the way of primary sources presenting the subject's words and no references to mental health journals or approaches. This methodology is too far removed from both key historical documents and literature on psychology to offer any real degree of insight into the minds of the individuals in question.

Most psychological assessments of historical personages have been undone for similar reasons, as historians, lacking credentialing degrees in psychology or psychiatry, have oddly felt empowered to assess and diagnose the emotional, psychological, and related social well-being of individuals of historical prominence. It has been purported, for example, that Harold T Parker's, 'The Formation of Napoleon's Personality: An Exploratory Essay,' was key to understanding Napoleon. Yet upon examination, it is little more than the musings of a historian regarding his interpretations of Napoleon's emotional development.[21] A trained psychologist played no formal role in this assessment, although one is thanked for his guidance in a footnote, severely limiting the article's value, then (1971) or now.

It remains unclear as to how these analyses, or others like them, illuminate the mental processes and disorders of these famous personages, given the authors' absence of professional training in either history or psychology; a firm grasp of historical methods or clinical experience using diagnostic tools like the DSM-5 appear to be in very short supply. These works of arm-chair psychology and history are either not grounded in professional literature related to psychological evaluation or in sound historical research methodologies, making them suspect across both disciplines. There were few exceptions to this problematic approach.

---

17 Coolidge, Davis, & Segal, pp.30–43. This approach of utilizing the *DSM-4* to assess Hitler's mental illnesses should be, nevertheless, the model for current studies. We discovered this parallel approach after the conclusion of our study.

18 Fromm, *Anatomy of Human Destructiveness,* pp.369–433.

19 Jablow Hershman and Julian Lieb, *A Brotherhood of Tyrants* (New York: Prometheus Books, 1994).

20 Nassir Ghaemi, *A First-Rate Madness* (New York: The Penguin Press, 2011).

21 Harold T Parker, 'The Formation of Napoleon's Personality: An Exploratory Essay,' *French Historical Studies* 7:1 (1971), pp.6–26.

For this study, it was decided to allow five trained psychologists to read and independently interpret primary source material. In addition, a decision was made to limit the historical research to either Napoleon's words or those of the men who were in the room, heard his words directly, and recorded them. This removed some of the biases of the external viewers, be he/she a contemporary of Napoleon who offered opinions on him or his conduct, or a historian who compiled select quotations within a larger work on the emperor. This restricted technique was intended to present Napoleon to the examining psychologists with as few barriers as was feasible, in hopes that the examiners might come as close as possible to hearing and weighing Napoleon's words as if he were in the room, alone. That, of course, was a difficult task as the volumes of his words preserved by his various secretaries were, themselves, the result of selective processing and conscious or unconscious editing by these men, all of whom had their own opinions as to how and what should reach the general public, as of course did Napoleon. He had three secretaries, two formal and one informal, who recorded and published his words, and one general and diplomat who accompanied him to Moscow and back during the Russian campaign: Louis Antoine Fauvelet de Bourrienne; Gaspard Gourgaud; Emmanuel-Auguste-Dieudonné, Comte de Las Cases; Armand-Augustin-Louis de Caulaincourt (Duc de Vicence)[22] In addition, a few other eyewitness accounts were consulted.[23] Each of these men had a certain rhythm to his writing and one

22 Louis Antoine Fauvelet de Bourrienne, *Memoirs of Napoleon Bonaparte* (New York: Thomas V. Crowell & Company, 2010). This is a reprint of the 1831 edition. Four volumes published between 1800 and 1821. Bourrienne was Napoleon's school days acquaintance. He became his private secretary in 1792. He remained loyal until he was accused of making profits off his insider knowledge, the same thing Napoleon did with relish. He was fired in 1802. Gaspard Gourgaud, *Talks of Napoleon at St. Helena with General Baron Gourgaud: together with the Journal kept by Gourgaud on their Journey from Waterloo to St. Helena*, translated by Elizabeth Wormeley (Chicago: A. C. McClurg & Company, 1904). Gourgaud was a French officer and Napoleon's *aide-de-camp* during the Waterloo campaign. He accompanied the emperor to St. Helena, where he remained until Napoleon's death. He later returned in 1840 to help bring home Napoleon's remains. Emmanuel-Augustin-Dieudonné-Joseph, Comte de Las Cases, *Memorial de Sainte Helene: Journal of the Private Life and Conversations of the Emperor Napoleon at Saint Helena*, (London: Forgotten Books, 2015). Three volumes. De Las Cases was a noble, historian, map maker, and writer who rallied to Napoleon's side in 1802 and accompanied Napoleon to St. Helena. He served faithfully as Napoleon's informal secretary, staying until Napoleon's death in 1821. Armand-Augustin-Louis de Caulaincourt, George Libaire, Jean Hanoteau (eds.), *With Napoleon in Russia: The Memoirs of General de Caulaincourt Duke of Vicenza* (New York: William Morrow and Company, 1935). De Caulaincourt was a French general, diplomat, and Napoleon's Master of the Horse throughout the Russia campaign, which Caulaincourt had advised against. He was one of the most loyal of all Napoleon's officers.

23 Louis Constant Wairy, Napoleon's First Premier Valet de Chambre from 1806 to 1814, wrote three volumes devotedly filled with praise. Louis Constant, *Recollections of the Private Life of Napoleon*, translated by Walter Clark (New York: The Saalfield Pub Co., 1911). Also, Louis-Joseph Marchand, the valet who replaced Constant in 1814, complied a narrative of his times with Napoleon. Louis-Joseph Marchand, *In Napoleon's Shadow; The Memoirs of Louis-Joseph Marchand, Valet and Friend of the Emperor 1811–1821* (Barnsley: Greenhill Books, 1998). In addition, Adam Zamoyski's new volume on Napoleon was examined in part, as Zamoyski's multilingual, multinational, and even-handed approach brought together in one work many observations of people who knew and closely interacted with Napoleon. Adam Zamoyski, *Napoleon: A Life* (New York: Basic Books, 2018). This work, while both critical and impartial in its analysis of Napoleon, sometimes causes research difficulties, as its citations can be hard to unravel and related translations occasionally seem off the mark. Thus,

could sense, in some cases, whether or not the conversations were recorded nearly as they happened, or if they were edited with a purpose. The large number of passages in question was in itself a challenge, not only because Napoleon could wax poetic on any number of topics, and enjoyed doing so in his times of stress, exhaustion, or loneliness, but because key revealing paragraphs were often buried in his sometimes long, rambling soliloquies. This was especially true of his last years at St. Helena. Memory is what it is: faulty and often self-serving. The sheer number of his declarations in these works helped to mitigate concerns that any of Napoleon's individual pronouncements might have been shaped too positively or too harshly by a secretary on any given day. In addition, some of his correspondence was examined, although most of it was official and directive in content.[24] Napoleon, due to his confidence and self-pride, was frequently unguarded in his pronouncements; whether truly angry, exalted, or playacting his recollections, Napoleon often presented unvarnished insights into his persona. The thousands of pages examined never failed, eventually, to present something startling.

These volumes were examined in detail; the histories and possible agendas of each secretary were presented, beforehand, to the psychologists to weigh as he/she wished. In the end, after consulting with the five professionals as to the type of material for which I should search, I passed on more than 400 observations or dictations. Each psychologist evaluated this evidence independently, making note of key passages as they would in any clinical situation, comparing his behaviours against the mental illnesses listed in the APA's *Diagnostic and Statistical Manual for Mental Disorders-5*. We looked for repeating patterns of behaviour, which were found in abundance. What is offered is not a definitive diagnosis, but an approximation offered by five mental health professionals, all following APA guidelines. Phrases like, 'it appears,' 'it might be conjectured,' 'perhaps,' 'it is likely that Napoleon might,' etc. will be used liberally and form the foundation for understanding the final diagnoses and this psychological/historical analysis.[25]

According to the *Diagnostic and Statistical Manual for Mental Disorders-5*, Narcissistic Personality Disorder is defined as:

> A pervasive pattern of grandiosity (in fantasy or behaviour), need for admiration, and lack of empathy, beginning by early adulthood and present in a variety of contexts, as indicated by FIVE (or more) of the following:
> 1. Has a grandiose sense of self-importance (e.g., exaggerates achievements and talents, expects to be recognised as superior without commensurate achievements).
> 2. Is preoccupied with fantasies of unlimited success, power, brilliance, beauty, or ideal love.

questionable quotations were traced back to the original French documents and retranslated. Errors in these reworked passages are mine, alone.

24 Napoleon Bonaparte, *Correspondance générale* (Paris: Fondation Napoléon, 2004–2017).

25 When assessing Napoleon, we do not state, definitively, for example, that he was completely lacking in empathy, just that in many cases he appeared to ignore the feelings and needs of those around him. So, while he may have given gold coins to an indigent woman, he also often exhibited little or no concern for many of the individuals with whom he interacted. Thus, the number of historical examples determined the direction of our general analysis. Marchand, *In Napoleon's Shadow*, p.83.

3. Believes that he or she is 'special' and unique and can only be understood by, or should associate with, other special or high-status people (or institutions).
4. Requires excessive admiration.
5. Has a sense of entitlement (i.e., unreasonable expectations of especially favourable treatment or automatic compliance with his or her expectations).
6. Is interpersonally exploitative (i.e., takes advantage of others to achieve his or her own ends).
7. Lacks empathy: is unwilling to recognise or identify with the feelings and needs of others.
8. Is often envious of others or believes that others are envious of him or her.
9. Shows arrogant, haughty behaviours or attitudes.'[26]

It is important to highlight two parameters: these characteristics must manifest themselves from an early age, being 'present in a variety of contexts,' and the threshold for diagnosis is exhibiting behaviours in at least five of the criterion categories. Through the lens of these nine benchmarks, a very human, and troubled, portrait of Napoleon emerges. To make this somewhat interactive, as was done at the War and Peace Conference, a few statements by or about Napoleon will be presented for each category, allowing the reader to assess and decide, in his/her mind's eye, whether the quotes seem to meet the standards for that criterion. The diagnoses of the psychologists will follow, thereafter.

1. Has a grandiose sense of self-importance (e.g., exaggerates achievements and talents, expects to be recognised as superior without commensurate achievements).

In this first criterion, Napoleon does not disappoint. He offers a multitude of self-aggrandizing opinions.

- After the battle of Lodi against the Austrians in northern Italy (1796), Napoleon remarked to Auguste de Marmont, his *aide-de-camp*, later a *maréchal* and the Duc de Ragusé, that 'They have not seen anything yet, and the future holds successes far superior to what we have already done … Fortune is a woman [mistress] and the more she does for me, the more I will demand of her.'[27]
- During his time in Egypt in 1798, Napoleon had, according to Adam Zamoyski, 'primarily from his reading of Voltaire, formed a view of the Prophet Muhammad as a kind of wise tyrant and thought he could understand how his followers responded to

26 APA, *Diagnostic and Statistical Manual for Mental Disorders*, pp.669–670. If, as you read this chapter, you find yourself ruminating on how this applies to yourself, loved ones, friends, or national leaders, please understand that this has been the norm wherever this topic was presented. Hopefully, no one you know will breach the five characteristics threshold.

27 Auguste Marmont, *Mémoires du Maréchal Marmont, duc de Ragusé de 1792 à 1841* (Paris: Perrotin Libraire-Editeur, 1857), I, pp.322–323. '*Ils n'ont encore rien vu,et l'avenir nous réserve des succès bien supérieurs à ce que nous avons déjà fait … Elle est femme, et plus elle fait pour moi, plus j'exigerai d'elle.*' Translation by author. Cited in Zamoyski, *Napoleon: A Life*, p.127.

authority.'[28] Napoleon commented that, 'I dreamed all sort of things ... I created a religion ... in my hand a new Koran, which I should compose according to my own ideas.[29]

- Thinking back on his time in the Middle East, Napoleon emoted on what might have been achieved, telling Gourgaud, Baron de l'Empire, his companion and informal secretary during his exile on St. Helena, 'Ah! If I had stayed in Egypt, I should have been at this moment Emperor of the Orient. But for Saint Jean d'Acre the whole population would have declared for me.'[30]
- In 1799, in a hall during his takeover of the French government, Napoleon was interrupted many times by various representatives. De Bourrienne watched Napoleon's growing agitation: 'Instead of giving an explanation of what he had said, he began to make fresh accusations; and against whom? The Council of the Five Hundred, who, he said, wished for "scaffolds, revolutionary committees, and a complete overthrow of everything." Violent murmurs arose, and his language became more and more incoherent and inconsequent ... Then by unaccountable transition, he spoke of "thunderbolts of war!" and added that he was "attended by the God of war and the God of fortune."'[31]
- In 1804, André François Miot de Mélito, French scholar and statesman, heard Napoleon tell his older brother Joseph, whom he later elevated to the throne of Spain, that Napoleon had been 'called to change the face of the world ... Perhaps some notions of predestination have affected my thought,' he admitted, 'but I do not reject them; I even believe in them, and that confidence provides the means of success.'[32]

Does Napoleon, therefore, meet the criteria for this first component? Given that we discovered well over 70 more discrete examples, the psychologists concluded, unanimously, that he appears, indeed, to exhibit grandiosity.

2. Is preoccupied with fantasies of unlimited success, power, brilliance, beauty, or ideal love.

This category illustrates the interconnectivity of these criteria. Assigning dialogue between psychologist and patient to a particular sub-trait is an art. Determining whether exchanges pinpoint that Napoleon 'exaggerates achievements and talents' as opposed to overlapping with his expression of 'fantasies of unlimited success' is a refined assessment, which is why the evaluations were done by professionals with decades of clinical practice. As in the first case, Napoleon did not disappoint.

28 Zamoyski, *Napoleon: A Life*, p.196.
29 Claire Remusat, *Memoirs of Madame de Rémusat. 1802–1808* (New York: D. Appleton and Company, 1880) pp.99–100.
30 Gourgaud, *Talks of Napoleon*, p.69.
31 De Bourrienne, *Memoirs of Napoleon Bonaparte*, I, pp.247–248.
32 André François Miot de Melite, *Memoirs of Count Miot de Melito, Minister, Ambassador, Councillor of State and member of the Institute of France, between the years 1788 and 1815* (New York: Scribner, 1881) Vol. II, p.241.

- In 1799, Napoleon shared his views with de Bourrienne on what he would accomplish during the Egyptian campaign, 'I will announce to the people the abolition of servitude, and of the tyrannical governments of the pashas. I will arrive at Constantinople with large masses of soldiery. I shall overturn the Turkish empire, and found in the East a new grand empire, which will fix my place in the records of posterity.'[33]
- Napoleon also told de Bourrienne what attracted and repelled him about women: 'One thing that gave Bonaparte great pleasure when in the country was to see a tall, slender woman, dressed in white ... To fat women he had an invincible antipathy, and he could not endure the sight of a pregnant woman.'[34]
- Reminiscing about his truncated expedition to India, following the path of Alexander, Napoleon told Gourgaud that 'I would thus have marched to the Indus, and have destroyed the power of the English in India. It would have been a march of three thousand miles ... If I had stayed in the East I should have founded an empire, like Alexander.'[35]
- On St. Helena, Napoleon, selectively looking back on the totality of his time as emperor and the missed opportunity to commission a series on the histories of Europe, told de Las Cases that, '"My reign," he observed, "would have been a perfect epoch for that object. The superiority of France, its independence, and regeneration, enabled the actual government to make such a publication, without inconvenience. It would have resembled the publication of ancient history. Nothing could have been more valuable."'[36]
- This next passage is disturbing and it bears careful examination, exhibiting as it does Napoleon's unbridled fantasies regarding *amour* and his unrestrained access to whatever struck his fancy; in this case his caprice involved young girls and his proposed idea ran counter to the norms and laws of most European nations. Even the emperor should not have considered 'devotion' along these lines, conveyed many years later to Gourgaud in a seemingly wistful recollection: 'I have a tender remembrance of the young girls who were chosen in all the cities of France to present me flowers. The Empress always offered some gift, and I paid them compliments, by which they were extremely flattered, and their little heads grew full of enthusiasm for me. At Amiens one of these girls, who on a previous occasion had presented me with flowers, sprang forward, exclaiming, "Ah, Sire, how much I love you!" ...Had I wanted a *seraglio* [harem] I might easily have formed one out of these young girls.'[37]

The reader, likely, has an inclination whether he/she believes Napoleon's words seem to fit this second DSM-5 criterion for Narcissistic Personality Disorder. It must be recognised,

33 De Bourrienne, *Memoirs of Napoleon Bonaparte*, Vol. I, p.190. Instead, Napoleon abandoned his army in Egypt and returned to France to deal with political upheaval due to a failed *coup d'état*. Gueniffey addresses the question of whether Napoleon might be labeled a deserter or someone betting on his own political destiny. Gueniffey, *Bonaparte*, p.521.

34 Gueniffey, *Bonaparte*, p.289.

35 Gourgaud, *Talks of Napoleon*, p.67.

36 Las Cases, *Memorial de Sainte Helene*, Vol. III part V, p.161. Las Cases felt a real affinity for Napoleon, commenting that 'I was present at his abdication; and when the question of his removal was agitated, I requested permission to participate in his fate.' Ibid., Vol. I, p.9.

37 Gourgaud, *Talks of Napoleon*, p.249.

though, that Napoleon, at times, might have been trying to convince his subordinates, *pour encourager les autres*, during times of stress and uncertainty that his visions were vast in scope, yet attainable. Over 50 distinct examples were found, however, convincing all the examining psychologists that Napoleon was, perhaps, often preoccupied with fantasies that were ideal or infinite in scope.

3. Believes that he or she is 'special' and unique and can only be understood by, or should associate with, other special or high-status people (or institutions).

Again, some of Napoleon's statements that worked to place him in either of the first two categories might also apply to this third aspect of the disease; to be careful, though, once a passage was used for a specific criterion, it was rarely used for a second. This proved not to be an issue, however, as Napoleon unreservedly offered scores of examples for most of the nine standards.[38]

- In Egypt, the bubonic plague infected his army. To his credit, Napoleon visited the soldiers in the hospital. Most people ran from an infected person; Napoleon, instead, tried to comfort them believing that something safeguarded him. He moved among his men, even touching one of the men's buboes. One of his men responded to Napoleon's entreaties by saying, 'You are right, General, your grenadiers are not made to die in a hospital.'[39]
- On the return journey from the disastrous Russian campaign in 1812, Napoleon seemingly had a detached and severely flawed impression of nearly every combat variable. He failed to grasp that his army was in desperate state: its logistical train was non-existent, the weather was horrendous and hampering his retreat, and the relentless and aggressive Russian army shadowed the French, attacking whenever and however they wanted. Armand-Augustin-Louis de Caulaincourt, Napoleon's Master of the Horse, was astounded that Napoleon still spoke of victory: 'The interval left between the departure of the various corps … proves the extent to which the Emperor deluded himself in regard to the army's situation and the dangers that threatened it. Did he flatter himself that he would once more bend Fortune to his use, and bring the cold within the compass of his will as he so often had brought victory?'[40]
- Caulaincourt also recorded Napoleon's refusal to accept that he could not conjure up logistics and allies, inventing circumstances by which he might yet turn debacle into victory, as he had almost always done before. Caulaincourt observed that 'The Emperor

38 The psychologists informed me that this was not unusual for someone with Narcissistic Personality Disorder, noting that in therapy sessions an individual might talk almost endlessly about him/herself as long as the monologues were not interrupted by probing questions requiring the patient to reflect on his/her actions and possibly consider them to be anything other than ideal. When that occurred, the session could end abruptly and there was a high probability that the patient would not return for further counseling.

39 De Bourrienne, *Memoirs of Napoleon Bonaparte*, Vol. I, p.199.

40 Caulaincourt, *With Napoleon in Russia*, p.225.

was convinced that more supplies could be got together in eight days at Wilna to resist the Russians than they would be able to collect in a month. In his mind's eye he saw Poland arming all her peasants to drive away the Cossacks, the French army tripling in size because it had food and clothing, and because its reinforcements were now within reach, whereas the Russians were leaving theirs farther and farther behind. The Emperor, as at Moscow, refused to take into account the fact that the climate favoured the Russians more than us. Already he saw our cantonments [in his imagination] ...'[41]

- Napoleon exclaimed his worth to Caulaincourt on the return journey from Moscow: 'Whether as First Consul or as Emperor, I have been the people's king; I have governed for the nation and its interest, without allowing myself to be turned aside by the outcries or the private interests of certain people. This is well-known throughout France, and the French people love me.'[42]
- After Napoleon took the throne as emperor in 1804, he believed it proper to reinstitute court protocols, reviving 634 articles from 1710. More than just rituals that established guidelines for exchanges between individuals of various levels of power and rank or granting access to the Napoleon's person, these rules elevated Napoleon's questionable status from a general who had seized power through a *coup d'état* to the new, leading noble in France. Pride, a desire for unassailable standing, and a burning need to be recognised as emperor likely played a role in the restoration of these court rules. He apparently believed that special treatment when interacting at court might give him added credibility through detailed etiquette, especially since he had just re-established the noble classes. The formality, however, was not embraced by all the soldiers who attended these proceedings. *Colonel* Louis-François Lejeune, who later rose to *général de brigade*, observed the rituals and recorded the absurdity: 'On entering, we made three bows, for which we had been taking lessons with Mr. Gardel, the ballet master at the Opera. This study greatly entertained us; but in general, it gave very little of the flexibility of courtiers to most of us who had remained fairly rough soldiers, and still Republicans.'[43] Napoleon, having married Louis XVI's niece, went so far as to adopt the Bourbon waddle; he also had the Revolutionary slogan 'Liberty, Equality, Fraternity'

41 Caulaincourt, *With Napoleon in Russia*, p.267. When the army reached Wilna, neither supplies nor soldiers awaited it. This example and the preceding one seem to allude to Napoleon's belief that he could will something to happen, shaping every situation according to his needs. None of the psychologists considered this to be outright delusion; instead, they commented that Napoleon's experiences seemed to reinforce his self-belief that he was unique and unrivaled. He appeared to think that he could anticipate events in ways that others could not.

42 Caulaincourt, *With Napoleon in Russia*, p.364.

43 Louis-François Lejeune, Baron, *Mémoires du Général Lejeune* (Paris: Librairie de Firmin-Didiot et Cie, 1895) p.252. *'En entrant, nous faisions trois saluts, dont nous avions été prendre la leçon chez M. Gardel, maître des ballets de l'Opera. Cette étude nous divertissait beaucoup; mais en général, elle donnait très peu de la souplesse des hommes de cour à al plupart de ceux d'entre nous qui étaient réstes d'assez rudes soldats, et encore républicains.'* Translation by author. There was, of course, great intricacy and purpose behind the protocols of courts in early modern Europe; all could be shaped by the desires of the monarchs to produce whatever ends were deemed necessary. See John Adamson, *The Princely Courts of Europe 1500–1750* (London: Orion, 1999); Jeroen Duindam, *Vienna and Versailles: The Courts of Europe's Dynastic Rivals, 1550–1780* (Cambridge: Cambridge University Press, 2008); Hannah Smith, 'Court Studies and the Courts of Early Modern Europe,' *The Historical Journal*

painted over on all public buildings.[44] Given the emotional weight of these words and the events that brought them to life, this last action would seem to be a gratuitous gesture of self-aggrandisement, one that appears to disavow the Revolution in favour of what Napoleon believed would be the brilliance of his reign.

- On St. Helena, Napoleon shared his view with Las Cases regarding how Napoleon's legacy was above reproach. Las Cases recorded that 'The Emperor concluded with the following statement: "I concern myself but little about the libels that have been written about me. My acts, and the events of my reign, refute them more completely than the most skilful arguments that could be employed. I seated myself on an empty throne. I arrived at supreme power, unsullied by the crimes that have usually disgraced the chiefs of dynasties. Let history be consulted, let me be compared with others! If I have to fear the reproaches of posterity and history, it is not for having been too wicked, but perhaps for having been too good."'[45]

After the reader ponders Napoleon's eligibility for this third criterion, it should be noted that an additional 40 passages were found. The psychologists were, again, unanimous that Napoleon likely believed that he was 'special and unique and ... could ... only be understood' by gifted people of similar status.

4. Requires excessive admiration.

This standard was challenging, as quantifying, in any sense, what constituted *excessive* admiration was an aspect we had to consider. It was decided that the sheer number of examples we initially assumed we were likely to find would provide a body of evidence that might allow us to parse out similar examples and, thereby, come to grips with *excessive.* Quantity did, indeed, offer us insight, just not in the way we anticipated.

- After the *coup d'état* of 18 *Fructidor,* (4 September, 1797), which entailed the removal of counterrevolutionaries and royalists from the national legislature by *Général* Charles Augereau, later 1st Duc de Castiglione, who was sent by Napoleon to aid the Jacobins (and his brother's ambition to sit as deputy for the province of Liamone), Napoleon felt slighted by the Directory regarding this key contribution. De Bourrienne recorded Napoleon's indignation two days later: 'I beg of you to receive my resignation, and appoint another to my place. No power on earth shall make me continue in the service after this shocking mark of ingratitude on the part of the government, which I was far from expecting.' He later stated that he was fatigued from riding on campaign and would need 'some years of repose.'[46]

49:4 (Dec., 2006); and Louis François Joseph De Bausett, *Private Memoirs of the Court of Napoleon* (Philadelphia: Carey, Lea & Carey, 1828).

44 Zamoyski, *Napoleon: A Life*, p.498.

45 Las Cases, *Memorial de Sainte Helene*, Vol. II, p.133.

46 De Bourrienne, *Memoirs of Napoleon Bonaparte*, Vol. I, pp.87, 96.

- Napoleon's need to re-establish 634 court protocols, addressed above, also appears to be a fair indicator that he may have demanded disproportionate esteem from those at the highest levels of society.
- Comte François Nicolas Mollien, recalled that in 1808 he was struck by Napoleon's 'in a word, *insatiable*, need to be the center of all, the single principle [point] of action and force on every person and everything.'[47] This passage may speak to Napoleon's grandiosity or it might hint at his need to be admired.
- On St. Helena, Las Cases told a story about how Napoleon allowed himself to be doted upon by his servants. This episode may indicate his need for admiration or, possibly, his realization of how far he had fallen and that this pitiable tribute was all the adoration he was ever likely to receive: 'One of the shoe-buckles fell out and we all eagerly strove [on hands and knees] to put it in again; he who succeeded, considered himself the most fortunate. The Emperor, who would not have allowed us to behave so at the Tuileries, seemed here to feel a kind of satisfaction at our conduct; he let us do as we liked ...'[48]

As the reader weighs these passages, it is worth mentioning that these were the only four examples in the thousands of pages examined that might fall under the umbrella of this fourth DSM-5 category. This was the only criterion that saw even mild disagreements between the examining psychologists. Some of the issue revolved around the word *excessive*. The majority of the team stated that the historical record did not present a clear-cut case of Napoleon needing gratuitous approbation. One of the psychologists, though, argued that because of Napoleon's dominant personality and hierarchical expectations, many people obeyed and praised him lavishly without prompts, thus providing all the levels of admiration he needed. The ways in which he rewarded loyalty and success guaranteed a coterie of loyal admirers. Additionally, it was suggested that this would explain the lack of examples in the historical record, as copious praise flowed continually in Napoleon's direction, eliminating the need to discuss or record exchanges. But as history relies on evidence, rather than conjecture, however enticing, the group concluded that Napoleon did not appear to manifest behaviours consistent with those needed for inclusion in this standard.

5. Has a sense of entitlement (i.e., unreasonable expectations of especially favourable treatment or automatic compliance with his or her expectations).

This is also a difficult assessment because Napoleon, as emperor, would have expected compliance. Many of these examples, though, predate his elevation to that position.

- After receiving news from the Directory following Napoleon's success at Lodi (1796) that his army and his command were to be divided, he sent off three letters – to the Directory, to Paul Barras, then its chief executive, and Lazare Carnot, one of its five

---

47 François Nicolas Mollien, Charles Gomel, (ed.), *Mémoires d'un Ministre du Trésor Public 1780–1815* (Paris: Guillaumin et Cie, Paris, 1898) p.40.'... *en un mot son insatiable d'être le centre de tout le principe unique d'action et d'impulsion sur toute personne et sur toute chose.*' Translation by author.

48 Las Cases, *Memorial de Sainte Helene*, Vol. III Part V, p.29.

leading members – threatening to resign because he brooked no interference on campaign, even though this strategic repositioning of forces and command were within their purview and not his. He would control the army, not the Directory from Paris. He wrote: 'If I have lost the trust I enjoyed at the beginning of the campaign, I entreat you to let me know. In that case, I would be asked to resign.'[49] He then commented on what the directory should look for regarding the qualities of his potential replacement, 'And finally a general who has his confidence in commanding the army, because I couldn't find anyone who could replace me in all of these three missions, all equally interesting.'[50] There is a condescending tone in these remarks as he feigns a desire to step down, then offers advice about the needed qualities of his replacement. He seemingly believed that no one was his equal; he might set boundaries and demand whatever he wanted from the Directory because he likely deemed that he was indispensable and deserving of every consideration.

- De Bourrienne was with Napoleon in 1797 when he reacted with 'extreme displeasure' after hearing that orators and pamphlets criticised his efforts, decisions, and the 'national glory' he believed he brought to France fighting the Austrians in Italy. De Bourrienne recorded that Napoleon 'was quite indignant at the suspicions which it sought to create respecting his conduct and ulterior views.'[51]
- That same year, Napoleon found himself guiding peace talks with Austria, which he was brazenly negotiating despite not having been granted authority by the Directory to do so. Gourgaud watched as Napoleon was dictating terms. When the Austrian negotiator, Count Ludwig Cobentzel, tried to make a counterpoint, Napoleon rose and stated, 'Compte Cobentzel, have you given us your ultimatum? Well, before three months are over I shall break your monarchy in pieces, as I now break the china cups upon this table. Our negotiations are at an end.'[52] He then upturned the table, causing Cobentzel's prized china set to be shattered. Napoleon left the room in dramatic fashion, shouting curses.[53]
- De Bourrienne noted, in 1799, that Napoleon became very angry after an exchange with *Général* Jean-Baptiste Bernadotte regarding Napoleon's decision to leave his army behind in Egypt, remarking, 'He actually reproached me for not having brought the army back from Egypt!'[54]
- While conversing with Napoleon about whether or not Hugues-Bernard Maret, 1st Duc de Bassano, his Minister of Foreign Affairs, had the necessary resources to complete his important negotiations, Caulaincourt voiced his doubts. Napoleon, who had stated in

---

49 Napoleon, *Correspondance générale*, Vol. I, pp.397–400. Originally cited by Zamoyski, *Napoleon: A Life*, p.126.

50 Napoleon, *Correspondance générale*, Vol. I, p.449. '*Et enfin un generale qui ait sa confiance pour commander l'armee, car je ne cannais personne qui puisse me remplacer dans l'ensemble de ces trois mission, toutes egalement interessantes.*' Translation by author.

51 De Bourrienne, *Memoirs of Napoleon Bonaparte*, Vol. I, p.61.

52 Gourgaud, *Talks of Napoleon*, p.63.

53 Zamoyski, *Napoleon: A Life*, p.171.

54 De Bourrienne, *Memoirs of Napoleon Bonaparte*, Vol. I, p.231. Napoleon's decision was, in fact, a political one. It is not surprising that a general might object to such a blatant disregard of command responsibilities.

the affirmative that Bassano had all that he needed, irritably snapped, 'When I tell you something, you've got to believe it.'[55]

When deciding how well these conversations align with the fifth benchmark, the reader should consider not only the role Napoleon's dominance as a general and emperor might play in these exchanges, but whether any of these examples might blend into previous standards: grandiosity, 'unlimited' expectations of power and success, or being 'special.' While it was difficult to find and assign passages specific to this criterion, a total of 15 stood out with such clarity that the team reached a consensus that it might be conjectured that Napoleon exhibited behaviours that met this fifth aspect of Narcissistic Personality Disorder.

6. Is interpersonally exploitative (i.e., takes advantage of others to achieve his or her own ends).

The challenge when considering passages for inclusion in this criterion came from trying to ascertain Napoleon's motives behind his efforts to shape the behaviour of others. Most military leaders are aware of how to use their personalities to motivate their subordinates. The question is who benefits from the interactions: the individual soldier, the collective unit, or the officer who initiates the exchange. It can be all three; this dynamic is fluid and often difficult to assess in the moment. Make no mistake, Napoleon was highly skilled in his interactions with his men, being apparently authentic and giving just the right praise or reward, leaving his soldiers wanting more and willing to do his bidding to earn the additional rewards. Sometimes, though, Napoleon lets his guard down just a bit; in these instances, a discerning eye might make out the theatrical and openly manipulative nature of his machinations.

- In 1796, Napoleon confided to Gourgaud that the 'Thirty-second half-brigade would have died for me because after [the battle of] Lonato, I had reported: "The Thirty-second brigade was there, and my mind was easy."' He then added, 'It is astonishing what power one can exert over men with words.'[56]
- Believing that his Egyptian campaign was nearing its political end, Napoleon decided to leave his army behind to return to Paris. De Bourrienne observed Napoleon as he gathered the soldiers one last time. As he was leaving the men, Napoleon told them, 'I leave the command of the army to General Kleber. The army shall hear from me forthwith ... It costs me much pain to quit troops to whom I am so strongly attached. But my absence will be temporary ...'[57] Kleber tried to lift the men's morale by telling them that Napoleon would return with reinforcements. He never did; he left his men behind. Napoleon then used the expedition for propaganda purposes.
- Speaking in 1800 to de Bourrienne about how religion could be exploited, Napoleon summed up how he saw it: 'In every country religion is useful to the Government,

55 Caulaincourt, *With Napoleon in Russia*, p.320.
56 Gourgaud, *Talks of Napoleon*, p.261.
57 De Bourrienne, *Memoirs of Napoleon Bonaparte*, Vol. I, p.207.

and those who govern ought to avail themselves of it to influence mankind. I was a Mahometan in Egypt; I was a Catholic in France.'[58]

- Twenty years later Napoleon confided to Gourgaud that his willingness to change religion to please the Muslims in and around Egypt had a purpose other than personal or religious: '"There is no God but God, and Mohammed is his Prophet." I said that to make myself popular among the Orientals.'[59]
- After offending Bourrienne in 1802, Napoleon quickly changed tack and tried to sweet talk him: 'The First Consul came up to me smiling, and pulling me by the ear, as he did when he was in the best of humours, said to me, "Are you still in the sulks?" and leading me to my usual seat he added, "Come, sit down."'[60]
- Caulaincourt understood how Napoleon tried to dissuade anyone who posed a dissenting view, noting that Napoleon pulled his ear every time Caulaincourt tried to speak the truth about the campaign: 'He tweaked my ear, with weak protests that it [my idea] was not so. He then gave me free leave to say whatever I desired, and accepted with utmost good humour everything I said. Whenever I touched a sore spot he pinched my ear again, giving me a gentle tap on the nape of my neck – especially when I seemed to him to be going rather far.' After Napoleon continued to call him a 'Russian' because Caulaincourt was persistent in presenting opinions that differed from Napoleon's, Caulaincourt offered to resign his post. Napoleon brought him in close, 'Who is doubting your fidelity? ... I was only joking. You are too touchy; you know perfectly well that I hold you in esteem.'[61]
- Embarking on the Russian campaign, with so many variables unknown, Caulaincourt observed how Napoleon 'never failed to shift the centre of argument when he encountered opposition ... No woman was ever more artful than he in making you want, or agree to, his own desire, when he thought it was in his interest to persuade, or merely want to do so ...[this] explains better than any other phrase could have done the price he was ready to pay for success: "When I want anyone," he said, "I don't make too fine a point about it; I would kiss his ——"'[62]

As the reader mulls over the evidence for this sixth criterion, it is only fair to reveal that, along with the first two standards of Narcissistic Personality Disorder, this benchmark was the easiest to assess. There are numerous examples of Napoleon's politically astute actions, small and large, that were done purposely so that they would be recalled by generations: standing guard for the sleeping grenadier, moving plague victims in Jaffa, pinching cheeks, offering snuff, recalling names of particular soldiers, etc. Napoleon knew how to bend a man to do his will. After reading more than 40 examples, described by the psychologists as 'clear' and 'enlightening,' the team unanimously determined that Napoleon appeared to present the required behaviours.

58 De Bourrienne, *Memoirs of Napoleon Bonaparte*, Vol. II, p.53.
59 Gourgaud, *Talks of Napoleon*, p.70.
60 De Bourrienne, *Memoirs of Napoleon Bonaparte*, Vol. II, p.132.
61 Caulaincourt, *With Napoleon in Russia*, pp.25, 55.
62 Caulaincourt, *With Napoleon in Russia*, pp.27–28.

7. Lacks empathy: is unwilling to recognise or identify with the feelings and needs of others.

This proved to be a particularly revealing and straightforward appraisal.

- In 1784, when Napoleon was 15 years old, his brother Lucien followed Napoleone, as he spelled his name at the time, to the military college at Brienne. There Lucien stated that Napoleone received him 'without the slightest show of tenderness … there was nothing amiable in his manner, either towards me or towards the other comrades of his age who did not like him.'[63]
- When asked by de Bourrienne about his decision at Jaffa in 1799, when he ordered the killing of somewhere between 3,000 and 4,500 prisoners of war, Napoleon said, 'It is not true that there were so many. I ordered about a thousand or twelve hundred to be shot, which was done … Indeed, to have acted otherwise than I did would probably have caused the destruction of my whole army.'[64]
- De Bourrienne wrote objectively about Napoleon's apparent tendencies to mistreat others: 'In his social relations Bonaparte's temper was bad … His violent language and bitter imprecations were frequently premeditated. When he was going to reprimand anyone he liked to have a witness present [to give him confidence]. He would then say the harshest things, and level blows against which few could bear up.'[65] To Napoleon's credit, de Bourrienne noted that Napoleon's 'fits of ill-humour passed away like a cloud, and spent themselves in words.'[66]
- In 1800, when he was 31, Napoleon shared with de Bourrienne his worldview regarding emotional intimacies: 'Friendship is but a name; I love nobody. I do not even love my brothers. Perhaps Joseph, a little, from habit. For my part, I know very well that I have no true friends. As long as I continue what I am, I may have as many pretend friends as I please. Leave sensibility to women.'[67]
- On St. Helena, Napoleon told Las Cases, with apparent relish 10 years after the fact, the sad circumstances of Louis-Alexandre Berthier, a *maréchal* of the Empire and his chief of staff. Berthier's plight concerned his wish to marry Madame Visconti, whose husband still lived. Napoleon convinced Berthier to marry a Bavarian princess in 1808, instead, which he reluctantly did. Then Madame Visconti's husband died, leaving her free. Las Cases recalled that Madame Visconti and Berthier 'were inconsolable. Berthier came with tears in his eyes to communicate his wretched fate to the Emperor, who laughed

---

63 Zamoyski, *Napoleon: A Life*, p.28. This was recalled years later by an embittered Lucien, whose recollections might have been inflammatory. Or, perhaps, this was how Napoleon routinely treated others.

64 De Bourrienne, *Memoirs of Napoleon Bonaparte*, Vol. I, pp.180–181. Napoleon's defense falls short on all counts, as his army had more than enough grain to feed and soldiers to guard the prisoners. His army was in no immediate danger. He was trying to justify his conduct, which given the rules of war then, or since, was unlawful. See Major Brian Carr, 'Napoleon Bonaparte's Decision to Execute Ottoman Prisoners of War was a War Crime at the Siege of Jaffa in 1799' (unpublsihed, 2020). This extraordinarily precise and convincing paper deconstructs all of Napoleon's excuses.

65 De Bourrienne, *Memoirs of Napoleon Bonaparte*, Vol. I, p.287.

66 De Bourrienne, *Memoirs of Napoleon Bonaparte*, Vol. I, p.287.

67 De Bourrienne, *Memoirs of Napoleon Bonaparte*, Vol. I, p.287.

at his misfortune. "To what a miserable condition," he exclaimed, "was he [Berthier] reduced; with a little more constancy, Madame V... might have been his wife!"'[68]

- Only once in the material examined for this study did Napoleon show real emotion for someone. This occurred after Jean Lannes, his daring *maréchal*, died in 1809. Joseph Fouché, Napoleon's Minister of Police, wrote that Lannes was 'the only friend of Napoleon who remained capable of telling him the truth.'[69] Charles-Louis Cadet de Gassicourt, the Emperor's personal pharmacist, observed the death scene, recording that even when he was dying, Lannes warned Napoleon that 'insatiable ambition will end you; you sacrificed unnecessarily, without care, without regrets.' He told Napoleon that: 'Your ingratitude keeps away from yourself those who admire you; you only have around you "flatterers"; I don't see a friend who dares to tell you the truth'... The marshal, in finishing, extended his hand to him, and the Emperor kissed him crying.[70]
- This exception, aside, what Napoleon does not say to any of his secretaries speaks volumes: during his time at St. Helena he never mentions the million men who died under his command. He expresses no acknowledgment of their service or sacrifice, no remorse for spending their lives, no regret that his naked ambitions had caused France to pay the ferryman so many times, over all those years.

The reader may be taken back, as we were, by the starkness of Napoleon's antipathy. This is the same leader who offered pensions, soldier homes, medical treatment, medals, and made the men proud of their service. One is left to decide: was he authentic in his sentiments underlying these emoluments or was he so lacking in empathy that he used these remunerations strictly to entice the soldiers to do his bidding and revere him, as might a master manipulator. After all, none of the perks were paid to dead soldiers. This appears to be a very strong trait in Napoleon's personality. What is staggering is the loyalty shown by so many of his soldiers to a man who seemed to care little about their fate, or that of hundreds of thousands of combatants and civilians. Because we found 40 additional passages that were illuminating, the psychologists agreed, to a person, that they thought it highly likely that Napoleon lacked empathy, qualifying him for this seventh category.

8. Is often envious of others or believes that others are envious of him or her.

Below is the passage that comes closest to illustrating criterion 8, although it might speak to Napoleon's feelings of grandiosity, as well.

68 Las Cases, *Memorial de Sainte Helene*, Vol. III Part V, p.22.

69 Joseph Fouché, *Mémoires de Joseph Fouché, duc d'Otrante, ministre de la police générale* (Paris: Chez Le Rouge Libraire, 1824) p.387. *'Lannes, le seul ami de Napoléon qui fût resté en possession de lui dire la vérité.'*

70 Charles-Louis Cadet de Gassicourt, *Voyage en Autriche, en Moravie et en Bavière fait à la suite de l'armée française pendant la campagne de 1809* (Paris: Chez L'Huillier Libraire, 1818) p.127. *'Ton ambition insatiable te perdra; tu sacri fies sans nécessité, sans ménagement, sans regrets, les hommes qui te servent le mieux . Ton ingratitude éloigne de toi ceux – mêmes qui l ' admirent; tu ' as plus autour de toi que des flatteurs; je ne vois pas un ami qui ose te dire la vérité.* Translations by author.

- Napoleon recounted to Las Cases on St. Helena that '... everybody has loved me and hated me: everyone has been for me and against me by turns. I may truly say that there is not a single Frenchman in whom I have not excited interest. All must have loved me ... I was like the sun crossing the equator ... I was blessed and adored ... but when I departed, when I was no longer understood, unfavourable sentiments arose.'[71]

Owing to the fact that we uncovered only four examples, none of them clear or insightful, the reader is correct in assuming that the team cleared Napoleon of meeting the requirements for this benchmark.

9. Shows arrogant, haughty behaviours or attitudes.

For this last standard, Napoleon presented scores of examples.

- De Bourrienne wrote down the following episode in Egypt in 1799, regarding the 4,000 prisoners captured during the siege of Jaffa: 'I was walking with General Bonaparte, in front of his tent, when he beheld this mass of men approaching, and before he even saw his *aide de camp* he said to me, in a tone of profound sorrow, "What do they wish me to do with these men? Have I food for them? – ships to convey them to Egypt or France? Why in the devil's name, have they served me thus? ... [to his aides] It was your duty to die rather than bring these unfortunates to me. What do you want me to do with them?" These words were pronounced in the most angry tone.'[72] The prisoners were all shot six days later.
- De Bourrienne commented that as early as 1800, Napoleon exhibited regular condescending and disdainful behaviours: 'Gallantry to women was by no means a trait in Bonaparte's character. He seldom said anything agreeable to females, and he frequently addressed to them the rudest and most extraordinary remarks. To one he would say, "Heavens, how red your elbows are!" To another, "What an ugly head-dress you have got!" At another time he would say, "Your dress is not the cleanest ... Do you ever change your gown? I have seen you in that twenty times!"'[73]
- That same year, de Bourrienne noted what was an obviously hasty intelligence report put together by *Général de brigade* Jean-Andoche Junot that was in part false but also more truthful than Napoleon wanted known regarding his ambitions to be First Consul. De Bourrienne shared the bulletin with Napoleon and observed him erupt: '"What an ass that Junot is"– "It is a long time that I have known that ... Tell him to come here." When Junot appeared [with others present] Bonaparte began – "Imbecile that you are! How could you send me such reports as these? Do you not read them?"'[74]
- On the trek into Russia, Caulaincourt preserved a revealing moment, recording Napoleon's reaction as much of Smolensk was burning to the ground: '"An eruption of

71 Las Cases, *Memorial de Sainte Helene*, Vol. III Part VI, p.9.
72 De Bourrienne, *Memoirs of Napoleon Bonaparte*, Vol. I, pp.177–179.
73 De Bourrienne, *Memoirs of Napoleon Bonaparte*, Vol. I, pp.180–181.
74 De Bourrienne, *Memoirs of Napoleon Bonaparte*, Vol. I, pp.328–330.

Vesuvius!" shouted the Emperor, clapping me on the shoulder and waking me from my stupor. "Isn't that a fine sight [he asked], *Monsieur le Grand Ecuyer*?" "Horrible, Sire!" [I responded.] "Bah!" he said. "Gentlemen, remember the words of a Roman Emperor: 'A dead enemy always smells sweet!'"[75]

- Napoleon reflected on his understanding of religion, conveying his contradictory ideas to Gourgaud on St. Helena: 'I have dictated thirty pages on the world's three religions; and I have read the Bible. My own opinion is made up. I do not think Jesus Christ ever existed. I would believe in the Christian religion if it dated from the beginning of the world. That Socrates, Plato, the Mohammedan, and all the English should be damned is too absurd. Jesus was probably put to death, like many other fanatics who proclaimed themselves to be prophets or the expected Messiah.'[76]
- The number of instances in which Napoleon blamed his officers for his losses and exile are legion. In Gourgaud's work, alone, there are 31 pages wherein Napoleon espoused the rightness of his conduct, while he excoriated his generals and marshals, vilifying them for his failures.[77]
- In early 1809, Napoleon was in a state of prolonged pique after discovering letters by Joseph Fouché, Napoleon's Minister of Police, and Charles Maurice de Talleyrand, his former Foreign Minister, that laid out contingency plans should Napoleon be killed, communiqués that united these two rivals. After a parade and while in council, Napoleon suddenly lost his temper and rounded on Talleyrand: 'You are a thief, a coward, a man without faith, you do not believe in God ... you would sell your father. I have showered you with good things, and there is nothing you can do against me ... Here, sir, you are nothing but shit in a silk stocking.'[78]

Appraising these passages, the reader must determine whether the actions exhibited therein may be attributed to the expected behaviours of someone sitting on a throne or, on the other hand, more likely ascribed to an individual of an exceptionally conceited and disdainful nature. Our research uncovered an additional 80 examples, leading the team to conclude, with no dissenting voices, that it is highly probable that Napoleon's behaviours meet the requirements for this last criterion.

75 Caulaincourt, *With Napoleon in Russia*, p.77.

76 Gourgaud, *Talks of Napoleon*, pp.276–277. The inherent oddness and nonlinear logic of this passage makes one wonder about Napoleon's mental state at the time.

77 Gourgaud, *Talks of Napoleon*, pp.118, 163–165, 185–190, 206–228, 264–265, 276–277.

78 Emmanuel de Waresquiel, *Talleyrand, Le Prince Immobile* (Paris: Le grand livre du mois, 2003) p.400. *'Vous êtes un voleur, un lâche, un homme sans foi, vous ne croyez pas de Dieu; ... vous vendriez votre père. Je vous ai comblé de biens, et il n'y a rien dont vous soyez capable contre moi ... Tenez, monsieur, vous n'êtes que de la merde dans un bas de soie.'* Translation by author. Waresquiel then hedges his bet, admitting that Napoleon may or may not have said this, but certainly thought it. These letters outlined plans to place Joachim Murat on the throne should Napoleon expire on campaign. The documents also detailed potentialities for Fouché and Talleyrand should this come to pass. One might better understand Napoleon's anger had these men been plotting against him. They were not; yet even the hint of anything other than absolute loyalty was enough for Napoleon to publicly embarrass Talleyrand.

Final clinical assessments by the team of psychologists

The following table shows the degree to which the five independent diagnoses were aligned. After deliberation, it became clear that Napoleon had personality traits that could be construed as meeting the standards for a Narcissistic Personality Disorder diagnosis. Napoleon exhibited behaviours in seven categories, two more than the DSM-5 requires for identifying someone with this disorder. This conclusion came only after sharing assessments, careful debate, and the recognition of the limits of this study, acknowledging that the team members were never in the room with Napoleon and that the appraisal could never be definitive.

Even this tentative judgment brought with it a recognition that Narcissistic Personality Disorder quite possibly had an enormous impact on Napoleon, colouring every relationship, interaction, and decision. Considering Napoleon's stature and historical import, the team, almost reluctantly, came to this diagnosis, largely because the evidence for each criterion was usually overwhelming, in content and quantity.

Table 1.1: Judgements of the Army psychologists who participated in this study

Traits	1 Grandiose	2 Fantasies of unlimited success, love...	3 Believes he/she is special	4 Requires excessive admiration	5 Has a sense of entitlement	6 Interpersonally exploitative	7 Lack Empathy	8 Envious	9 Arrogant
Razuri	✓	✓	✓		✓	✓	✓	✓	✓
Schrader	✓	✓	✓	✓	✓	✓	✓	✓	✓
Krauss	✓	✓	✓		✓	✓	✓	✓	✓
Ford	✓	✓	✓		✓	✓	✓	✓	✓
Preston	✓	✓	✓		✓	✓	✓	✓	✓

There is an irony that is an inherent part of this disorder: the individual is outwardly so haughty, but internally so vulnerable. He/she are susceptible to narcissistic injuries, which are perceived threats to the person's perceptions of self or his/her world construct. The Mayo Clinic provides a key piece of information regarding the narcissist's fragile mental make-up, noting that 'People with narcissistic personality disorder have trouble handling anything they perceive as criticism, and they can:

- Become impatient or angry when they do not receive special treatment*
- Have significant interpersonal problems and easily feel slighted*
- React with rage or contempt and try to belittle the other person to make themselves appear superior*
- Have difficulty regulating emotions and behaviour*
- Experience major problems dealing with stress and adapting to change
- Feel depressed and moody because they fall short of perfection*
- Have secret feelings of insecurity, shame, vulnerability and humiliation'*[79]

79 N.A., 'Narcissistic Personality Disorder,' Mayo Clinic, <https://www.mayoclinic.org/diseases-conditions/narcissistic-personality-disorder/symptoms-causes/syc-20366662>, accessed 8 July 2020.

The asterisked statements seem to apply to Napoleon. One of the team members, Major Stacey Krauss, focused on a person's inability to cope with any sort of negative feedback, writing, 'There is a section from the DSM-5 specific to Narcissistic Injury. It is of interest as a potential consideration: true depression upon exile versus massive narcissistic injury or perhaps both, which is the direction in which I would lean. The DSM-5 states that 'Vulnerability in self-esteem makes individuals with narcissistic personality disorder very sensitive to "injury" from criticism or defeat. Although they may not show it outwardly, criticism may haunt these individuals and may leave them feeling humiliated, degraded, hollow, and empty. They may react with disdain, rage, or defiant counterattack.'[80]

Napoleon certainly seemed to have behaved in ways that line up the symptoms starred above. It was important, though, to distinguish this disease from other similar ailments. The DSM-5 notes that 'The most useful feature in discriminating narcissistic personality disorder from histrionic, antisocial, and borderline personality disorders, in which the interactive styles are coquettish, callous, and needy, respectively, is the *grandiosity characteristic* of narcissistic personality disorder.'[81] This was the delineating characteristic, one that Napoleon manifested from an early age and throughout his life. Why this should matter from a historical standpoint will be addressed in the conclusion, as the team considered much more than Napoleon's Narcissistic Personality Disorder issues.

The original purpose of this work was to determine whether Napoleon may have been burdened by Post Traumatic Stress Disorder, given that he was at war, almost continuously, for nearly two decades. Due to the complexity of this disease, the APA presents the pathology of the disease in great detail, running two full pages.[82] We were surprised at how few of the criteria applied to Napoleon, even though he experienced, repeatedly, the first two major criteria: '1. Directly experiencing the traumatic event(s). 2. Witnessing, in person, the event(s) as it occurred to others.'[83] Napoleon seemed to exhibit symptoms related to only three of the sub-standards, out of a possible 24, far fewer than we originally surmised: '1. Irritable behaviour and angry outbursts (with little or no provocation) typically expressed as verbal or physical aggression toward people or objects'; '2. Reckless or self-destructive behaviour'; and '6. Sleep disturbance (e.g., difficulty falling or staying asleep or restless sleep).'[84]

Napoleon, though, appeared to have few to none of the dreams, flashbacks, or distress when presented certain stimuli related to the battlefield; he never seemed unable to articulate events related to the initiating trauma [dissociative amnesia], exhibit 'persistent and exaggerated negative beliefs [about self or others],' or, of particular interest, experience a 'persistent negative emotional state (e.g., fear, horror, anger, guilt, or shame).'[85] Napoleon gave the impression that he was free of all these symptoms. Neither did he present either of

80 Major Stacey Krauss, email to author, 'RE: Progress on that troublesome patient, Napoleon,' 12 June 2019. APA, *Diagnostic and Statistical Manual of Mental Disorders*, p.671.
81 APA, *Diagnostic and Statistical Manual of Mental Disorders*, p.672. Italics added by author.
82 APA, *Diagnostic and Statistical Manual of Mental Disorders*, pp.271-272.
83 APA, *Diagnostic and Statistical Manual of Mental Disorders*, p.271. This differentiates personally enduring the traumas of war and observing others experiencing its horrors.
84 APA, *Diagnostic and Statistical Manual of Mental Disorders*, p.272.
85 APA, *Diagnostic and Statistical Manual of Mental Disorders*, p.272.

the required dissociative indicators: 'Depersonalization: Persistent or recurrent experiences of feeling detached' or 'Derealization: Persistent or recurrent experiences of unreality of surroundings ...'[86] This is especially astounding given that Napoleon personally experienced at least 21 close calls in combat or on campaign, not to mention seeing, first hand, the battle carnage inflicted on the millions of wounded and dead soldiers, friendly and foe alike, during his decades at war.[87]

This gave the team of psychologists pause, as somewhere between 11 to 20 percent of the soldiers in the American Army, today, present symptoms consistent with PTSD.[88] They deemed it highly unusual, if not impossible, for an individual to experience war for so many years and not be traumatised. We shared potential explanations for this disconnect and wondered if we were missing some key underlying factor that allowed Napoleon to escape the kinds of psychological damage usually related to prolonged exposure to war. We were. What we had overlooked was that a near-total lack of empathy acted to shield Napoleon from the kinds of sadness, regret, and guilt that most soldiers experience. This human failing, this inability, according to *Psychology Today*, to 'experience another person's point of view, rather than just one's own' and which is 'crucial for establishing relationships and behaving compassionately' protected Napoleon's psyche.[89] The more than 80 examples that were gathered for criterion 7 of Narcissistic Personality Disorder ('Lacks empathy') revealed that Napoleon presented behaviours consistent with this benchmark; this flaw in his emotional make-up meant that the needs and experiences of others did not have a significant impact on his emotional state. This helps explain how he avoided being wracked by remorse at St. Helena for all the deaths, French and otherwise, caused by his choice of using warfare as his favourite instrument of national power to achieve his ambitions. Such a revelation merits further examination by Napoleonic scholars.

In addition, four of the psychologists independently came to the conclusion, from their reading of the passages related to Napoleon and Narcissistic Personality Disorder, that he was likely somewhere on the bipolar-depression continuum.[90] The APA defines the manic side of this illness as: 'A distinct period of abnormally and persistently elevated, expansive, or irritable mood and abnormally and persistently increased goal-directed activity or energy ... [that includes] mood disturbance and increased energy or activity ... Inflated self-esteem or grandiosity... Decreased need for sleep (e.g., feels rested after only 3 hours of sleep)... More talkative than usual ... Increase in goal-directed activity (either socially, at work or school, or sexually) or psychomotor agitation ... Excessive involvement in activities that have a

86 APA, *Diagnostic and Statistical Manual of Mental Disorders*, p.272.

87 The list ran from the siege of Toulon in 1793, where he was slashed in the head with a bayonet, through to 1814 when he walked his horse over an unexploded shell, losing his horse but not his life. It is estimated that Napoleon had approximately a score of horses killed under him during battle.

88 'Operations Iraqi Freedom (OIF) and Enduring Freedom (OEF): About 11–20 out of every 100 Veterans (or between 11–20%) who served in OIF or OEF have PTSD in a given year.' U.S. Department of Veterans Affairs, PTSD: National Center for PTSD, 'How Common is PTSD in Veterans?' <https://www.ptsd.va.gov/understand/common/common_veterans.asp>, accessed 7 July 2020.

89 Anon, 'Empathy,' *Psychology Today*, <https://www.psychologytoday.com/us/basics/empathy>, accessed 8 July 2020. Also, see APA, *Diagnostic and Statistical Manual for Mental Disorders*, p.670.

90 The fifth psychologist did not disagree; she just did not respond to our emails regarding this topic. Army officers are always busy.

high potential for painful consequences, among other symptoms.'[91] These descriptions seem to include some of the behaviours outlined in the first three criteria of the Narcissistic Personality Disorder (grandiosity, fantasies of unlimited success and power, belief that he is special/unique). It is, perhaps, within the realm of possibility that some of Napoleon's drive and related successes may have been related, in part, to manic episodes. Louis-Mathieu Molé, the French statesman, may have touched on the manic side of Napoleon, remarking that, 'The strange thing is that Napoleon, whose common sense was equal to that of a genius, could never discern at which point possibility ended.'[92] This seems an apt description of the main problem undermining his Russian campaign, in particular, and his diplomacy and attempted alliances with European allies and enemies, in general.

There was also a Major Depressive aspect present. The APA's clinical definition is as follows: 'Depressed mood most of the day, nearly every day ... Markedly diminished interest or pleasure in all, or almost all, activities most of the day ... Insomnia or hypersomnia ... Fatigue or loss of energy nearly every day.'[93] The historical record provides some insights. Behaviours meeting those in the APA's diagnostic criteria for 'Depressive Disorder,' seemed to be manifested with great frequency. Napoleon showed flashes of uncontrolled anger dating back to 1797, throughout the Egyptian campaign, and well into the 19th-century.[94] He also exhibited swift shifts in his moods as early as 1799 while he was in Egypt. He could also be violent with a subordinate who had displeased him.[95] He slept little and refused food. He slipped into ennui during the Battle of Borodino, in 1812, for example.[96] He did almost nothing near the end of the Leipzig campaign a year later, even as the French army was being entrapped. Antoine Marie Chamans, Comte de Lavalette, wrote that he found Napoleon 'so prostrate, so despondent, that I was horrified.'[97] During the campaign Napoleon prevented French cavalry from routing by moving his mount directly over a shell that had landed in their midst. His horse was disemboweled, but he was untouched.[98] This may have been an effort to commit suicide. Napoleon also twice attempted suicide with poison, once on the Russian campaign and another time after losing at Leipzig in 1814.[99]

Before the Battle of Waterloo in 1815, August Petiet, the *Adjoint* of the Imperial Headquarters was struck by Napoleon's physical condition: '... no soldier of his army could understand how a body so frail, and an appearance so sickly could survive such fatigues!'[100] During the battle, Napoleon appears to have issued few orders and slipped into inactivity,

91 APA, *Diagnostic and Statistical Manual for Mental Disorders*, p.124. Psychomotor agitation includes fidgeting, pacing, talking quickly, among other symptoms.

92 Zamoyski, *Napoleon: A Life*, p.599.

93 APA, *Diagnostic and Statistical Manual for Mental Disorders*, p.125.

94 Gourgaud, *Talks of Napoleon*, p.63; De Bourrienne, *Memoirs of Napoleon Bonaparte*, Vol. I, pp.140, 287, 329–330.

95 De Bourrienne, *Memoirs of Napoleon Bonaparte*, Vol. I, p.193.

96 Zamoyski, *Napoleon: A Life*, pp.546–547.

97 Zamoyski, *Napoleon: A Life*, pp.596–597.

98 Zamoyski, *Napoleon: A Life*, p.606.

99 Charles de Montholon, *Récits de la captivité de l'empereur Napoléon à Sainte-Hélène* (Paris: Paulin, Libraire-Editeur, 1847), Vol. II, pp.418–419. Both times he was administered emetics, which saved his life. The strength of the poisons he took has been questioned. Nevertheless, in the second instance aides took no chances and quietly took away Napoleon's pistols. Zamoyski, *Napoleon: A Life*, pp.616–617.

100 Andrew Field, *Waterloo: The French Perspective* (Barnsley: Pen and Sword Military, 2012) p.56.

allowing *Maréchal* Michel Ney to make most of the tactical decisions, while Napoleon sat exhausted, sometimes with tears running down his cheeks.[101] He was unable to concentrate; he was depressed and lifeless.[102] There are scores of recollections that Napoleon was prone to enervation; Jean-Paul Kauffmann writes that Napoleon at St. Helena 'spent most of his day alone in his room, leafing through a few books or more often than not, doing nothing ... It was easy to see that he no longer had any preoccupation with the future, did not reflect on the past, nor care about the present.'[103] Napoleon's private secretaries noted Napoleon's mood cycles, expressing energy one day and disinterest with life the next, as well as his bouts of chronic pain. Las Cases, in particular, recorded dozens of these episodes.[104]

Because all these behavioural episodes appear to align with those delineated in the DSM-5 for bipolar-depression or Major Depressive Disorder, it would be fair to speculate that Napoleon may have struggled with one or both of these mental illnesses, in addition to Narcissistic Personality Disorder. The psychologists certainly believed that this was a real possibility.

Lieutenant Colonel Sam Preston wrote: 'Though I do not know enough about Napoleon to make a formal read, my hunch is that the dissociation and depression he had leading up to his final defeat was associated with the realization that he was not omnipotent and quite mortal. Without that belief, he went forward with insincerity. The legend around him was simply too great. He had dug himself so far into a hole with his (now false) beliefs of his historical legacy and his near-godlike abilities; he had no choice but to move forward, however diminished. There was no escape, no opting-out. He failed at suicide, twice.'[105]

Major Stacey Krauss, concurred: 'With Napoleon's suspected prevailing diagnosis, he was [psychologically self-] tortured at St. Helena. Largely, the symptoms represent anhedonia (lack of pleasure in typically enjoyed activities), visible psychomotor slowing (it is obvious to the layperson observer that he seems behaviourally inert), persistent depressed mood, diminished sleep and appetite, concentration problems (which seem to be unique to the periods of low mood), and suicidality ...'[106]

---

101 Zamoyski, *Napoleon: A Life*, p.643; David Chandler, *The Campaigns of Napoleon* (New York: Macmillan, 1966) p.1084; Mark Atkin, *The Waterloo Companion* (London: Stackpole Books, 2001) p.79. There remains a small controversy as to the degree of Napoleon impairment that day. Charles Esdaile and Gareth Glover argue against any real issues. The first-hand accounts of Napoleon's behaviour that day, however, would seem to lean towards him experiencing some of the euphoria, irritability, loss of energy and focus, and other symptoms of bi-polar disorder or, possibly, Major Depressive Disorder. This is not meant to imply that Napoleon was incapacitated, just that he was, quite possibly, diminished. There is little doubt from various other witnessed accounts that he was just physically and mentally exhausted on 18 June.

102 Zamoyski, *Napoleon: A Life*, p.644; Field, pp.50-51.

103 Jean-Paul Kauffmann, *The Black Room at Longwood* (New York: Four Walls Eight Windows, 1999) p.xv.

104 De Bourrienne, *Memoirs of Napoleon Bonaparte*, Vol. I, p.193; Gourgaud, *Talks of Napoleon*, pp.47, 63, 245, 249, 265, 266; Las Cases, *Memorial de Sainte Helene*, Vol. II, pp.151, 165, 182, 247, 249, 253; Part V, 23, 70–71, 91, 94, 161, 187, 233, 234–235, 238; Part VI, 8, 20, 101, 146, 366.

105 Lieutenant Colonel Sam Preston, email to author, 'RE: Progress on that troublesome patient, Napoleon,' 19 May 2019.

106 Kraus, emails to author, 'RE: Progress on that troublesome patient, Napoleon,' 26–27 June and 'RE: Napoleon,' 3 July 2019.

Major Patricia Razuri also affirmed the findings of her colleagues: 'He seems to meet the diagnosis for a Major Depressive Disorder. I believe the more prudent working diagnosis would be an Unspecified Depressive Disorder to account for the other possible aetiologies. The text provided indicates a fragile ego who built grandiose personal defences to protect him from some reality or shortcoming. When epically defeated, reality set-in, his humanity exposed, and the shredding of his defences likely resulted in his suicidal depression.'[107]

Major Angela Shrader agreed, writing that, 'There were signs and symptoms of depression noted in many of the examples. These aspects stood out: long-standing sleep issues; attempts to harm self on multiple occasions; mood disturbances ('melancholy'); descriptions of poor self-care; chronic pain; and many instances of anger/explosive outbursts.'[108]

This tentative diagnosis emerged concomitantly as the team considered the possibilities that Traumatic Brain Injury (TBI) may have played a role in some of Napoleon's behaviours. Mild to major neurocognitive issues can be caused by impacts to the head, which damage the brain at the collision point, but also to other areas as the brain, as well, when it is driven into the skull case on the side opposite the original blow, such as in a car wreck when rapid and sudden deceleration propels the brain against the cranium. The APA's guidelines state that in addition to 'neurocognitive deficits, there may be associated neurophysiological, emotional, and behavioural complications.[109]

The duration of the loss of consciousness helps determine the severity of related symptoms. Less than 30 minutes is classified as *mild* severity, with related neurocognitive issues usually clearing up in days to weeks, with three months being the metric for near-full recovery. Unconsciousness lasting from 30 minutes to a full day is categorised as a *moderate* TBI episode; in this case, up to two years may needed to recovery, with the chance that there may be some permanent deficits. The APA warns, 'With moderate and severe TBI [being knocked out for more than 24 hours] … [side effects] include seizures (particularly in the first year), photosensitivity, hyperacusis, irritability, aggression, depression, sleep disturbance, fatigue, apathy, inability to resume occupational and social functioning at pre-injury level, and deterioration in interpersonal relationships. Moderate and severe TBI have been associated with increased risk of depression, aggression, and possibly neurodegenerative diseases such as Alzheimer's disease.'[110]

Napoleon is known to have been knocked out at least twice, once for an extended period. The first incident occurred on 30 October 1799, just 10 days before the Coup of 18 *Brumaire* saw the overthrow of the Directory, replaced by the Consulate, and the rise of Napoleon to First Consul. In this case, Napoleon's horse stumbled, throwing him violently to the ground. He lost consciousness for several hours. When he regained himself, he brushed off the incident and returned to Paris for a dinner with Paul Barras, who was attempting to win Napoleon's support in the upcoming coup. Napoleon reacted violently and declined further dealings. They made amends the next day, but even then Napoleon complained of physical and mental exhaustion, which he blamed on the Egyptian campaign.[111] Instead, it might

107 Major Patricia Razuri, email to author, 'RE: Progress,' 20 June 2019.
108 Major Angela Shrader, email to author, 'RE: Napoleon,' 10 June 2019.
109 APA, *Diagnostic and Statistical Manual for Mental Disorders*, p.626.
110 APA, *Diagnostic and Statistical Manual for Mental Disorders*, p.626.
111 Zamoyski, *Napoleon: A Life*, p.226.

be conjectured that this outburst, and even possibly Napoleon's erratic behaviour and near psychological collapse during the coup, could be the result of TBI, for as the APA outlines, 'Neurobehavioural symptoms tend to be most severe in the immediate aftermath of the TBI.'[112] The long-term effects of this moderate concussion could have debilitated Napoleon for the rest of his life. No one who suffers such an accident can avoid some short and long term deterioration in physical, affective, and cognitive capacities.

The second instance in 1803 at St. Cloud was triggered when Napoleon insisted he could drive his six-horse calash (carriage). The horses were startled by an aide and, as Napoleon related to Las Cases on St Helena, 'set off at full speed, and the calash which rolled along with extreme velocity, struck a railing. The Emperor was thrown out to the distance of eight or 10 feet, and lay stretched on the ground with his face downwards. He was, he said, dead for a few seconds. He felt the moment at which his life became extinct ...'[113] In this case, a light touch brought Napoleon back to consciousness. Even so, this constituted a mild concussion, which are serious events because they can engender long-term neuro-physiological issues.[114] Because the outcomes of a concussion were not understood at the time of Napoleon's injuries, no one looked for or recorded changes in his behaviour. Nevertheless, this offers a tantalizing insight into Napoleon's psychological make-up over time. One can only speculate that TBI may have played a role in Napoleon's declining psychological state.

The team held one surprise for the end, one that was unexpected to say the least. The psychologists were troubled by several of Napoleon's behaviours that resulted in his tentative Narcissistic Personality Disorder diagnosis but that were also underlying symptoms for Antisocial Personality Disorder, which was formerly referred to as *sociopathy* or *psychopathy*. The APA defines this illness as 'A pervasive pattern of disregard for and violation of the rights of others, occurring since age 15 years, as indicated by three (or more) of ...' seven criteria.[115] Napoleon, the team indicated, exhibited behaviours possibly aligning with four of them, which was not anticipated. The four were:

1. Deceitfulness, as indicated by repeated lying, use of aliases, or conning others for personal profit or pleasure.
2. Irritability and aggressiveness.
3. Reckless disregard for safety of self or others.

112 APA, p.626. See Gueniffey, *Bonaparte*, pp.552–569.

113 Las Cases, *Memorial de Sainte Helene*, Vol. II p.168. Napoleon was also thrown violently from his horse several times. One does not need to be knocked unconscious to have TBI issues. Micro-concussions, as they are called, can result from blows to the head, the 'seeing stars' episodes or what is now called 'shaken brain' syndrome, that soldiers and athletes have been ignoring until recently. Thus, it is possible that Napoleon experienced other head traumas in addition to the two mentioned. See Jeff Victoroff and Erin D. Bigler, (eds.), *Concussion and Traumatic Encephalopathy: Causes, Diagnosis and Management* (Cambridge: Cambridge University Press, 2019).

114 Dr. Alex Bornstein, Neuroscience Department, The Ohio State University Wexner Medical Center, explained that once a patient experiences a concussion, they are twice as likely to have a second concussion, and four times as likely to have a third due to the damage caused to the delicate fibers anchoring the brain to the skull. Interview with author, 12 December 2005.

115 APA, *Diagnostic and Statistical Manual for Mental Disorders*, p.659.

4. Lack of remorse, as indicated by being indifferent to or rationalizing having hurt, mistreated, or stolen from another.[116]

The psychologists, however, cautioned that there is often a comorbidity between Narcissistic Personality Disorder and Antisocial Personality Disorder and that Napoleon's behaviours matching the third criterion were borderline and difficult to gauge; there was more conjecture, here, than in other evaluations. Still, Napoleon's actions seem to meet three benchmarks. While the team thought it unlikely that Napoleon presented for this disorder, the group believed it important to consider the historical evidence and acknowledge the possibility. Two team members thought this was worth exploring. Without further substantiation, though, especially during Napoleon's teenage years, the team was reluctant to assign this affliction to Napoleon.

It has been posited, all too often, that Napoleon exhibited a stable personality throughout his reign. He is portrayed as a man of unwavering intellectual prowess and emotional actualization. The most renowned biographies of Napoleon all have one thing in common: they largely overlook deviations in Napoleon's cognitive, affective, or psychomotor functioning, either in the moment or over time.[117] Few of these works explore underlying psychological causes for Napoleon's behaviours when he deviated from the norm, and deviate he did, as we have seen. His dynamism, charm, impatience, violent temper, mood swings, sleeplessness, manic-depressive episodes, and inability or unwillingness to establish close personal relationships seem to be accepted at face value.[118] Even his suicide attempts somehow manage to acquire a rationale veneer.[119] Napoleon's aberrant behaviours, his 'spectacular fits of rage' are attributed to posturing for 'posterity' or as a means of shifting blame.[120] His propensity to lie when it suited him is mentioned, but not examined, missing this key component of Narcissistic Personality Disorder.[121] Napoleon's defeat at Waterloo is presented as the outcome of a series of what Carl von Clausewitz later termed as 'fictions,' not in any way related to a decline in Napoleon's cognitive and psychological competencies or, possibly, his TBI-related mishaps.[122] His mental and emotional capacities are presented as no different

116 APA, *Diagnostic and Statistical Manual for Mental Disorders*, p.659.

117 The examined works were Chandler, *The Campaigns of Napoleon*; Alan Schom, *Napoleon Bonaparte* (New York: Harper Collins, 1997); Andrew Roberts, *Napoleon: A Life* (New York: Viking, 2014); Gueniffey, *Bonaparte 1769-1802*; and Zamoyski, *Napoleon: A Life*. None of this analysis is meant as criticism. Its purpose is to illustrate that Napoleon's mental state has largely escaped scrutiny even by the best scholars. In addition, some of psychological methodologies used herein are out of the norm in history. In addition, some of the issues are fairly new. TBI, for example, and the ties between concussive events and short and long term cognitive/emotional wellbeing, has only recently become a key consideration in medicine. Due to space limitations, this historiographical analysis has been condensed.

118 Gueniffey, *Bonaparte 1769-1802*, pp.359–360.

119 Roberts, *Napoleon: A Life*, pp.715, 772.

120 Chandler, *The Campaigns of Napoleon*, p.325.

121 Schom, *Napoleon Bonaparte*, pp.30, 163, 177, 179, 389, 568.

122 Carl von Clausewitz, *On War*, edited and translated by Michael Howard and Peter Paret (Princeton: Princeton University Press, 1976) pp.119–121. Schom, *Napoleon Bonaparte*, pp.752–760.

at Waterloo in 1815 than they were at Toulon in 1793.[123] Even when Napoleon's behaviours are described as 'bizarre,' juxtaposing his 'indefatigable' energy against his 'profound, languishing repose,' or when his violent histrionics are explicated in detail, no psychological considerations are proffered as potential explanations for these variations in the emperor's behaviour.[124] This seems to be a missed opportunity to fathom why Napoleon succeeded and why he stumbled. Context would seem to matter a great deal, here, as do Napoleon's possible mental health indicators.

It is assumed that Napoleon's capacity to reason and act was always based on thorough and measured analyses, largely devoid of inhibiting personal eccentricities. By implication, the cult of personality that grew up around him must be an indicator of his unwavering talents, faculty for solving thorny problems, constancy, charisma, and the reciprocating concern and affection between the emperor and those who served him. Napoleon is never portrayed as erratic or damaged, despite all his years at war and the enormity of failed campaigns in Spain and Russia.

This depiction of Napoleon may be as flawed as was the emperor. While it is difficult to ascertain with certitude details about Napoleon's mental state so far removed from the psychologist's examination room, the consensus opinion of five American Army psychologists, using the *Diagnostic and Statistical Manual for Mental Disorders, Fifth Edition*, is that Napoleon likely exhibited behaviours consistent with psychological illnesses as outlined by the APA. Though his lack of empathy may have protected Napoleon from PTSD, he was probably plagued by Narcissistic Personality Disorder, bi-polar or Major Depressive issues, and problems related to possible TBI incidents. These maladies may have impaired, to some extent, his capacity to reason and interact. Understanding that varying degrees of cognitive and emotional impairment may have shaped Napoleon's life, day to day, allows us to examine his words and deeds with some degree of psychological insight, a thing of no little import for readers, soldiers, and historians exploring the enigma that is Napoleon.

Napoleon remains a genius at war, but one more encumbered by psychological limitations than has been previously acknowledged. He was a gifted, charismatic, fragile, and manipulative leader. It is hoped that the material in this chapter might act as a lens for future examinations of this complex and, sometimes, troubled individual.

Bibliography

American Psychological Association. *Diagnostic and Statistical Manual of Mental Disorders, Fifth Edition* (Virginia: American Psychiatric Publishing, 2013)

Atkin, Mark, *The Waterloo Companion* (London: Stackpole Books, 2001)

Bonaparte, Napoleon, *Correspondance générale* (Paris: Fondation Napoléon, 2004–2017)

Chandler, David, *The Campaigns of Napoleon* (New York: Macmillan Company, 1966)

123 Of the five biographers, Zamoyski offers the most insight regarding Napoleon's failings; with a keen eye Zamoyski identifies scores of instances wherein Napoleon's conduct is unusual, troubling, inconsistent, or aberrant. His work, however, misses the connections between these behaviours and Napoleon's possible on-going mental health issues.

124 Schom, *Napoleon Bonaparte*, p.377; Roberts, *Napoleon: A Life*, p.149.

Clausewitz, Carl von. *On War*, edited and translated by Michael Howard and Peter Paret (Princeton: Princeton University Press, 1976)

Constant (Wairy, Louis Constant). *Recollections of the Private Life of Napoleon*, translated by Walter Clark (New York: The Saalfield Pub Co., 1911)

De Bourrienne, Louis Antoine Fauvelet. *Memoirs of Napoleon Bonaparte* (New York: Thomas V. Crowell & Company, 2010)

De Caulaincourt, Armand-Augustin-Louis, George Libaire, Jean Hanoteau (eds) *With Napoleon in Russia: The Memoirs of General de Caulaincourt Duke of Vicenza* (New York: William Morrow and Company, 1935)

De Gassicourt, Charles-Louis Cadet, *Voyage en Autriche, en Moravie et en Bavière fait à la suite de l'armée française pendant la campagne de 1809* (Paris: Chez L'Huillier, Libraire, 1818)

De Waresquiel, Emmanuel, *Talleyrand, Le Prince Immobile* (Paris: Le grand livre du mois, 2003)

Field, Andrew. *Waterloo: The French Perspective.* (Barnsley: Pen and Sword Military, 2012)

Fouché, Joseph, *Mémoires de Joseph Fouché, duc d'Otrante, ministre de la police générale* (Paris: Chez Le Rouge, Libraire, 1824)

François Miot de Melite, André, *Memoirs of Count Miot de Melito, Minister, Ambassador, Councillor of State and member of the Institute of France, between the years 1788 and 1815* (New York: Scribner, 1881)

Gourgaud, Gaspard, *Talks of Napoleon at St. Helena with General Baron Gourgaud: together with the Journal kept by Gourgaud on their Journey from Waterloo to St. Helena*, translated by Elizabeth Wormeley (Chicago: A. C. McClurg & Company, 1904)

Gueniffey, Patrice, *Bonaparte 1769-1802* (London: The Belknap Press of Harvard University Press, 2015)

Kauffmann, Jean-Paul, *The Black Room at Longwood* (New York: Four Walls Eight Windows, 1999)

Kroll, Jerome and Pouncey, Claire, 'The Ethics of APA's Goldwater Rule,' *Journal of the American Academy of Psychiatry and the Law*, 44:2 (June 2016), pp.226–235

Las Cases, Emmanuel-Augustin-Dieudonné-Joseph, *Memorial de Sainte Helene: Journal of the Private Life and Conversations of the Emperor Napoleon at Saint Helena* (London: Forgotten Books, 2015)

Lee, Bandy (ed.), *The Dangerous Case of Donald Trump: 37 Psychiatrists and Mental Health Experts Assess a President* (New York: Thomas Dunne Books, 2017)

Lejeune, Louis-François, *Mémoires du Général Lejeune* (Paris: Librairie de Firmin-Didiot et Cie, 1895)

Marchand, Louis-Joseph, *In Napoleon's Shadow; The Memoirs of Louis-Joseph Marchand, Valet and Friend of the Emperor 1811–1821* (Barnsley: Greenhill Books, 1998)

Marmont, Auguste, *Mémoires du Maréchal Marmont, duc de Ragusé de 1792 à 1841* (Paris: Perrotin, Libraire-Editeur, 1857)

Mollien, François Nicolas comte, Charles Gomel (ed.), *Mémoires d'un Ministre du Trésor Public 1780–1815* (Paris: Guillaumin et Cie, 1898)

Montholon, Charles de, *Récits de la captivité de l'empereur Napoléon à Sainte-Hélène* (Paris: Paulin, Libraire-Editeur, 1847)

Remusat, Claire, *Memoirs of Madame de Rémusat 1802–1808* (New York: D. Appleton and Company, 1880)

Roberts, Andrew, *Napoleon: A Life.* (New York: Viking, 2014)

Schom, Alan, *Napoleon Bonaparte* (New York: Harper Collins, 1997)

Trump, Mary, *Too Much and Never Enough: How My Family Created the World's Most Dangerous Man* (New York: Simon & Schuster, 2020)

Zamoyski, Adam, *Napoleon: A Life* (New York: Basic Books, 2018)

2

'A Melville Expedition': Sir Home Popham's Political Networks and the Walcheren Expedition of 1809

Jacqueline Reiter

Towards the end of July 1809, the little coastal town of Deal in Kent thronged with men taking part in an amphibious expedition to destroy the French navy and dockyards at Flushing, on the Dutch island of Walcheren, and at Antwerp. As one contemporary described it, they formed a part of 'the largest [British] army ever sent to the continent.'[1] This campaign, which went down in history as the Walcheren Expedition, was Britain's main contribution to the Fifth Coalition against Napoleonic France. As part of a treaty of alliance with Austria in May, Britain had pledged to provide her new ally with a £2.5 million down-payment, £400,000 a month in subsidies, and a military diversion.[2] Antwerp, part of the French-controlled Kingdom of Holland, was the second-largest enemy naval base after Toulon and a perennial invasion threat. Focusing on it made strategic sense, and 1809 was neither the first nor the last time Britain focused on the importance of the Scheldt River basin. Nevertheless, the 40,000 troops embarking aboard the 600 vessels attached to the expedition were destined for disaster. A third were struck down by 'Walcheren fever' by mid-September, and one in 10 of the entire force was dead by February.[3]

In July 1809, however, this lay in the future. As might be expected, the majority of the individuals fighting for a billet along the Kentish coast were present in a professional capacity, but many people had made special trips to the coast just to watch the unprecedentedly

---

1 National Records of Scotland (NRS): Melville MSS, GD51/2/412/4, William Budge to Lord Melville, 27 June [1809].

2 Jacqueline Reiter, *The Late Lord: The Life of John Pitt, 2nd Earl of Chatham* (Barnsley: Pen and Sword, 2017), p.100.

3 'Walcheren fever' is thought to have been a combination of malaria, typhus, dysentery, and typhoid. For more, see Martin R. Howard, *Walcheren 1809: The Scandalous Destruction of a British Army* (Barnsley: Pen and Sword, 2011), pp.164–66; see also Gordon C. Bond, *The Grand Expedition* (Athens, GA: University of Georgia Press, 1979), pp.133, 205 n.38.

large armament sail to death or glory. Perhaps more surprisingly, a sizeable group of civilians accompanied the expedition. Some were looking for a safe passage to the continent to pursue their business ventures, such as the merchant David Irving; others were keen to play a military role, like Lord Yarmouth, who volunteered the services of his private yacht to boost the strength of the enormous fleet. Still others were there because they had never had an opportunity to see Antwerp before and were anxious not to miss '*the Fun*'.[4] One of the latter was the 23-year-old Lord Lowther, whose diary and letters home to his father provide a transparent and increasingly petulant window into the manoeuvrings underpinning the ill-fated expedition. These men had one thing in common: they had been invited to join the expedition because they were influential and belonged to strong political and social networks. Lowther, for example, was the son of the Earl of Lonsdale, a prominent Tory peer who controlled nine boroughs in Parliament and was close friends with Lord Mulgrave, the First Lord of the Admiralty.

The individual responsible for the presence of these men was Captain Sir Home Popham of HMS *Venerable*. Popham was perfectly within his rights to invite guests aboard his own ship, but the presence of men like Lowther throughout the early part of the Walcheren campaign – a campaign intended to be swift, stealthy, and above all secret – reveals an interesting facet to Popham's career. Popham was attracted by Lowther's political connections, for he was very much a politician afloat. He had been a Member of Parliament since 1804 and had long-standing ambitions to obtain a seat on the Board of Admiralty, or at least on the Navy Board.[5] He was not unique in this: Evan Wilson points out that 100 naval officers sat in Parliament between 1790 and 1820, but 80% of those officers were likely to have some family interest that had brought them to Parliament.[6] Popham had no such interest. He punched far beyond his weight in terms of his rank and social status, as Walcheren demonstrated extremely well. He corresponded directly with the Secretary of State for War Lord Castlereagh and the military commander, the Earl of Chatham; and yet he was certainly not Captain of the Fleet, as he had been during the Copenhagen expedition of 1807, although many contemporaries assumed he was.[7] As Lord Lowther made clear in a letter to his father, there had been a difficulty in securing Popham's appointment: 'It was supposed that [Lieutenant General] Sir John Hope would have commanded the troops with Sir Richard Strachan as Admiral, and Sir Home Popham as Captain of the Fleet; but this would have borne too much the appearance of a Melville expedition.'[8] In other words, the expedition would have been too closely connected with the 1st Viscount Melville – Strachan's fellow Scotsman, Hope's brother-in-law, and Popham's main political patron.

4 Cumbria Record Office: Lonsdale MSS, DLONS/L1/2/70, Lord Lowther to Lord Lonsdale, [July 1809], emphasis in original.

5 As is clear from NRS: Melville MSS, GD51/1/565, Popham to Lord Melville, 13 January 1806.

6 Evan Wilson, *A Social History of British Naval Officers* (Woodbridge: Boydell and Brewer, 2017), p.118.

7 For example, Sir William Dillon, *A Narrative of my Professional Adventures (1790–1839),* ed. Michael A. Lewis (London: Navy Records Society, 1956), vol.2, p.128; and Robert Stafford Clover in H.G. Thursfield (ed.), *Five Naval Journals, 1789–1817* (London: Navy Records Society, 1951), pp.368–369.

8 Cumbria Record Office: Lonsdale MSS, DLONS/L1/2/70, f.2, extract of a letter enclosed by Lord Lowther to his father, 14 July 1809.

Popham's connection with Melville sits at the heart of this chapter, which aims to illuminate the extent to which political networking buttressed Popham's rise (and fall). He made up for a lack of traditional naval contacts by deliberately laying himself at the disposal of a series of political champions, bringing himself opportunities that might not come the way of normal naval captains through undertaking 'services of a nature distinct and different from the naval service'.[9] However, as the men who protected him fell from grace or died, Popham became increasingly vulnerable, and Walcheren brought this to a head. This 'Melville expedition', which Popham helped plan and execute, brought out the exposed nature of his place both in the Navy (where he had few friends) and in political circles (where he had outlived his usefulness). Popham's experience therefore represents a fascinating vignette into an alternative form of patronage that was not necessarily available to most naval officers, and which relied heavily on Popham remaining both active and useful. Operating at the very edges of political, naval, and even moral respectability, Popham demonstrated all too clearly what could happen to an officer when he stretched those limits to their fullest extent.

Naval Versus Political Patronage

Before turning to Popham's experience at Walcheren, however, a short explanation of the patronage context for officers in the Royal Navy is necessary. The early 19th century Navy throve on patronage – the networks of influence harnessed in the chase of what one hopeful referred to as 'that *long desired object, promotion*, without which my life will be a dreary journey of disappointment and sorrow'.[10] In this the Navy was no different from the rest of British society, and professional networks were by far the most valuable to have in a service that relied so much on the ability of the men appointed to command. Captaining a man of war was no sinecure: in Evan Wilson's words, 'Talent mattered; incompetence and a poor recommendation were ... deadly to a career'.[11]

The quality of one's connections, however, was also tremendously important, especially with so many officers crowding for promotion and so few opportunities for distinction through battle or acts of conspicuous heroism. The First Lord of the Admiralty and the Admiralty Board had the final say in promotions and appointments, but they were open to suggestion or pressure from a number of different sources. Commanders-in-chief of foreign stations were able to appoint officers to certain vacancies within their remit; captains could bring their protégés aboard their own ship in various capacities. Royal Navy officers with a strong professional family background were thus at a double advantage; conversely, the social elite (who were more likely to have access to networks that might help a man advance

9 See the proceedings of Popham's court martial: Anon., *A Full and Correct Report of the Trial of Sir Home Popham ...* (London: J. and J. Richardson, 1807), p.164.

10 Wiltshire and Swindon Record Office: Ailesbury MSS, 9/35/383, Lieutenant Joseph Bullen to Lord Ailesbury, 24 August 1792.

11 Wilson, *A Social History of British Naval Officers*, p.122. See also Charles Consolvo, 'Prospects and promotion of British naval officers', *Maritime Mirror* 91(2) (2015), pp.137–159, 149.

in a land-based career) did not do noticeably better afloat than the middle or commercial classes.[12]

Royal Navy patronage, therefore, combined traditional patronage routes with personal competence, professional connections, and influence. While influence was not enough to overcome a lack of skill, simple ability did not get a naval officer far without some sort of influence to back it up.[13] This often makes it difficult to unpick an officer's rise through the ranks, which is even more true when trying to trace the role of politics in the process. 'The balance between political and professional influences on officers' careers remained uncertain,' writes N.A.M. Rodger, and Evan Wilson agrees.[14] But if politics played a lesser role in the average naval officer's career than might be expected, this did not mean it was unlikely to have any weight at all, particularly where an ambitious officer had very few alternatives.

Popham is an excellent example of this. Had he relied on traditional naval patronage networks and promotion routes, his career might never have taken off. As a younger son in the large family of a minor British civil servant, he did not necessarily have a strong professional advantage. His first naval patron did have some impressive connections, amongst them Admirals Keppel and Howe, but he died at the beginning of Popham's career. Popham's lack of alternative interest contributed to his being placed on half-pay during the 1780s; his decision to leave the Royal Navy and pursue private trading opportunities did not help him when he returned to the profession at the outset of the wars with France. He then became a Transport Agent – usually a dead-end job.[15] Nevertheless, despite this unpromising start, he became a post-captain in April 1795. By the time of the Walcheren Expedition in 1809, he had been almost continuously employed on a string of high-profile and often delicate assignments and had become one of the most notorious men in the Royal Navy.

Zeal, Controversy, and Politics

Popham's career progression was not unique: as Evan Wilson has shown, many of his naval peers were also 'active participants who could earn promotion based on their merit'.[16] Where Popham differed from his colleagues was that the exploits that got him noticed and promoted were conducted on land and attracted the attention of men more accustomed to dispensing military, not naval, patronage (such as the Duke of York, responsible for Popham's promotion to post-captain). Popham's naval achievements were solid but hardly stand-out material. He was an acclaimed hydrographer and his system of telegraphic signals remained the basis of Royal Navy and even United States Navy signals well into the 20th

12 Wilson, *A Social History of British Naval Officers*, pp.84–86.

13 Wilson, *A Social History of British Naval Officers*, p.110.

14 N.A.M. Rodger, *The Command of the Ocean* (London: Allan Lane, 2004), p.391; Wilson, *A Social History of British Naval Officers*, p.127.

15 Rodger, *Command of the Ocean*, p.216; Moira Bracknall, 'Lord Spencer, Patronage and Commissioned Officers' Careers, 1794–1801', PhD Thesis, University of Exeter, January 2008, p.92.

16 Wilson, *A Social History of British Naval Officers*, p.120.

century.[17] He made a name for himself as an expert in amphibious warfare, which required a combination of skill, administrative ability, diplomacy, and quick wits – all of which Popham had in abundance – but was not especially glamorous and left Popham in a sort of no man's land between the two services. One anonymous naval commentator recalled: 'I can never think of [him] … without bringing to mind the showman's description of the hippopotamus: "This 'ere is the ippopotamos or river orse, an amfiberous hanimal, wot cannot live on the land, and wot dies in the water."'[18] Many historians agree he was more bluster than substance: Roger Knight describes Popham as one of those 'showy egotists' who 'made fools of themselves'.[19] In the words of W.H. Fitchett, 'Probably no man in that generation got himself talked about so much, and did so little.'[20]

This is not entirely inaccurate, but then Popham's missions were often of a nature that meant they could not be 'talked about'. Popham was just as comfortable in the world of politics and high strategy as he was on the quarterdeck – probably more so, given the paucity of his experience in action. His correspondence regularly found its way onto the desk of some of the most important men in Napoleonic-era Britain. These plans and ideas were seriously read, circulated, and considered, and even regularly solicited, giving Popham an *entrée* at the highest decision-making levels in the country. He made the most of the opportunity and had a talent for telling his superiors what they wanted to hear. Although he was a post-captain for all but the first and last years of the long wars with France, Popham had fingers in many pies of many flavours – military, naval, political, diplomatic – and was interested in everything from military science and logistics to grand strategy. Although undeniably brave and enterprising, thinking and planning were his forte. His official assignments came through a variety of departments: although never fully accepted by a Royal Navy that valued obedience to orders and had little place for unpredictability, he was often employed by the Foreign Office or the War Department, and even on occasion by the prime minister himself.

Popham was not shy about his qualifications, nor did he have any doubt of his own genius. In 1815 he wrote to the Under-Secretary of the Admiralty that his whole life had 'been devoted to my country, and I will not allow that my zeal has ever been behind anyone in the service of the Navy.'[21] Popham was nevertheless so brash at least in part because he knew many felt his poor personal reputation outweighed his achievements. His life had been a long string of controversy, and he was lucky to have attracted the attention of men in high places, for he needed their protection. Litigation and accusations of pecuniary misconduct dogged his every step; his love of money, and the questionable lengths he went to obtain it, were a byword. Contemporaries were well aware of the lingering Admiralty Courts case regarding the *Etrusco*, the private trading vessel Popham had owned before the wars with France, which had been seized by a British ship in 1793 as a prize while sailing under Tuscan

17 William Davis Miller, 'The Background and Development of Naval Signal Flags', *Proceedings of the Massachusetts Historical Society* (3rd s.) 68 (October 1944–May 1947), pp.60–71, p.67.

18 'W.', 'Expedition to Walcheren in 1809, Part I', *United Service Journal*, 3 (1838), p.53. The quotation is transcribed as printed in the *Journal*.

19 Roger Knight, 'After Trafalgar', in Quentin Colville and James Davey (eds.), *Nelson, Navy and Nation* (London: National Maritime Museum, 2013), p.225.

20 W.H. Fitchett, *How England Saved Europe: The Story of the Great War, 1793–1815* (New York: Charles Scribner's Sons, 1900), Vol. 3, p.107.

21 Hugh Popham, *A Damned Cunning Fellow* (Tywardreath: Old Ferry Press, 1991), pp.184, 190.

colours. Only government pressure ensured the case was eventually settled in Popham's favour in 1805: he received £18,000 from the transaction, sparking several acrimonious debates in Parliament. This immediately followed official investigations into the exorbitant funds Popham had spent refitting his squadron while employed in the Red Sea. Again, a select committee of the House of Commons cleared all charges against him.

When Popham deserted his station off the Cape of Good Hope in 1806 for an apparently entirely unauthorised invasion of Spanish South America, many immediately made the connection between this land of silver and the fabulous amount of prize money Popham was likely to secure.[22] His notorious court martial in the wake of this highly embarrassing adventure (which had led to 15 months of almost continuous military disaster) should have destroyed him, but if Popham was undoubtedly controversial, he was also versatile. The court martial inevitably found him guilty of abandoning his post, but Popham got away with being 'severely reprimanded'. Lady Hester Stanhope, Pitt's niece, thought Popham had got off because his fruitful brain would make him 'a dangerous weapon in the hands of enemies'.[23] Apparently the government agreed. A handful of months after his court martial, Popham was appointed Captain of the Fleet[24] during the expedition to Copenhagen in the teeth of an official protest from several other Royal Navy officers disgusted 'at seeing a Man ... so improperly upheld by those they have been brought up to venerate & obey'.[25]

The Political Patronage of Henry Dundas, 1st Viscount Melville

Popham enjoyed the patronage of numerous influential politicians, including Lord Moira (personal friend of the Prince of Wales), the Duke of York (the Army's Commander-in-Chief), and prime minister William Pitt. This chapter, however, focuses on Popham's connection with Henry Dundas, elevated to the peerage in December 1802 as Viscount Melville. As Secretary of State for War (1794–1801) and First Lord of the Admiralty (1804–05), Dundas was central to the wartime decision-making process and one of Pitt the Younger's most trusted lieutenants. He was also Popham's longest-running political patron: almost all Popham's employment between 1796 and 1805 came through this man.

At a time when 'no General Staff existed' and there was no 'unified command', Dundas (as Secretary of State for War) was a central, vitally important figure in the creation of military strategy.[26] A civilian himself, he relied on a broad network of advisors and political

22 Ben Hughes, *The British Invasion of the River Plate, 1806–07* (Barnsley: Pen and Sword Military, 2013), pp.71, 89; Ian Fletcher, *The Waters of Oblivion: the British Invasion of the Rio de la Plata, 1806–07* (Stroud: Spellmount, 2006), pp.2–3; Chris Coelho, *Pirates in Uniform: The Conspiracy to Invade Buenos Aires that Triggered a War* (self-published, 2019, eBook edition).

23 Lady Hester Stanhope to Lord Grenville, undated but [1809], quoted in Winifred Stokes, 'Popham, Sir Home Riggs (1762–1820), of Titness Park, Berks.', in R. Thorne (ed.), *The History of Parliament: The House of Commons 1790–1820* (London: Boydell and Brewer; History of Parliament Trust, 1964–2019), <http://www.histparl.ac.uk/volume/1790-1820/member/popham-sir-home-riggs-1762-1820>, accessed 11 August 2020.

24 A Captain of the Fleet is the naval version of a chief of staff, equivalent in status to a Rear-Admiral.

25 British Library (BL): Wellesley MSS, Add MS 37887, f.108.

26 Michael Fry, *The Dundas Despotism* (Edinburgh: University Press, 1992), pp.189–190.

contacts and was well known for seeking advice from military men whom he considered capable of thinking holistically about the needs of the war – in short, professionals who were able to look beyond the European theatre and who shared his 'blue-water' vision focusing on Britain's imperial holdings around the globe. For Dundas, 'Navigation and commerce [were] inseparably connected': as a result, Britain needed to increase her colonial strength and attempts to wrest colonies from the enemy 'ought to admit of no limitations'.[27] Popham – with his familial connections in the East India Company, his trade networks in the City, and his personal conviction that 'the golden object of India' and the Middle East ought to be the fulcrum for British grand strategy – echoed Dundas's belief that trade networks and maritime power could ensure Britain's final victory.[28]

Between 1796 and 1805, Dundas and prime minister William Pitt used Popham in a variety of ways unconnected with Popham's official naval character: as a defence strategist, as an unofficial strategic adviser, and occasionally as a confidential agent. Popham was sent on diplomatic missions to Russia and the Middle East; he was tasked with planning (and carrying out) raids on French coastal towns, including Ostend, Brest, and Calais; and he presided over the testing of Robert Fulton's prototype torpedoes. Popham enjoyed privileged access to top secret information and acted as a middleman between the British government and disaffected parties in France and Spain, from South American troublemaker Francisco de Miranda to disgraced French naval officer Baron d'Imbert. While Popham provided the politicians with unquestioning loyalty and service, they in turn provided him with the protection he needed against his (numerous) enemies. When Popham's credentials and background were questioned, Dundas brushed such criticism aside in no uncertain terms:

> I am well aware that Sir Home Popham is an object of envy with some, of jealousy with others, but in proportion as he is attempted to be run down, it is the duty of the Government to run him up. To the conviction of us all he has served Government for many years in various capacities zealously and well. Anything therefore that little jealousness or captious observations may throw out with regard to Sir Home Popham individually I feel perfectly indifferent about ... If any person feels the service [of working alongside him] cumbersome, there will be no doubt many others to supply their places.[29]

By 1805, willing as he was to take on any number of jobs that required brains, talent, and discretion, and with Dundas (now Lord Melville) as First Lord of the Admiralty, Popham probably believed he had managed to make himself indispensable. He may also have believed himself invulnerable – a conclusion that must have been strengthened by his court martial acquittal in 1807, with Melville himself appearing as a witness in Popham's favour.

27 Piers Mackesy, *War Without Victory: The Downfall of Pitt* (Oxford: Clarendon Press, 1984), pp.7–8, 11–12, 38–39; Fry, *The Dundas Despotism*, pp.194–195, 198–199, 209–210. The quotation from Dundas comes from Fry, p.227.

28 Popham to Lord Melville, 10 September 1808, BL: Melville MSS, BL Loan 57/108, f.9.

29 C.C. Lloyd (ed.), *The Keith Papers* (London: Navy Records Society, 1955), Vol. 3, p.95, Lord Melville to Lord Keith, 7 Oct 1804.

Although he denied Popham had received official government sanction to attack South America, by getting Melville to spell out how useful he had been to government – literally by Melville's mere appearance before the court – Popham had placed his connection with some of the most important political names in the country on record. A footnote in the published proceedings of the court martial pressed the point: 'It is known what degree of influence Mr Pitt and Lord Melville had over His Majesty's government at the time. If an officer acted under such influence, can he be deemed culpable?'[30]

This questionable position, however, was tenable only so long as Popham's political patrons were in power or able to speak on his behalf. Tying himself so explicitly to Melville exposed Popham to the winds of political change. By the time he was 'severely reprimanded' aboard HMS *Gladiator* on 11 March 1807, the wheel of fortune had already turned against him. Popham's golden career as a 'Melville man' suffered a strong blow when Melville was impeached in 1805 following accusations that he had engaged in the embezzlement of huge sums of money while Treasurer of the Navy in the 1790s. Although Melville was acquitted, his political reputation – and he had always been viewed as something of a fixer and corrupt *eminence grise* – never recovered.

After 1805, Popham not only had his own poor reputation hanging about his neck: his well-publicised closeness to Melville also meant he was associated with politically damaged goods. More ominously, many of the other men Popham cited in his March 1807 trial were not really in a position to help him either. Pitt had been dead for over a year; within weeks of Popham's acquittal another former employer, Lord Grenville, resigned as prime minister and was succeeded by the Duke of Portland. Popham, a perennial optimist, always retained the hope that Lord Melville would overcome the blot of his impeachment to return to office; he certainly anticipated that Melville would experience a revival under his former colleague Portland, whose government was never very stable.[31] What Popham did not realise was that this very instability made Portland and his colleagues less, and not more, likely to call on Melville's assistance, as recruiting such a controversial colleague, however experienced, might lay them open to attack.

Melville, therefore, was kept at arm's length, and complained that he 'had no communication of any sort, neither have I received … a letter of any kind from any of the King's servants or anybody in any respect connected with them.'[32] Popham's hopes for Melville turned first to frustration, and then to anger: as he put it, with as much reference to his own case as to Melville's, 'there is a damn'd deal of ingratitude in the World.'[33] He badgered Melville to return to London and oppose Portland's ministry, particularly in 1809 when the government seemed likely to fall. He devoted so much effort to this, in fact, that Melville had to tell him in no uncertain terms to drop it.[34] When Popham tried to get some friends to publish pamphlets or newspaper articles in Melville's favour, Melville argued the point

30 Anon., *Full and Correct Report*, pp.159, 161, 163 n.
31 Melville himself believed this: Fry, *The Dundas Despotism*, p.299.
32 NRS: Buccleuch MSS, GD224/38/8, f.12, Lord Melville to the Duke of Buccleuch, 15 October [1807].
33 BL: Melville MSS, Loan MS 57/108, no. 8, Popham to Lord Melville, 23 November 1807.
34 NRS: Melville MSS, DG51/151/2, Lord Melville to Popham, 6 November 1809.

more strongly: 'I am certain your Judgement & Discretion will suggest to you that nothing ought to be published which has not been submitted to previous Perusal & Revision.'[35]

How much of Popham's devotion to his patron was due to genuine attachment and how much to self-interest is open to question, but one thing is certain: he was not afraid of being associated with a man whom he was convinced would rise like a phoenix from the ashes of disgrace. 'You are I am satisfied convinced that neither persecution, nor the consequences of persecution, can affect my attachment to you,' he told his patron.[36] Popham clung to his Melville connection because it enabled him to erase his humble beginnings, it helped brush his unpalatable past under the carpet, and it underlined the fact he had made his reputation through his abilities. To others, however, being Melville's trusted acolyte emphasised the fact that the duties Popham performed were often unofficial and (as such) unscrutinised. Popham's most significant enemy was Lord St Vincent, First Lord of the Admiralty between 1801 and 1804, who viewed Popham as little more than an unscrupulous buccaneer. Among the many 'persecutions' St Vincent's Admiralty had perpetrated against Popham was an inquiry into the materials he had required to repair his ship, HMS *Romney*, while serving in the Red Sea between 1801 and 1803 – the implication being that Popham had sold most of those supplies and pocketed the profits. A print dated 1805 shows Lord Melville as a drooping Scottish thistle bending before the onslaught of the political opposition. He is protected by a blunderbuss labelled 'Popham's defence' – but beyond this are references to some of the accusations of peculation levelled at Popham himself. Against the side of a ship labelled *Romney* is a placard reading 'Wanted Supply of naval Stores – Inquire within'. In other words, the servant was just as bad as the master.

Walcheren: Mystery and Subterfuge

By the time of the Walcheren Expedition in 1809, therefore, Popham's close connection with Melville (a disgraced politician) and his own unsavoury reputation were well established. Little wonder, then, that Lord Mulgrave resisted any proposal to make Popham Captain of the Fleet at Walcheren. Lord Lowther's use of the phrase 'a Melville expedition' to describe the arrangements for the Walcheren Expedition was far from positive: not only was Melville in the political wilderness, but the term also made reference to the well-known fact that he had been angling for office under Portland for some time. The government was moving swiftly towards internal crisis, with Foreign Secretary George Canning manoeuvring against Secretary of State for War Lord Castlereagh. Under these circumstances, appointing a man like Popham, with explicit links to Melville, to a prominent command in Britain's most significant military effort to date would not have been politic.

Yet the First Lord of the Admiralty, Lord Mulgrave, could hardly keep him away from Walcheren, for three major reasons. The first was, quite simply, expertise. Popham was an authority in amphibious operations and facilitating inter-service relations. His *curriculum vitae* made him one of the best-qualified officers to go to Walcheren, the success of which

35 NRS: Melville MSS, DG51/151/2, Lord Melville to Popham, 6 November 1809.
36 NRS: Melville MSS, DG51/151/1, Popham to Lord Melville, 2 November 1809.

'The Brewer and the Thistle', aquatint by James Sayer, 1805. (Wellcome Collection). Attribution 4.0 International (CC BY 4.0)

relied so much on seamless combined operations. The second reason was equally obvious: Popham was an excellent hydrographer, and a man who had spent many years operating a private trading vessel out of Ostend. He thus knew the area around the Scheldt exceedingly well. These two arguments were, however, not the *only* reasons for his appointment, despite the assertion of one historian that Popham's role at Walcheren was limited to giving advice and assisting the advance of the fleet: 'He simply had a difficult job of seamanship to do, and did it supremely well.'[37] Popham did spend some time surveying the complicated navigation of the Scheldt, but even a superficial examination of the manuscript evidence, not to mention the frequency with which his name crops up in contemporary accounts of the expedition, demonstrates this was far from his only role.

The third and main reason for Popham's appointment, despite all the political and logistical obstacles in the way of it, is that he was largely responsible for suggesting Walcheren to the War Department as a suitable destination for an expedition in the first place. Popham later downplayed his role in the planning process before the parliamentary inquiry that followed the expedition's failure: 'I certainly was accessary to the arrangements of the Expedition from having been examined a good deal by the commanders-in-chief of the army and navy, with respect to my local knowledge of that country.' But even Popham had to admit he had been called upon for advice in part because of a plan he had drawn up in 1798 for an attack on Walcheren, and that he had been pushing for an assault on the islands for many years.[38]

Popham's role in the planning of the expedition was not secret. It was much discussed after the expedition failed, partly, of course, because of the need to seek a convenient scapegoat for the disaster. According to John Barrow, 'The contriver of this scheme was said to be – as indeed it turned out to be – Sir Home Popham; who, by his insinuating and plausible address, had prevailed on [the Secretary of State for War, Lord Castlereagh] ... to undertake it.'[39] Barrow was Secretary of the Admiralty and was almost certainly seeking to shift blame for Walcheren off the shoulders of the members of the Admiralty Board (which must also have agreed to undertake a venture relying so much on amphibious cooperation). A more favourable writer, however – Lord Lowther – made the same assertion before the expedition had even sailed: 'The whole plan from the Beginning to end is Popham's.'[40] One of the first things the military commander at Walcheren, Lord Chatham, did after being officially appointed was to make contact with Popham; his desire 'not to be separated from Sir Home Popham' in the run-up to departure led to considerable logistical juggling to allow Chatham and the naval commander, Sir Richard Strachan, to sail together in Popham's ship.[41] This

37 Popham, *Damned Cunning Fellow*, pp.184, 190. It may be worth noting that Hugh Popham, the author of this biography, was a descendant and therefore possibly less likely to be critical of his subject.

38 William Cobbett, *Parliamentary Debates from the Year 1803 to the Present Time* (London: Longman, Hurst, Rees, Orme, and Brown, 1812), Vol. 15, col.clxviii.

39 Sir John Barrow, *An Auto-Biographical Memoir of Sir John Barrow, Bart., Late of the Admiralty ...* (London: John Murray, 1847), p.304.

40 Cumbria Record Office: Lonsdale MSS, DLONS/L1/2/70, f.4, Lord Lowther to Lord Lonsdale, [20 July 1809].

41 House of Commons, *A Collection of Papers Relating to the Expedition to the Scheldt, Presented to Parliament in 1810* (London: A. Strahan, 1811), Sir Richard Strachan to William Wellesley Pole, 24 July 1809, p.371.

certainly points towards the centrality of Popham's role in the expedition: clearly, he was not simply a professional man caught in the wrong place at the wrong time.

The full extent of Popham's role at Walcheren has to be pieced together from various sources, and no explicit instructions or appointment of any sort have yet been found. It is therefore difficult to know exactly what Popham was doing, or to whom he was reporting. Strictly speaking, therefore, he was correct when he stated to the parliamentary inquiry that he had been no more than 'captain of the *Venerable*'.[42] Yet even this was something of a white lie for, while Popham had certainly been *appointed* captain of HMS *Venerable*, he was not *technically* captain of the *Venerable*, at least not when he sailed with the expedition. According to the ship's muster books, the date of Popham's commission was given as 10 May 1808, but he had been absent on Admiralty orders ever since his appointment. In practical terms, the actual captain of the ship was Andrew King, at least up to 30 July 1809, when Popham attempted to assert his authority. Curiously, Popham's entry in the muster book is marked with the following note: 'Not to be paid during any part of the time as Captain' (although it appears this decision was overturned in 1817, when he was finally paid retrospectively for the period up to 1 October 1809).[43]

The correspondence between Sir Richard Strachan and Lord Chatham sheds more light on why Popham's authority aboard the *Venerable* may have been in question. Nearly a week after the expedition sailed from the Downs, Strachan told Chatham he had made a disturbing discovery:

> I came to Camveer [Veere, one of the most important fortified towns on the island of Walcheren] in the hopes of seeing Sir Home Popham, but he is not here and I have heard nothing from him[.] I am concern'd at this irregularity of his more particularly as I find he has never taken command of the Venerable and cannot be recognised as being in actual employ[.] Consequently he can have no authority in the Fleet ... I am sorry he has not communicated with me to day because there were many points that required explanation.[44]

Clearly Popham had failed to have his commission read on taking command of the *Venerable*, which at the very least placed him in violation of the official regulations and instructions by which officers in the Royal Navy were bound to abide – without even considering the implications of his leaving his station without informing Strachan, nominally his commanding officer, of his whereabouts.[45]

Either Popham made an honest mistake, or there was another reason for this serious breach of naval protocol. Strachan's wording, and subsequent events, imply the latter. A few months after the expedition to Walcheren had failed, when those involved in it were wading through the political fall-out, an anonymous pamphlet appeared in circulation. The author claimed not to have accompanied the expedition in any naval or military capacity, but to judge from the pamphlet's contents he was allowed full access to Lord Chatham's private

42 *Parliamentary Debates*, Vol. 15, col.clxxxii.
43 The National Archives (TNA): ADM 53/1236, muster book of HMS *Venerable*.
44 TNA: Chatham MSS, PRO 30/8/369, f.72, Sir Richard Strachan to Lord Chatham, 2 August 1809.
45 I am grateful to Peter Leech for pointing this out to me.

correspondence. The author drew attention to 'the mysterious circumstance of [Popham] not publishing his commission … and detaching himself upon other very inferior services.' 'Why violate the rules of the service?' the pamphlet asked. 'Why keep two Captains on board [the *Venerable*]?' The pamphlet's conclusion appeared to be that Popham had manoeuvred himself into position as *de facto* Captain of the Fleet by a process of subterfuge, taking advantage of the fact that his commanding admiral was, to be candid, not the sharpest knife in the drawer: 'Why commit one [captain] to the service of the ship, in order to leave to the other the guidance of the Admiral?'[46]

This relied overmuch on Lord Chatham's extremely poor opinion of Strachan's talents as a naval commander, but it nevertheless draws attention to another mystery arising from Strachan's 2 August letter. Clearly, Strachan had no idea where Popham was or what he was doing, but assumed Chatham did – which begs the question of whether Popham might have been conducting duties on Chatham's behalf, which he may have been able to do if he was not *officially* captain of the *Venerable* (and therefore only accompanying the expedition as a private individual).

The supposition that Popham's appointment involved subterfuge designed to bypass the usual chain of naval command appears to have been reasonably widespread. Suspicions were voiced that the whole arrangement had been designed to allow Popham to act either as unofficial Captain of the Fleet or as a sort of naval director of operations (with Strachan as a complacent, if not complicit, figurehead). One of Popham's naval colleagues, Captain Pulteney Malcolm, remarked on 'the singular mode of appointing Sir R[ichar]d Strachan to the command of the Expedition in order that Popham should have power and rule all in conjunction with Lord Chatham.'[47] Chatham's supporters naturally denied this, but this may have glossed over his own obvious reliance on Popham's expertise.[48] Whatever the truth, Popham was certainly not always present at his station as captain of the *Venerable*. It is not clear what Popham was doing when Strachan could not find him; nor is it clear whether he was reporting directly to the Admiralty in all his activities. Perhaps, as had happened so many times in the past decade, Popham was reporting directly to the War Department and Lord Castlereagh; but if he was, there is no evidence of it. The only conclusion that can be drawn with any confidence is that Popham was carrying out duties far beyond his limited role as captain of HMS *Venerable*.

Popham's behaviour at Walcheren was significant in one other respect, which again had only a tangential connection with his 'official' reasons for being there. One of Popham's many talents was as a publicist. Ever since his court martial, and probably before then, he had seen the value of manipulating public opinion through newspaper articles and polemical publications (some widespread, others privately circulated to influential friends and patrons). Popham's networks were thus not limited to seeking out and exploiting high political patronage: he also had contacts with the press, many of them questionable at best.

46 Anon., *Brief Remarks Upon the Public Letter of Sir Richard Strachan and the Narrative of the Earl of Chatham* (London: T. Becket and J. Porter, 1810), pp.17, 25.

47 National Library of Scotland (NLS): Pulteney Malcolm MSS, Acc. 6684/2, Pulteney Malcolm to his wife, [February 1811?]. Many thanks to Paul Martinovich for this reference.

48 TNA: Chatham MSS, PRO 30/8/369, f.170, memorandum of a conversation with Lord St Vincent by 'Mr B—g', 7 February 1810.

Amongst the more respectable connections was his long-standing friendship with Thomas George Street of the *Courier*, who had already worked with Popham during the invasion of Buenos Aires to spread messages of the likely benefit of a South American adventure to British trade. In 1809 and 1810, the *Courier* took instructions from Popham on how to present Walcheren to the public – first as an expedition that was likely to succeed, and then (as things started to go wrong) as a well-planned and well-intentioned enterprise, the failure of which could not be blamed on the Navy.

Popham may have written some of these articles himself; he certainly appeared in the newspaper columns thanks to the speeches he made as MP for Ipswich, a role that allowed him a front-row seat during the debates over Walcheren and the inquiry in 1810. As Alexander Hope, Quarter-Master General at Horse Guards, noted balefully regarding Popham's public speeches: 'Sir Home Popham at once a planner & Actor ... is perfectly qualified to protect the Executive on the part of the Navy.'[49] Popham continued to rely on his press contacts throughout his career: while serving off the north coast of Spain in 1812, he may have been responsible for placing a large number of articles in various British newspapers detailing his exploits.[50] As late as 1816, he was still able to influence the stories that appeared about him in the press, and he probably wrote some of them himself.[51]

Popham undeniably helped manipulate the way the Walcheren story got told. Some contemporaries thought he deserved much of the blame for its failure, but, given the nebulous nature of his role in the expedition, it was difficult to prove he had been anything other than 'captain of the *Venerable*'. The parliamentary inquiry did not even try to challenge that assertion; indeed, based on how little attention historians have focused on his role at Walcheren, he may escaped with less than his fair share of the blame – at least in the short term. Of the two men who might have drawn him more deeply into the bitter recriminations that followed the campaign's collapse, the first, Strachan, was no threat. Popham may have described him as 'the Child of Lord St Vincent', but he and Strachan nevertheless made common cause in navigating the complicated political minefield of the Walcheren inquiry.[52] Popham helped Strachan with the evidence he provided to Parliament and assisted him in writing his official narrative in March 1810.[53] The second man, Lord Chatham, was so completely destroyed by Walcheren he could do Popham little harm.[54] At the end of the

49 TNA: Chatham MSS, PRO 30/8/367, f.157, Alexander Hope to Sir Robert Brownrigg, 14 February 1810.

50 Silvia Gregorio Sainz has compiled a list of the articles Popham inserted in the press regarding his exploits in 1812: Silvia Gregorio Sainz, 'The Royal Navy in Santander: Sir Home Popham's logistics centre in the Peninsular War (1812)', conference paper delivered at 'War and Peace in the Age of Napoleon', King's College London, 13 September 2019.

51 'Popham ... perhaps put the paragraph in the paper himself': NLS, Pulteney Malcolm MSS, Acc. 6990/1, Pulteney Malcolm to his wife, [15 February 1816]. Many thanks to Paul Martinovich for this reference.

52 BL: Melville MSS, Loan MS 57/108, no. 11, Popham to Robert Dundas, [13 October 1809].

53 *Parliamentary Debates*, Vol. 15, col.5xl, Strachan's testimony, 15 March 1810. The two men became so close, in fact, that Popham named his youngest son Strachan.

54 For the effect of Walcheren and the following inquiry on Chatham's reputation, see Chapters 10 and 11 of Reiter, *The Late Lord*.

whole episode in April 1810, with Chatham neutralised and the Royal Navy vindicated, Popham must have believed he had emerged unscathed.

After Walcheren: The Burden of the Past

Yet Walcheren was Popham's last major active employment during the war. He did spend six months between July and December 1812 off the north coast of Spain, assisting the Spanish *guerrillas* and aiding Wellington's operations in the Peninsula, but perhaps the only reason he was sent to Spain in the first place – as Christopher D. Hall notes, his appointment 'was quite contentious' – was that the First Lord of the Admiralty at the time was none other than Robert Dundas, 2nd Viscount Melville, son of Popham's greatest political patron.[55] Popham's attachment to the second Melville was a hereditary one, as he made clear in a letter that also underlined his growing sense of isolation: 'I have neither a claim on, or an attachment to, any member of [the government] but Your Lordship.'[56] Melville's relationship with his father had not been easy, particularly in the last couple of years of his father's life when their political ambitions had come into conflict, but whatever the private damage to the son–father relationship, in public the second viscount's 'filial piety was heroic' and there is no indication that family feuding influenced his attitude towards Popham.[57] Nevertheless, Melville's political tastes were significantly different from his father's, and Popham's flamboyance may have irritated and embarrassed him.[58] Popham was recalled in December 1812, ostensibly because Wellington's movements made his activities off the Spanish coast both more dangerous and less useful, but probably also because he had managed to annoy nearly everyone he was meant to be working with. Whereas the first Lord Melville might have swept aside criticism of his protégé's methods, the second quietly sent Popham to take the Marquess of Hastings to India as governor general, a lengthy mission far from any field of war.

The reasons for Popham's fall from grace were thus partly due to changes in political personnel. Popham had become accustomed to using his close association with important politicians to advance his unusual career and to protect himself against accusations of unscrupulousness and corruption. Walcheren was the last time he was successfully able to do this. By 1810 Popham had lost his main political patrons through death, disgrace, or resignation, and their successors in government knew his association with the failed expedition all too well. Teaming up with Popham on a scheme like Walcheren had already been

55 Christopher D. Hall, *Wellington's Navy: Seapower and the Peninsular War, 1807–1814* (London: Chatham Publishing, 2004), p.200.

56 BL: Loan MS 57/108, no. 29, Popham to Robert Dundas, 2nd Lord Melville, 19 July 1812.

57 For the difficult relationship between the two Viscounts Melville, see Fry, *The Dundas Despotism*, pp.285, 289, 294, 299–304, and the quotation regarding the second viscount's 'filial piety' on p.313. See also R.G. Thorne, 'Dundas (afterwards Saunders Dundas), Robert (1771–1851), of Melville Castle, Edinburgh', in R. Thorne (ed.), *History of Parliament: The House of Commons 1790–1820* (London: Boydell and Brewer; History of Parliament Trust, 1964–2019), <https://www.historyofparliamentonline.org/volume/1790-1820/member/dundas-%28afterwards-saunders-dundas-%29-robert-1771-1851>, accessed 13 August 2020.

58 Fry, *The Dundas Despotism*, p.294.

a risk for the weakened and internally divided Portland ministry; had they won the gamble things might have been different, but the result had been a debacle, and the Perceval and Liverpool governments that followed were unwilling to make the same mistake. Popham's service in Spain in 1812 was an epilogue to a career that was already spent. Isolated and vulnerable, he found, to his dismay, that the politicians were more than happy to distance themselves from him – and it was Walcheren, again, that provided the opportunity.

Amidst the atmosphere of political opportunism that surrounded George III's final descent into mental illness in February 1811, Spencer Perceval's weak government fought for its life. It had already narrowly lost one crucial vote in the House of Lords on the Regency Bill, introduced to make the Prince of Wales Regent in the event of the King's illness being permanent. Robert Plumer Ward, one of the Lords of the Admiralty, was watching one of the critical debates in the Upper House from behind the throne when he ran into Sir Home Popham. Ward recalled Popham 'had lately complained to me of being not only ill-treated, but insulted, by the Admiralty, in being sent on a special mission to the coast of Spain, but immediately recalled. ... He was much affronted at being reduced to act as a private Capt[ai]n of his ship, the *Venerable*, in the Channel service.'[59] Popham had been approaching Ward for some time to seek active employment away from the coastal blockade of the French ports. Kicking his heels was not something Popham was accustomed to doing, and he felt his country owed him more than he was getting.

Recent events, however, had once more reinforced Popham's unfortunate connection with Walcheren. One of his numerous press contacts was a man named Peter Finnerty, who had taken the official shorthand account of Popham's court martial. For reasons known only to himself, Popham had invited Finnerty to Walcheren to report back to his paper, the *Morning Chronicle*, as a semi-official war correspondent. A number of problems were likely to arise from this scenario, but the most obvious was that Finnerty was an Irish radical who had previously been convicted of sedition.[60] When Finnerty was inevitably found out and sent home, he wrote a lengthy article in the *Morning Chronicle* lambasting Lord Castlereagh, using some choice language that landed him back in prison for libel.[61] Unfortunately for Popham, Finnerty brought his name up during his trial as evidence in his favour.[62] No wonder, then, that when Popham came up to Robert Plumer Ward in the House of Lords begging to be employed, he received a stern rebuff:

> The late declaration of Finnerty ... involved Popham very much, not in the libel, but in the most glaring indiscretion (only equalled by the vanity which prompted it) in connecting himself with such a *polisson*. ... When he now came up to me in the Lords, to complain as usual of the Admiralty, I said to him ... 'Sir Home, I

59 Edward Phipps, *Memoirs of the Political and Literary Life of Robert Plumer Ward ...* (London: John Murray, 1850), Vol. 1, p.396.

60 For Finnerty, see Ivon Asquith, 'James Perry and the *Morning Chronicle*, 1790–1821' (PhD thesis, University of London, 1973), p.241 n.3; see also Elias Duran de Porras, 'Peter Finnerty, an ancestor of modern war correspondents', *Textual and Visual Media*, 7 (2014), pp.41–62, 46, 53.

61 Peter Finnerty, 'Lord Castlereagh and Mr Finnerty', *Morning Chronicle*, 23 January 1810.

62 Anon., *The Case of Peter Finnerty, Including a Full Report of All the Proceedings Which Took Place in the Court of King's Bench Upon the Subject ...* (London: J. McCreery for M. Jones, 1811), pp.17–18.

> won't hear you, I will never speak to you again' ... He seemed disconcerted, and asked why not? I said ... for a man that pretended to any sense, talents, or loyalty, to invite the blackest incendiary in the kingdom to accompany the troops on any expedition, but especially to Walcheren, was what nobody would have believed![63]

Popham had inadvertently handed the government an excellent reason to cut all ties with him – something it may have been trying to do for some time.

But the incident with Ward is not sufficient to explain why a man like Popham sank so far and virtually without a trace. No doubt Popham's association with Finnerty contributed part of the reason why he was only actively employed for six months between October 1809 and the end of the war in 1815, but other factors were at play. Popham's career was a roller-coaster combination of skill, intelligence, and occasionally almost unbelievable *chutzpah* balanced by underhand dealings, behind-the-scenes manoeuvring, and having the ear of the right people. Although underpinned by solid service (mostly in the field of amphibious operations), Popham made up for a lack of professional contacts and became adept at getting political decision-makers to consider, and often adopt, his plans and ideas. He was useful, and therefore protected – vital for a man like Popham, with a shady past and many enemies.

His career also rode, however, on luck and, with Walcheren, that luck finally ran out. The 1st Lord Melville's habit of taking private advice for government policy from a personally picked circle of professional advisers was falling out of fashion, perhaps partly because of the effects of relying on controversial men like Popham. The episode with Peter Finnerty was important because it showed Popham's influence at the highest levels had effectively come to an end. The men who had been willing to overlook Popham's transgressions were gone; the new set were all too keen to distance themselves from what had come before. Popham was no longer useful and – because he relied almost exclusively on being useful – he had nothing to fall back on.

Pitt's niece Lady Hester Stanhope, who knew Popham well, remarked:

> One of the great faults in the education of modern statesmen is a want of practical knowledge, which makes it necessary for them when in office to constantly call for the assistance of an *underling* who has knowledge and experience; these low men take advantage of the confidence placed in them and make public men in high stations pay dear for the information they receive.[64]

She was not the only contemporary to reach such a conclusion. Melville's own brother-in-law Sir John Hope drove in the point bitterly at the very end of the Walcheren debacle: 'It is a melancholy fact ... that our administration ... eagerly embraced the visionary schemes of any Projector, & having once allowed themselves to be caught by a plausible story, they shut their Eyes & Ears to all sound Views, & rational counsel.'[65] He no doubt had Popham in mind.

63 Phipps, *Memoirs of Robert Plumer Ward*, Vol. 1, pp.396–397.
64 Stokes, 'Popham, Sir Home Riggs'.
65 NRS: Hope MSS, GD364/1/1190, Sir John Hope to Alexander Hope, 28 August 1809.

Bibliography

Manuscripts

British Library (BL)

Melville MSS, Loan MS 57/108

Wellesley MSS, Add MS 37887

Cumbria Record Office, Lonsdale MSS, DLONS

National Library of Scotland (NLS), Pulteney Malcolm MSS, Acc. 6684, Acc. 6990

National Records of Scotland (NRS)

Buccleuch MSS, GD224

Hope MSS, GD364

Melville MSS, GD51

The National Archives (TNA)

Admiralty MSS, ADM 53/1236

Chatham MSS, PRO 30/8

Wiltshire and Swindon Record Office, Ailesbury MSS, 9/35/383

Primary Sources

Anon., *A Full and Correct Report of the Trial of Sir Home Popham …* (London: J. and J. Richardson, 1807)

Anon., *Brief Remarks Upon the Public Letter of Sir Richard Strachan and the Narrative of the Earl of Chatham* (London: T. Becket and J. Porter, 1810)

Anon., *The Case of Peter Finnerty, Including a Full Report of All the Proceedings Which Took Place in the Court of King's Bench Upon the Subject …* (London: J. McCreery for M. Jones, 1811)

Barrow, Sir John, *An Auto-Biographical Memoir of Sir John Barrow, Bart., Late of the Admiralty …* (London: John Murray, 1847)

Cobbett, William, *Parliamentary Debates from the Year 1803 to the Present Time* (London: Longman, Hurst, Rees, Orme, and Brown, 1812), Vols.15–16

Dillon, Sir William, *A Narrative of my Professional Adventures (1790–1839),* ed. Michael A. Lewis (London: Navy Records Society, 1956), Vol.2

Finnerty, Peter, 'Lord Castlereagh and Mr Finnerty', *Morning Chronicle*, 23 January 1810

House of Commons, *A Collection of Papers Relating to the Expedition to the Scheldt, Presented to Parliament in 1810* (London: A. Strahan, 1811)

Lloyd, C.C. (ed.), *The Keith Papers* (London: Navy Records Society, 1955), Vol.3

Phipps, Edward, *Memoirs of the Political and Literary Life of Robert Plumer Ward …* (London: John Murray, 1850), Vol.1

Thursfield, H.G. (ed.), *Five Naval Journals, 1789–1817* (London: Navy Records Society, 1951)

'W', 'Expedition to Walcheren in 1809, Part I', *United Service Journal*, 3 (1838)

Secondary Sources

Asquith, Ivon, 'James Perry and the *Morning Chronicle*, 1790–1821' (PhD thesis, University of London, 1973)

Bond, Gordon C., *The Grand Expedition* (Athens, GA: University of Georgia Press, 1979)

Bracknall, Moira, 'Lord Spencer, Patronage and Commissioned Officers' Careers, 1794–1801', PhD Thesis, University of Exeter, January 2008

Coelho, Chris, *Pirates in Uniform: The Conspiracy to Invade Buenos Aires that Triggered a War* (self-published, 2019, eBook edition)

Colville, Quentin, and Davey, James (eds.), *Nelson, Navy and Nation* (London: National Maritime Museum, 2013)

Consolvo, Charles, 'Prospects and promotion of British naval officers', *Maritime Mirror* 91(2) (2015), pp.137–159.

Duran de Porras, Elias, 'Peter Finnerty, an ancestor of modern war correspondents', *Textual and Visual Media*, 7 (2014)

Fletcher, Ian, *The Waters of Oblivion: the British Invasion of the Rio de la Plata, 1806–07* (Stroud: Spellmount, 2006)

Fry, Michael, *The Dundas Despotism* (Edinburgh: University Press, 1992)

Hall, Christopher D., *Wellington's Navy: Seapower and the Peninsular War, 1807–1814* (London: Chatham Publishing, 2004)

Howard, Martin R., *Walcheren 1809: The Scandalous Destruction of a British Army* (Barnsley: Pen and Sword, 2011)

Hughes, Ben, *The British Invasion of the River Plate, 1806–07* (Barnsley: Pen and Sword Military, 2013)

Mackesy, Piers, *War Without Victory: The Downfall of Pitt* (Oxford: Clarendon Press, 1984)
Miller, William Davis, 'The Background and Development of Naval Signal Flags', *Proceedings of the Massachusetts Historical Society* (3rd s.) 68 (October 1944–May 1947), pp.60–71
Popham, Hugh, *A Damned Cunning Fellow* (Tywardreath: Old Ferry Press, 1991)
Reiter, Jacqueline, *The Late Lord: The Life of John Pitt, 2nd Earl of Chatham* (Barnsley: Pen and Sword, 2017)
Rodger, N.A.M., *The Command of the Ocean* (London: Allan Lane, 2004)
Sainz, Silvia Gregorio, 'The Royal Navy in Santander: Sir Home Popham's logistics centre in the Peninsular War (1812)', conference paper delivered at 'War and Peace in the Age of Napoleon', King's College London, 13 September 2019
Stokes, Winifred, 'Popham, Sir Home Riggs (1762–1820), of Titness Park, Berks.', in R. Thorne (ed.), *The History of Parliament: The House of Commons 1790–1820* (London: Boydell and Brewer; History of Parliament Trust, 1964–2019), <http://www.histparl.ac.uk/volume/1790-1820/member/popham-sir-home-riggs-1762-1820>, accessed 11 August 2020
Thorne, R.G., 'Dundas (afterwards Saunders Dundas), Robert (1771–1851), of Melville Castle, Edinburgh', in R. Thorne (ed.), *History of Parliament: The House of Commons 1790–1820* (London: Boydell and Brewer; History of Parliament Trust, 1964–2019), <https://www.historyofparliamentonline.org/volume/1790-1820/member/dundas-%28afterwards-saunders-dundas-%29-robert-1771-1851>, accessed 13 August 2020
Wilson, Evan, *A Social History of British Naval Officers* (Woodbridge: Boydell and Brewer, 2017)

3

Sir Home Popham's Mission in 1812: Santander, A British Logistics Centre?[1]

Silvia Gregorio Sainz

Introduction

The British Government was aware of the strategic importance of modern-day Cantabria, and particularly the port city of Santander, from the outset of the Peninsular War. Cantabria's central position on the Bay of Biscay, and at the north end of the River Ebro, made its control vital to commanding the southern part of the country, as it blocked the route from France to Madrid via Burgos.[2] British officers and engineers described Santander port as one of the safest, not only to undertake operations but also to ensure sea communications with Great Britain and deliveries along the coast. Its routes with the interior of Spain also allowed relatively easy contact with the capital. The general course of events did not render Santander useful in the first years of the conflict. However, Wellington's advance inland in 1812 renewed British interest in the Cantabrian port. As the main theatre of operations moved eastwards across the Iberian Peninsula, the control of the major French fortresses along the Northern coast from Bayonne to Gijón (San Sebastián, Bilbao, Santoña and Santander) became essential. This led the British Government to send Commodore Sir Home Popham of the Royal Navy there in May of that year. He soon understood the importance of Santander port for his mission and turned it into his main logistics base.

This essay aims to bring to light both the relevance of Cantabria in Wellington's plans for the 1812 campaign, and the decisive impact of Popham's presence there. Special attention

1 The information presented in this chapter is part of a broader research about Anglo-Spanish relations during the Peninsular War, which concluded with the work 'Relaciones hispanobritánicas durante la Guerra de la Independencia (1808-1814). El caso de Cantabria: estudio y repertorio documental' (PhD thesis, University of Oviedo, 2017).

2 Rafael Palacio Ramos, 'Importancia estratégica de Cantabria durante la Guerra de la independencia: vías de comunicación y plazas fuertes', in Rafael Palacio Ramos (coord.), *Monte Buciero 13. Cantabria durante la Guerra de la Independencia* (Santander: Ayuntamiento de Santoña, 2008), pp.223, 233 and 239. This author emphasises the strategic importance of Cantabria from the French perspective.

will be paid to the role of Santander as a British logistics hub in 1812 and the effect this had on the inhabitants' everyday life. It draws mainly on both Wellington's and Popham's dispatches, on the Cantabrian authorities' minute books and other local documents.[3] Critical examination of these sources provides a new perspective on the importance of Cantabria in the general development of the Peninsular War.

From 1810 to 1812: a growing importance

Sir Home Popham was one of the British officers that established longer and closer contacts with Cantabria during the Peninsular War. He had first heard about its advantageous qualities during his mission in Corunna in 1810, where he had to agree with the *Junta* of Galicia on combined diversionary operations along the Northern coast. His orders also required him to investigate the most effective ways in which the Royal Navy could conduct those operations, by determining the best ports which could be used to either meet with and supply local Spanish guerrilla forces, or that could be developed into logistics centres for the British.[4]

When Popham arrived at Corunna, he immediately contacted both the Galician *Junta* members and Captain Robert Mends, of the *Arethusa,* who as commander of a squadron on the Northern coast was already co-operating with the Spanish authorities. In their conversations, Mends pointed out the coastal village of Santoña for those purposes, and invited Popham to participate in some operations planned by the *Mariscal de Campo* Francisco M. Renovales to capture it.[5] The Commodore could not accept the invitation as he was surprisingly recalled by the Admiralty shortly after his arrival. Sir Home therefore returned to England as soon as he had compiled the necessary information. In his concluding report, Popham drew his superiors' attention to San Sebastián instead due to its proximity to the road leading to France.[6] In fact, Cantabria did not interest him at that time.

Two years later circumstances changed. By January 1812 over 25,000 French soldiers had been withdrawn to participate in the Russia campaign and the main theatre of operations in Spain moved towards the country's centre.[7] Wellington's pursuit of *Maréchal* Marmont into Old Castile increased the importance of operations on the Northern coast as a means of diverting *l'Armée du Nord*'s attention. It was essential to control the main sea fortresses

3 Most of the documents analysed come from The National Archives (hereafter, TNA) and local archives such as the *Archivo Histórico Provincial de Cantabria* (hereafter, AHPCan) and the *Archivo Municipal de Santander* (hereafter, AMS).

4 Hugh Popham, *A Damned Cunning Fellow. The eventful Life of Rear-Admiral Sir Home Popham KCB, KCH; KM, FRS. 1762–1820* (Cornwall: The Old Ferry Press, 1991), pp.193–194.

5 TNA: War Office (hereafter, WO) 1/261, p.1099, Popham to the *Junta* of Galicia, 5 September 1810; pp.1095–1098, Mends to Popham, 6 September 1810; pp.1103–1106 and 1106–1109, the *Junta* of Galicia to Popham and *vice versa*, 7 September 1810; pp.1110–1111 and 1115–1120, Renovales to Popham and *vice versa*, 8 September 1810. Also, Foreign Office (hereafter, FO) 72/99, pp.312–313, the *Junta* of Galicia to Richard Wellesley, 7 September 1810; and, pp.41–43, George White to William Hamilton, 7 September 1810.

6 Popham, *A Damned Cunning Fellow*, pp.193–194.

7 Charles Esdaile, *The Peninsular War: A New History* (Suffolk: Penguin Books, 2003), p.370.

along the Cantabrian coast to prevent French communications and supply deliveries. The command of those strongholds would also make the transportation of British dispatches and stores along that shore easier. The British Government therefore supported diversionary operations in spring, and at the end of May the Admiralty sent Popham to the Northern coast with that mission. The proposal made by Lieutenant Colonel Sir Howard Douglas, British liaison officer with the Spanish army in Galicia, seems then to have been accepted.[8] Sir Home's orders involved capturing a seaport which would provide safe anchorage for the squadron, whilst enabling him to meet the guerrillas regularly.[9] Wellington emphasised the importance of those operations even before they had started and recommended that his superiors support them in every possible way.[10] The initial squadron, which consisted of two ships-of-the-line (*Venerable* and *Magnificent*), a troopship (*Diadem*), five frigates (*Medusa, Surveillante, Hostpur, Rhin* and *Iris*) and two sloops (*Rover* and *Lyra*), was reinforced with a battalion of marines and an artillery battery.[11]

The British press quickly relayed Popham's new mission and the convoy's departure from Great Britain without offering their readers many details. The first paper to announce the operation appears to have been the daily evening paper the *Star*. On 8 June it reported in the 'Naval Intelligence Section' that 700 marines were aboard the *Diadem* and a convoy had set off from Portsmouth to Plymouth where they were to join Sir Home on a secret mission to conduct diversionary attacks on the Northern coast of Spain. This is an example of what Wellington complained about in March 1812 when he accused newspapers of revealing too much information about military operations.[12] Unsurprisingly, in the following days various regional papers also included that news with only slight changes: the *Bury and Norwich Post*, the *Stamford Mercury*, the *Nottingham Journal*, the *Norfolk Chronicle*, and the *Aberdeen Press and Journal*.[13] Unlike the *Star*, they generally published that news in prominent pages among other relevant information about the Peninsular War. More importantly,

8 Arsenio García Fuertes, *No sin nosotros: La Aportación Militar Española a la Victoria Aliada en las Campañas de 1811 y 1812 de la Guerra Peninsular* (Madrid: CSED, 2016), p.308.

9 William G. Perrin and Christopher Lloyds (eds.), *The Keith Papers: Selected from the Papers of Admiral Viscount Keith* (London: Navy Records Society, 1927–1955), pp.267–268, Popham to Keith, 30 May 1812. This document is also mentioned in Joshua Moon, *Wellington's Two Front War. The Peninsular Campaigns, at Home and Abroad, 1808–1814* (Oklahoma: University of Oklahoma Press, 2011), pp.124–125. For Popham's instructions on the Northern coast see Popham, *A Damned Cunning Fellow*, p.197.

10 Moon, *Wellington's Two Front War*, p.125, Wellington to Lord Liverpool, 10 June 1812.

11 This information in British Library, Loan 57/108, Melville Papers. Access has been possible thanks to Dr Jacqueline Reiter (2019), 'Questions about Popham'. Email (27/12/2019). Briefly explained in Popham, *A Damned Cunning Fellow*, p.197; and, William James, *The Naval History of Great Britain: From the Declaration of War by France in February 1793, to the Accession of George IV in January 1820* (London: Harding, Lepard and Co., 1826), p.89.

12 Hannah Barker, 'England, 1760–1815,' in Hannah Barker and Simon Burrows (eds), *Press, Politics and the Public Sphere in Europe and North America, 1760–1820* (Cambridge: Cambridge University Press, 2009), p.99.

13 *Star* (London), 8 June 1812, p.3; *Bury and Norwich Post* (Suffolk), 10 June 1812, p.2; *Stamford Mercury* (Lincolnshire), 12 June 1812, p.2; *Nottingham Journal* (Nottinghamshire) and *Norfolk Chronicle* (Norfolk), 13 June 1812, p.1 and p.2, respectively; and, *Aberdeen Press and Journal* (Aberdeenshire), 17 June 1812, p.3.

they omitted the nature of that secret mission highlighting, instead, the names of the officers involved in it.

This marked the beginning of Popham's constant presence in the British press. A short analysis of *The British Newspaper Archive* website's catalogue shows that during Sir Home's mission in 1812 British periodicals included news on his actions regularly between July and August. The number of references made during this period reaches 180 of which around 25% belongs to national papers. These figures reveal a sharp increase in those months. From the six references already mentioned in June, they multiplied by fourteen in July (to approximately 84), and in the following month 96 were identified. Such attention by the press at that moment is not surprising as it coincided with Wellington's success in Old Castile.[14] Popham's operations in support of the Anglo-Spanish Army were of interest to the press as well. Although newspapers relayed mainly official dispatches received in the Admiralty and published in *The London Gazette*, private correspondence from officers in the squadron on the Northern coast was occasionally printed.

Despite their varying political ideologies, all editors coincided in repeatedly using positive terms ('success', 'successful', 'brilliant', etc.) to introduce those reports or information about Popham. His manoeuvres were then either directly, or in more subtle ways, praised. This, together with the frequency of those references to his operations, suggests an attempt to maintain readers' interest in the Peninsular War at a time when news was encouraging and positive. Also, as papers were arguably generators of public opinion, it might be seen as a way to sustain support to British involvement in the Spanish cause. This theory is also supported by the fact that in September, when the Siege of Burgos was at a stalemate, references dropped drastically, by around 81 per cent.

A more personal interest could be inferred as well. The Commodore's prestige had been damaged after his assumed connections with Peter Finnerty, and his mission on the Northern coast might have been seen as an opportunity to boost it again.[15] The anticipated results did not entirely emerge, however, due to a poetical creation, according to *The Spirit of Public Journals for 1812,* published in an unspecified paper on 3 September. Although it is difficult to know with certainty British readers' interest in the operations, that poem, entitled 'Sir Home Popham's exploits', shows not only that they were followed but also a less positive vision of that figure.[16]

Once in Corunna, on 9 June, Popham together with Sir Howard Douglas and *Teniente General* Castaños started planning the forthcoming operations to neutralise *l'Armée du Nord*. The combined attacks with the Seventh Army, under *Teniente General* Gabriel Mendizábal's orders, were launched a week later.[17] They focused, quite successfully for

14 Zack White, 'From Cintra to Salamanca: Shifting Popular Perceptions of the War in the Iberian Peninsula, 1808–1812,' *British Journal for Military History*, 1:3 (2015), pp.60–79.

15 Popham, *A Damned Cunning Fellow*, p.195.

16 Stephen Jones (ed.), *The Spirit of Public Journals for 1812. Being an Impartial Selection of the most Ingenious Essays and Jeux D'Esprits that appear in the Newspapers and Other Publications. With Explanatory Notes and Anecdotes of Many of the Persons Alluded to* (London: S. Gosnell, 1812), Vol. 16, p.296.

17 In 1812 Spanish regular forces were organised in seven smaller armies. The Seventh was composed of the guerrillas in the Cantabrian mountains and in Navarre. They were organised in five divisions: *División de Vanguardia Cántabra* [Cantabrian Advance Guard] (commanded by *Brigadier* Juan Díaz

a month, on the main French sea fortresses along the Basque coast (Lequeitio, Bermeo, Portugalete, Bilbao and Guetaria). The operations moved westward into Cantabrian ports in July. After Douglas sent a circular to the guerrilla leaders (now part of the Seventh Army) to co-operate with the British squadron,[18] Sir Home and the commander of the Iberian Division, Francisco de Longa, organised an action at Castro Urdiales for 6 July. On 29 June Popham had communicated with Admiral George Keith about this operation and also how important it was for the Spanish, not for him yet, to regain control of Santoña that, in his own words, 'has become one of the strongest positions on the North Coast of Spain'.[19] The occupation of Castro, which could also be used as a logistics hub, would make a subsequent gradual attack on Santoña easier.

When Popham arrived in Castro on 6 July, Captain George Collier, of the *Surveillante*, had already ordered a company of marines to disembark to assist Longa. However, the approach of French reinforcements made them withdraw. Operations were resumed the following day and, after a fierce attack on the castle, the French garrison surrendered.[20] Once Castro had been liberated, Sir Home sought the advice of the Spanish generals on the suitability of the town as a base for communicating and supplying Wellington's forces but was advised that Santander was more appropriate.[21] This marked a turning point in Popham's view of Cantabrian ports and their usefulness for his mission. Castro, as Rear Admiral Robert Deans said, 'was not the sheltered harbour to support Wellington Popham was looking for, but it was a useful foothold'.[22] As Santander was in enemy hands, Castro was essential to cut off an eventual French withdrawal from Santoña and also to prevent supplies from Bayonne from reaching that port. Therefore, Sir Home recommended that it be fortified. Nonetheless, he still preferred Guetaria to coordinate his diversionary operations and, consequently, together with the forces commanded by Francisco Espoz y Mina and those of Gaspar Jáuregui, tried to free it.[23]

Two important pieces of news made Popham change his plans in the Basque Country: first, rumours of a French evacuation of Santander on 25 July and, secondly, *Brigadier* Juan

---

Porlier), *1º División Castellana* [1st Castilian Division] (Colonel Jerónimo Merino Cob), *2ª División Iberia* [2nd Iberian Division] (Colonel Francisco de Longa), *3ª División Vascongada* [3rd Basque Division] (Field Marshal Mariano Renovales), and, *4ª División Navarra* [4th Division from Navarre] (Brigadier Franscisco Espoz y Mina). García Fuertes, *No sin nosotros*, pp.417–418.

18 Stephen W. Fullom, *The Life of General Sir Howard Douglas, BART., G.C.B., G.C.M.G., F.R.S., D.C.L., from his notes, conversations and correspondence* (London: John Murray, 1863), pp.169–170. Included in García Fuertes, *No sin nosotros*, pp.665–666.

19 TNA: WO 1/263, pp.33–39, Popham to Keith, 29 June 1812.

20 *The London Gazette* (London), n.16626, 25–28 July 1812, pp.1440–1441, Keith to J.W. Croker, 28 July 1812. Also, in James Stanier Clarke and John McArthur, *The Naval Chronicle for 1812: containing a General and Biographical History of the Royal Navy of the United Kingdom: with a variety of original papers on nautical subjects* (London: Joyce Gold and John Ralfe, 1812), Vol. 28, pp.164–165.

21 TNA: WO 1/263, pp.61–62, Popham to Keith, 26 July 1812.

22 Popham, *A Damned Cunning Fellow*, pp.200–201.

23 Carmen Gómez Rodrigo, 'Ayuda inglesa a Santander durante la Guerra de la Independencia', in *XL Aniversario del Centro de Estudios Montañeses* (Santander: Diputación Provincial, 1976), Vol. 1, p.407, Francisco de Longa to Mendizábal, 10 July 1812.

Díaz Porlier's plans to attack that city.[24] Sir Home decided to cooperate with the Spanish brigadier, as he informed Mina on 21 July, so as to prevent a possible retreat of the enemy that could reinforce *l'Armée du Portugal* and hinder Wellington's actions.[25] Thus, Popham's presence in Santander was not due to his initial interest in the city as a safe port. The general development of events brought him there. The *Venerable* arrived in Santander on 22 July. On that same day Wellington defeated Marmont in Salamanca, achieving his most important victory that year. As Wellington himself acknowledged, this was partly possible thanks to the operations on the Northern coast preventing Caffarelli from reinforcing *l'Armée du Portugal* properly before the battle.[26] Popham's masterstroke, however, had not taken place yet.

Porlier was already besieging the city when Sir Home entered Santander port, but the attack was delayed due to a lack of artillery. A common plan was agreed and, though the squadron was able to gain control of La Magdalena peninsula and the port, the first Anglo-Spanish assault on the city on 27 July failed. Operations were therefore blocked for several days. Popham took the opportunity to then question the Spanish brigadier on the advantages of that port for Wellington's communications and the delivery of troops and supplies. The results of those discussions reinforced the benefits of using Santander as a logistics centre. Nonetheless, the anchorage in that port needed to be examined.[27] Three days later, *Teniente General* Mendizábal arrived in the area and a combined attack was planned. Aware of this, *Général de Brigade* Jean-Louis Dubreton ordered a complete evacuation on the night of 2 August.[28]

The following day, Wellington praised Popham's diversionary operations and encouraged him to continue them. This was the first of many dispatches they would exchange.[29] The capture of Santander, which Charles Oman defined as 'the most important event that had happened on the Northern coast since 1809', put the best port between Galicia and France into British hands.[30] For this reason, the event was widely covered by the papers.

The first papers to reveal that news were seemingly the London evening publication the *Globe*, and the provincial *Oxford University and City Herald* on 8 August. They briefly relayed

24 TNA: WO 1/348, p.3, Popham to Wellington, 4 August 1812. For that evacuation see José Simón Cabarga, *Santander en la Guerra de la independencia* (Santander: José S. Cabarga, 1968), pp.225–226.

25 TNA: WO 1/263, pp.89–92, Popham to Mina, 21 July 1812; and, p.3, Popham to Wellington, 4 August 1812. J. W. Fortescue, *A History of the British Army* (London: MacMillan and Co., 1917), p.554 also mentions the importance of Popham's operations.

26 Popham, *A Damned Cunning Fellow*, p.201, Wellington to General William Bentick, 28 July 1812. John Gurwood (ed.), *The Dispatches of Field Marshal the Duke of Wellington, K.G. during his various campaigns in India, Denmark, Portugal, Spain, the Low Countries, and France. From 1799 to 1818* (London: Parker, Furnivall and Parker, 1844), Vol. 5, pp.765–766, Wellington to Lord Henry Bathurst, 28 July 1812. This latter published in *The London Gazette Extraordinary*, n.16.633, 16 August 1812, p.1613.

27 See above, n.21.

28 Popham's operation in Santander is briefly described in Popham, *A Damned Cunning Fellow*, pp.201–202. Also, in more detail in Charles Oman, *A History of the Peninsular War* (Oxford: Clarendon Press, 1914), Vol. 6, pp.554–556.

29 Gurwood, *Dispatches*, p.329, Wellington to Popham, 4 August 1812. Moon, *Wellington's Two Front War*, p.126.

30 Oman, *Peninsular War*, p.555.

Popham's successful expedition in Santander according to the Commodore's dispatches which had just arrived in Plymouth. On the following days the *Salisbury and Winchester Journal*, the *Public Ledger and Daily Advertiser*, the *Star*, the *Perthshire Courier*, and the *Kentish Gazette* also published that same information.[31] More details on the operation were offered by the *Globe* on 13 August, when a private letter from an officer in the squadron was printed.[32] The first official information appeared two days later though. On 15 August, *The London Gazette* published, by order of the Admiralty, the reports about Popham's actions in Santander. The *Gazette* later went on, (on 18 August) to publish details of Wellington's and Keith's satisfaction with them.[33] After that, although it seems the press limited itself to copying the news in that official journal, some brief comments were added. These show that papers, regardless of their ideology, were not unanimous in offering an initially positive description of the operation and, like the *Star*, some presented it as a failure focusing on the French withdrawal from the Cantabrian city instead. In any case, Santander was not in the spotlight. The press did not consider the city and its port of much importance as a strategic position. On the contrary, it was simply mentioned peripherally and as the setting where those diversionary operations to favour Wellington were taking place.

Despite British papers' stance, Popham's involvement in the diversionary operations on the Northern coast was complete and efficient. Although the success of those attacks was hindered by the lack of a well-organised plan (in fact, a rather improvised one), his co-operation with the Spanish forces was crucial to freeing Santander. For this reason, Sir Home was received in the Cantabrian city with full honours and great expectation.

Popham in Santander: mixed feelings

Before going ashore on 3 August, the Commodore ordered his men to examine the safety of the anchorage which was, finally, confirmed.[34] The capture of Santander was not merely a notable achievement; the information gathered about its sea and land communications suggested that it met his need for a safe port, as he told Wellington on 4 August.[35] The collaboration of the inhabitants was, however, in question. Rumours spoke of a pro-French attitude in the city.[36] Consequently, on 3 August, Sir Home sent the city council a proclamation strongly recommending Santander inhabitants to keep calm. The local authorities, willing to cooperate with the British officer, immediately published an edict to maintain

31 The *Globe* (London) and *Oxford University and City Herald* (Oxfordshire), 8 August 1812, pp.3 and 4–5, respectively; *Salisbury and Winchester Journal* (Wiltshire), 10 August 1812, pp.3–4; *Public Ledger and Daily Advertiser* (London), 11 August 1812, p.1; *Star* (London), 11 August 1812, pp.2–3; *Perthshire Courier* (Perthshire), 13 August 1812, pp.1–2; and, *Kentish Gazette* (Kent), p.4.

32 The *Globe* (London), 13 August 1812, pp.2–3.

33 *The London Gazette*, n.16632, 11–15 August 1812, p.1584 and n.16.635, 15–18 August 1812, p.1643. The latter also included in Stanier Clarke and McArthur, *The Naval Chronicle for 1812*, Vol. 28, pp.171–172.

34 Popham, *A Damned Cunning Fellow*, p.202.

35 TNA: WO 1/348, p.3, Popham to Wellington, 4 August 1812.

36 Cabarga, *Santander*, pp.228–229.

public order.[37] Despite the underlying mistrust the latter's proclamation might have aroused among locals, Popham and the squadron disembarked and were warmly welcomed. An example of that reception can be seen in Deans's diary in which he described Santander as 'a pretty town' where he had enjoyed 'a great deal of pleasant company'. He also revealed that he entertained himself strolling around the place and attending the balls that were held soon after the liberation.[38] They were then actively involved in the city's everyday life. This points to the inhabitants' willingness to warmly receive British officers and soldiers in the early days.

Sir Home's proclamation had been accompanied by his first request for supplies, particularly 'a hundred bread rations of one-pound each, a hundred pints of wine and 20 pounds of meat'.[39] At that moment the Provincial *Junta* was still away from the city and the local authority had to take the responsibility for the contacts with the British allies.[40] Although the request was immediately accepted, Santander was in a wretched state. French requisitions and taxes had drained the public and private warehouses and to guarantee those supplies the Council had to ask neighbouring villages and civilians to collaborate. That same day, the mayor of Torrelavega, a neighbouring village, was asked to send to Santander the wheat stored there. The answer was not the expected one. The village warehouses were empty, and the wheat obtained that day was for the 1st Battalion of *Tiradores de Cantabria*, lodged there. The following day, the mayors of other neighbouring valleys were also invited to sell Popham 40 oxen to supply his crew with fresh meat. Evidence shows they did.[41]

These were not the only measures taken in the city to meet the squadron's needs. There are also several examples of locals buying other products at their own expense. On 4 August, for instance, León J. Eydelin Gayoso, who soon after would be officially appointed English interpreter for Santander,[42] at the request of the council, bought vegetables and fruit as a present for the squadron. That day local authorities also asked two well-known inhabitants, Sirs Uribarri and Hondal, to pay for a barrel of liquor for Popham's men. Taking into account the city records of payments, that month another three locals bought products for the same purpose, for instance the typical Basque white wine known as *txacolí*, beans, flour, bread, and meat.[43] The local authorities did not always return the money advanced or only did so after being sent a series of strong complaints.

Santander's willingness to collaborate with the allies was beyond doubt. For this reason, Sir Home's initial unsatisfactory opinion about the locals and their patriotism soon changed. Gayoso, the above-mentioned Spanish interpreter of English, was entrusted by the council

---

37 AMS: *Libro de Actas de Sesiones del Ayuntamiento*, año 1812, Pleno 25 n.1, pp.1–5, 3 August 1812.

38 Popham, *A Damned Cunning Fellow*, p.202.

39 My translation. See above, n.37.

40 Cabarga, *Santander*, pp.228–229 and 234.

41 AMS: Leg. A-66 n.1, Pantaleón Sánchez Bustamante to Santander Council, 3 August 1812; and, n.10, Santander council to the mayors of some neighbouring valleys, 4 August 1812.

42 AMS: Leg. 66 n.5, León Eydelin Gayoso to Mendizábal, 11 August 1812; Eydelin to Santander council and *vice versa*, 12 and 19 August 1812, respectively; *Libro de Actas*, Pleno 25 n.1, pp.23–26, 19 August 1812.

43 See above, n.37. AMS, Leg. A-79 n.191, Joaquín Gutiérrez, 23 October 1812; Leg. B-291 n.1, Luis del Campo, [August-September 1812]; Leg. A-43 n.48, José A. Prado to Santander Council, 22 August 1812.

to run the initial contacts with Popham. After some conversations on board the *Venerable*, the former collaborated in the Commodore's second proclamation to Santander inhabitants on 6 August. The relevance of this document lies in two facts. First, Popham justified his early recommendation for public order in an attempt to encourage the locals' patriotism owing to those rumours of a pro-French attitude in Santander. His meetings with respectable inhabitants made him realise, however, that he had been wrongly advised. Secondly, Sir Home announced his intention to turn Santander into his logistics centre and port of communication with Great Britain.[44]

During August, Santander council was in charge of supplying the British squadron and they did so with all the means at their disposal. However, good intentions were not enough and Popham's men had to buy some more basic products in local shops where prices had been shamelessly inflated. Sir Home had to intervene, reporting that unfair practice to the authorities, and some actions may have been taken, as there is no evidence of similar complaints subsequently.[45] Furthermore, to compensate Popham and the squadron, and also to encourage the city trade, on 12 August the circulation of British silver currency was accepted and its value fixed.[46]

Despite these episodes, coexistence was peaceful that month. There seemed to be a welcoming atmosphere in which the authorities sought to please the British allies in every possible way. Concessions were even made on traditional customs, for example, by allowing theatrical representations.[47] Being involved in the city's daily life, the squadron took part in some remarkable events such as the *Te Deums* held to celebrate the freeing of Santander and for marking the official oath to uphold the Spanish 1812 Constitution.[48]

However, everything changed from mid-August onwards and, especially, in September. Popham's squadron resumed their operations in the Basque Country and Santander started to be used as a logistics hub. British and Spanish soldiers began to assemble in the city to join operations, along with civilians returning home or who were attracted by the liberation of the place. For example, on 31 August, it was announced that 600 British soldiers would disembark in the city the following day, and the Provincial Government asked the local authorities to lodge and feed them.[49] In time, Santander became overwhelmed and the relationship with the allies started to cool down. The enemy's proximity also raised indifference or coldness among locals to British presence there. There was a growing fear

44 AMS: Leg. A-66 n.8, Popham's proclamation to Santander inhabitants, 6 August 1812. Also, in Cabarga, *Santander*, pp.230–231.

45 AMS: Leg. A-66 n.9, Popham to Santander Council, 6 August 1812.

46 AMS: Leg. A-66 n.134, Matheo Gordey, 12 August 1812; *Libro de Actas,* Pleno 25 n.1, pp.17–19, 12 August 1812; and, AHPCan, Sautuola, 11/58, Luis del Campo, 12 August 1812.

47 For the heated debate among local authorities, provincial government and Mendizábal regarding theatrical representations see AMS: *Libro de Actas*, Pleno 25 n.1, pp.79–83, 23 September 1812; and, Leg. A-69 n.29, Santander Council to Mendizábal and *vice versa*, 23 September, 20 November and 1 December 1812.

48 AMS: *Libro de Actas*, Pleno 25 n.1, pp.10–11 and 11–16, 8 and 9–10 August 1812, respectively. Also, AMS: Leg. A-66 n.138, and AHPCan, Sautuola, 11/55, p.1, Minute, 10 August 1812.

49 AMS: Leg. A-64 n.29, Junta of [Cantabria] to Santander Council, 31 August 1812.

of French reprisals for those who had collaborated with the British, if the city was reoccupied.[50] In addition, subsistence supplies for the inhabitants of Santander also began to dwindle, leading to clashes between local authorities and the provincial government on whose responsibility it was to manage the Anglo-Spanish troops' presence. The situation was so precarious that requisitions even had to be carried out to provide British soldiers with basic cooking utensils. Even so, the problem was not completely solved, and those demands just contributed to the locals' increasing frostiness towards the allies.[51]

The situation was similar when it came to lodgings. There was not enough accommodation either in public buildings or private houses and a few problems arose. On 29 September, Popham reported to the council that, due to some misunderstanding, several British officers had not been lodged the previous night. The person responsible for lodging them had a different story: the officers had refused the rooms offered as they did not suit their rank. Local authorities tried immediately to grant them proper places to stay by asking, without success, for all the Spanish cadets to be transferred to a neighbouring village. No solution came and in December the council had to ask Sir Home to make his men accept the lodgings assigned.[52] In short, local authorities in Santander tried to do their best.

Santander: a suitable British logistics centre on the Northern coast

From late August onwards, Popham's squadron was involved, together with the forces of the Seventh Spanish Army, in two main diversionary operations to support Wellington's movement forward: first, in Guetaria and, then, in Santoña.

In the first half of September, the Basque village of Guetaria was the main goal both to interrupt the enemy's communications through the main road from France to Madrid and to isolate the fortress of Santoña. Also, as Guetaria was considered a strong port by the French, an attack on it would draw the enemy's attention, thereby diverting reinforcements based at Vitoria.[53] The Anglo-Portuguese army's advance towards Valladolid increased the importance of those operations. Determined to capture Guetaria, Sir Home tried to organise a combined attack with Mendizábal. Three reasons though prevented the latter from getting directly involved in the action: a pressing lack of ammunition, the scattering of his forces involved in other operations and, mainly, the enemy's pressure on Bilbao. Despite this, the Spanish general ordered Renovales and Porlier to join the British squadron in the

50 University of Southampton, Hartley Library, Wellington Papers (hereafter, WP): 1/350/78, Popham to Wellington, 29 September 1812.

51 See, for example, AMS: *Libro de Actas*, Pleno 25 n.1, pp.61–67, 14 September 1812. For more information on British soldiers' need for cooking utensils see AMS, Leg. A-66 n.52, Santander Council to Antonio Joaquín Calera, provincial governor, 2 October 1812; n.51, Hermenegildo Hidalgo, war commissary, to Santander Council and *vice versa*, 3 October 1812; *Libro de Actas*, Pleno 25 n.1, pp.97–99, 3 October 1812.

52 AMS: Leg. A-66 n.15, Popham to Santander Council and this latter to Calera, 29 September 1812; Leg. A-67 n.32, Santander council to Mendizábal, 3 December 1812; and, *Libro de Actas*, Pleno 25 n.1, pp.150–152, 9 December 1812.

53 WP: 1/348/74, Douglas to Wellington, 15 August 1812. TNA: WO 1/262, pp.461–468, Collier to Douglas, 18 May 1812. TNA: WO 1/263, pp.121–123, Popham to Keith, 16 August 1812.

offensive.[54] Mendizábal's own problems with the commanders of the guerrilla divisions under his orders did not make co-operation easier.[55] Sir Home interpreted his words as lack of involvement and blamed him for the failed capture of Guetaria. As a consequence, the relationship between Mendizábal and Sir Home started to become strained. Although it had not been possible to capture that Basque village, the British squadron's combined actions with the guerrilla divisions (those of Gaspar, Renovales and the Cantabrian Juan López Campillo) were successful in diverting the enemy from Wellington's movements.[56] Popham's interest turned then to the Cantabrian coast.

By the time the siege of Burgos had started, all efforts were focused on Santoña. Due to Wellington's operations and the time of the season, Santander was the most important place to maintain for use as a British logistics centre and a port of communication on the northern coast. Control of Santoña therefore seemed vital. On 26 September Popham asked for Wellington's approval of his intended actions over the latter port and insisted on its benefits in consecutive dispatches to Lord Keith.[57] At the beginning of October Wellington authorised those actions on the grounds that it was crucial to prevent French forces crossing the Ebro to reinforce *Général de division* Clausel. His interest in the Basque port had not disappeared but circumstances prevented those operations.[58] Thus, in Santander Sir Home started preparing his co-operation in the siege of Santoña. In doing so, on 7 October he asked the city council for the workforce and wood to build carts with the intention of moving supplies and military equipment there.[59]

While those operations were underway, the Admiralty was considering the squadron's return to England due to the awful weather conditions on that coast in winter and the growing presence of American privateers. Curiously enough, at the same time Wellington was struggling with that department for a naval reinforcement to be sent to the Bay of Biscay.[60] In fact, on 16 September Popham informed Wellington of the squadron's orders to return. The former made it clear though that he disagreed with that measure. Remaining on the Cantabrian coastline had been proven safe for the fleet in winter provided that Santander was in allied hands. Sir Home emphasised again the good qualities of that port as a logistics hub for the operations of the Anglo-Portuguese army. Just one day after this announcement, 17 September, in another dispatch to Wellington Popham seemed resolved to keep his position as long as his presence there could be useful.[61] Wellington's complaints to the

54 TNA: WO 1/263, pp.299–301, Mendizábal to Popham, 23 August 1812; pp.347–354, Carrol to Wellington, 24 August 1812; and, pp.215–217, Mendizábal to Popham, 28 August 1812.

55 TNA: FO 72/133, pp.126–128, Carrol to Wellington, 1 August 1812.

56 WP: 1/350/15, Popham to Wellington, 8 September 1812; and, 1/350/69, Popham to Keith, 15 September 1812. The Spanish forces involved in the attack in Guetaria in Popham, *A Damned Cunning Fellow*, p.205.

57 WP: 1/350/69, Popham to Wellington, 26 September 1812; and, TNA: WO 1/263, pp.447–450 and 519–520, Popham to Keith, 28 September and 12 October 1812, respectively. These operations are briefly explained in Popham, *A Damned Cunning Fellow*, pp.205–208.

58 Gurwood (ed.), *Dispatches*, Vol. 6, p.101, Wellington to Popham, 2 October 1812.

59 AMS: Leg. A-66, n. 47, Popham to Santander Council, 7 October 1812.

60 Moon, *Wellington's Two Front War*, pp.115–116.

61 WP: 1/350/46 and 48, Popham to Wellington, 16 and 17 September 1812, respectively. TNA: WO 1/263, pp.475–478, Popham to Keith, 29 September 1812.

Admiralty to send more frigates to the northern coast and Lord Melville's inability to do so made Sir Home's stay the most sensible measure to take. As Keith explained to the Secretary of the Admiralty, J. W. Croker, on 5 October, Popham should remain in the Cantabrian port to favour the army's movement forward.[62]

Wellington's support of Sir Home's operations was decisive. Those actions and the Commodore's presence in Santander were necessary even in the event of an Anglo-Spanish withdrawal from Burgos. Otherwise, Caffarelli would reinforce *l'Armée du Portugal* complicating the retreat. According to Wellington, Popham had to be on that coast since he would give those harassment operations more credibility and, in consequence, their effectiveness would increase. This points to Wellington's high regard of Sir Home and his actions. Five days later, Wellington insisted on the need for Popham to remain on the northern coast and highlighted the importance of retaining Santander. It was the only port that could guarantee Sir Home's presence and, therefore, the operations to support the Anglo-Portuguese army. On no account should Popham risk the security of Santander in an attempt to capture Santoña. The loss of the former port would mean the squadron's withdrawal, with terrible consequences.[63] The importance of Santander for Wellington's operations therefore seems unquestionable. That is why Sir Home was finally allowed to remain and his squadron was reinforced with a ship-of-the-line, the *Abercrombie*, and a second battalion of marines.[64]

Diverting troops was not the only role assigned to Santander at that time. As Popham insisted, the qualities of that port made it essential also to ensure the reception and safe delivery of stores. Between September and early November 1812, supplies were conveyed to Santander to support Sir Home, the Spanish forces in that area and also Wellington. On 26 September Popham informed Keith that he had sent the *Surveillante* to Corunna to bring 'provisions and stores' to the Cantabrian port. Around that date, Wellington also gave orders for all the transports with musket ammunition on board in the Galician port to be sent to Santander.[65] British stores were therefore being gathered in Santander, which underlined the role the city could play as a logistics centre in supplying the army in northern Spain. Aware of this and due to Sir Home's presence in the city, on 26 September Wellington sent the former his first request for supplies to carry out the siege of Burgos. It included '40 barrels of gunpowder each containing 90 pounds' and also an appeal to local authorities in Santander for pack animals.[66] The following day, Wellington also asked Popham for biscuit.[67]

---

62 TNA: WO 1/263, pp.443–445, Keith to Croker, 5 October 1812.

63 Gurwood (ed.), Vol. 6, pp.116 and 122, Wellington to Popham, 12 and 17 October 1812, respectively. Moon, *Wellington's Two Front War*, pp.127–128. Popham, *A Damned Cunning Fellow*, pp.206–207. Robert K. Stucliffe, *British Expeditionary Warfare and the Defeat of Napoleon, 1793-1815* (Suffolk: The Boydell Press, 2016), p.138.

64 Moon, *Wellington's Two Front War*, p.250 states that the squadron was reinforced by the *Abercrombie*. However, it replaced the *Magnificient*, which had returned to England in August. See above, n.11.

65 TNA: WO 1/263, pp.423–425, Popham to Keith, 26 September 1812; Gurwood, *Dispatches*, Vol. 6, pp.114–115, Wellington to Bathurst, 11 October 1812.

66 Gurwood, *Dispatches*, Vol. 6, p.90, Wellington to Popham, 26 September 1812. Fortescue, *British Army*, pp.557–558 and Moon, *Wellington's Two Front War*, p.126 just mention this initial gunpowder request.

67 WP: 1/351/81, Wellington to Popham, 27 September 1812.

Sir Home received those requests on 29 September. On that date he immediately asked Santander council for mules and carts to urgently send Wellington the gunpowder at his disposal. However, Popham faced a severe lack of transportation assets in the city. As the biscuit was not available, he also sent a victualler to Corunna to bring it to Santander. The gunpowder in that initial request, which was repeated by Wellington on 2 October, did not arrive in Burgos until 5 October. It took it six days to get there whereas a single person could do that same journey, as Captain Bouverie had demonstrated, in just three.[68] Santander's main drawback was thereby revealed.

Four more requests of military supplies were sent to Popham in Santander including gunpowder (in particular, 40 barrels of 90 pounds each on October 5 and 14, and 200 barrels on 8 November) and the well-known 24-pounder long guns (2 October).[69] To handle these demands properly and anticipate Wellington's future needs, Sir Home asked his superiors at least four times to send gunpowder, muskets, ammunition and also provisions to Santander.[70] At the end of September, following Wellington's initial demand, Popham asked Keith to send 100 barrels of gunpowder to the Cantabrian port. In fact, there is evidence that this request, like the others made by Sir Home mentioned previously, were accepted and those supplies disembarked in Santander.[71]

On the whole, Wellington's needs were met except for those naval guns that were still in Reinosa when the siege of Burgos was lifted. Although Douglas and Popham had suggested it from the very beginning, Wellington's request for proper artillery to open a breach in Burgos castle was said to be made too late.[72] That was not the only determining factor though. Wellington was aware that Sir Home had to face a severe lack of transportation assets and security in his deliveries inland. Although Popham tried to have carts and mules available regularly in Santander, the shortage obliged Wellington to send his pack animals to Reinosa delaying deliveries further.[73] Wellington bitterly complained about that shortage because it prevented him from making use in Castile of the means available in Santander and Madrid.[74] Also, the difficulties inherent in the transportation of provisions and, above all, heavy guns by land did not make things easier. Despite that, Santander showed itself as a

68 WP: 1/350/78 and 77, Popham to Wellington, 29 September 1812. Gurwood, *Dispatches*, Vol. 6, pp.101 and 106, Wellington to Popham, 2 and 5 October 1812, respectively.

69 Gurwood (ed.), *Dispatches*,Vol. 6, pp.106 and 119, Wellington to Popham, 5 and 14 October 1812, respectively. Moon, *Wellington's Two Front War*, p.127 marks October 2 as the day when the naval guns request was submitted. Also, Carlos Santacara, *La Guerra de la independencia vista por los británicos* (Madrid: Machado Libros, 2005), p.488 makes reference to the request of those naval guns.

70 TNA: WO 1/263, p.487, Popham to Keith, 29 September 1812; pp.395–398, Bourke to Bathurst, 2 October 1812; pp.516–518, Popham to Keith, 14 October 1812; pp.595–598, Popham to Keith, 8 November 1812.

71 TNA: WO 1/263, p.487, Popham to Keith, 29 September 1812; pp.443–445 and 515–518, Keith to Croker, 5 and 20 October 1812, respectively.

72 See above, n.70.

73 WP: 1/350/78, Popham to Wellington, 29 September 1812. AMS, Leg. A-66 n.47, Popham to Santander Council, 7 October 1812. TNA: WO 1/263, pp.549–550, Popham to Wellington, 10 October 1812. Fortescue, *A History*, p.583 makes reference to Wellington's soldiers going to Reinosa to collect those naval guns.

74 Gurwood, *Dispatches*, Vol. 6, pp.172–175, Wellington to Liverpool, 23 November 1812.

key strategical location and, after Wellington broke up the Siege of Burgos, military supplies and provisions continued arriving in the Cantabrian port.

Santander was also identified to as a useful point of communication with Great Britain. From the very first moment and all along his stay on the northern coast, Popham emphasised the good qualities of that port for the British Government to contact Wellington and *vice versa*. In a dispatch to the latter on 4 August, Sir Home seemed certain that Santander would be made Wellington's port of communication.[75] In fact, British authorities tried to make the most of those advantageous characteristics. Later that month, on 15 August, Bathurst informed Wellington that instructions would be sent to him the following day via both Corunna and Santander. Bathurst admitted, however, Wellington would receive the ones by Santander sooner.[76]

Around the same date, 18 August, the Admiralty also officially allowed Popham to send his reports directly from Santander to England.[77] Sir Home had already done so on several occasions even before his superiors had granted him that permission. After their authorisation, he repeatedly offered that possibility to Wellington. On 17 September, for example, Popham re-emphasised this alternative to Corunna to Wellington and highlighted the rapidity of those communications through Santander port: 'Whenever your Lordship wishes an immediate conveyance to England if you will have the goodness to send [it] to Santander it shall sail immediately. We have had letters landed in three days from England'.[78] Wellington appears to have finally agreed to Sir Home's suggestion at least once, as Lieutenant Colonel Richard Bourke let Bathurst know on 25 September. However, the following day the former updated that information announcing that, in the absence of British ships in Santander at that time, Wellington had to send those dispatches through Galicia instead.[79]

Two conclusions can be drawn from the above: first, the benefits of the main Cantabrian port were well-known among the British allies and, second, bidirectional communications were occasionally taking place between Great Britain and Santander. Yet, it was not a systematic process. The official British operational base was still in Portugal and the closest official communication channel in Galicia. There was an important drawback which prevented Santander from being made an official port of communication in 1812: the enemy's proximity. The French army was still too close, and the control of the place would not be reliable, according to Wellington, until the Anglo-Portuguese army gained effective control of the Ebro. Santander could not be considered a completely safe port as long as Santoña was occupied by a French garrison. As a consequence, on 17 October Wellington turned

75 TNA: WO 1/262, pp.61–62, Popham to Keith, 26 July 1812; WO 1/348, p.3. Also, in WP: 1/348/23, Popham to Wellington, 4 August 1812. The same idea is repeated in WP 1/348/42, Popham to Douglas, 8 August 1812 and, later on, TNA: WO 1/263, pp.539–542, Popham to Wellington, 10 October 1812.

76 WP: 1/348/72 and 349/73, Bathurst to Wellington, 15 and 22 August 1812, respectively.

77 WP: 1/350/4, Melville to Popham, 18 August 1812.

78 WP: 1/350/15 and 48, Popham to Wellington, 8 and 17 September 1812, respectively.

79 TNA: WO 1/263, pp.371–374 and 387–390, Sir Richard Bourke to Bathurst, 25 and 26 September 1812, respectively.

down Popham's recommendation to make the Cantabrian port his official communications centre.[80] The fate of this city was again closely linked to the general development of events.

A mission coming to an end: discontent

After Wellington's retreat from Burgos, Sir Home remained in Santander in an attempt to divert *l'Armée du Nord* from chasing the Anglo-Portuguese troops.[81] The Admiralty instructions were clear on 27 October. Popham's diversionary operations on the northern coast had to continue for the sake of Wellington's withdrawal. The main Cantabrian port played thus a significant role as an operational hub guaranteeing at the same time the squadron's safety.[82] Sir Home, with Wellington's approval, focused then on the freeing of Santoña.[83] He also tried to prepare Santander for a possible French attack by asking the council again to collaborate in improving up its fortifications. Otherwise, Popham warned them that were the enemy to approach, he would retreat. It was also key to track French movements along the coast and to do so he recommended hiring spies. The city council's apparent reticence to help in the preparations due to the enemy's proximity, together with the problems in everyday life mentioned before, may have deteriorated Sir Home's relations with the local authorities still further.[84]

While trying to fortify the main Cantabrian port, Popham was actively involved in the siege of Santoña. On 2 December, for example, he asked Santander council and also the Royal Consulate in the city for spades and mattocks to be used in the blockade of the village.[85] The operations in Santoña were, however, stalled due to Mendizábal's lack of collaboration. At that moment the Spanish general appeared to be more concerned about political issues ensuring that all the freed territories in the Basque Country took the official oath to uphold

80 Gurwood (ed.), *Dispatches*, p.122, Wellington to Popham, 17 October 1812. Also, Fortescue, *British Army*, p.588.

81 To know more about the Siege of Burgos see Moon, *Wellington's Two Front War*, pp.126–129; Charles Esdaile, *The Duke of Wellington and the Command of the Spanish Army* (London: Macmillan, 1990), pp.59–84, and *id.*, 'Burgos (1812). El asedio de Wellington', in Gonzalo Butrón and Pedro Rújula (eds.), *Los sitios de la Guerra de la independencia: la lucha en las ciudades* (Madrid: Sílex and Universidad de Cádiz, 2012), pp.319–334. Also, Rory Muir, *Wellington. The Path to Victory 1769–1814* (New Haven: Yale University Press, 2013), pp.478–498.

82 TNA: WO 1/263, pp.555–558, Croker to Popham, 27 October 1812.

83 Gurwood, *Dispatches*,Vol. 6, pp.144 and 148–149, Wellington to Popham and Bathurst, 1 and 3 November 1812, respectively.

84 AMS: Leg. A-66 n.8, Popham to Santander Council, 6 August 1812; Leg. A-64 n.28, Provincial Government to Santander council and *vice versa*, 30 and 31 October 1812; Leg. A-66 n.41, Juan Antonio López, War Commissary, to Santander Council and *vice versa*, 30 and 31 October 1812; Leg. 66 n.60, López to the council and *vice versa*, 3 and 4 November 1812; Leg. A-67 n.29, Santander Council to Mendizábal and *vice versa*, 4 and 10 November 1812; *Libro de Actas,* Pleno 25 n.1, pp.119–121 and 122–124, 31 October and 4 November 1812.

85 AHPCan: Real Consulado, 79/75/2A, Popham's secretary to the Royal Consulate and *vice versa,* 2 December 1812; AMS: Leg. A-66 n.71, Popham to Santander Council and *vice versa*, 2 December 1812.

the 1812 Constitution.[86] His attitude exasperated Popham and the absence of an efficient plan to render the place might have made Sir Home withdraw the squadron to Santander, according to Deans, on 4 December.[87] The Spanish generals that were participating in that blockade were not aware of the reasons for the British sudden departure from Santoña, as Campillo explained to Longa on 18 December.[88]

Wellington's retreat to the Portuguese frontier and the lack of operations in the Basque Country and in Santoña meant that the British position in Santander became more precarious. Therefore, despite Wellington's insistence on controlling Santander, the government considered Popham's mission to be over. On 13 December, the *Fairy* arrived in Santander with orders for Sir Home and the squadron to return to Britain. Eight days later, the *Venerable* left the Cantabrian port as *The Morning Chronicle* and *The Morning Post* published at the beginning of January 1813.[89] Wellington bitterly regretted Popham's return to England, given the great benefits his stay in the Cantabrian city during winter would have had for the forthcoming Anglo-Portuguese operations.[90] The squadron's withdrawal meant, as Wellington foresaw, a new French occupation of Santander.[91]

Conclusion

This chapter has explored the references to Santander made by Wellington and Popham in their dispatches in 1812. Allusions to British presence and actions that year in the Cantabrian authorities' minute books and other local primary sources, most of them forgotten, have also been analysed. These documents not only provide a new perspective on Popham's stay in Cantabria, which has previously been oversimplified, but also shed light on the significance of Santander for the course of events elsewhere in the Iberian Peninsula.

In 1812 the strategic importance of that city and its port for Wellington's operations was unquestionable. It offered a strong position from which to support the Anglo-Portuguese advance and force the French to withdraw from the Northern coast. The freeing of Santander was thus not only a military success but also a morale boosting one. Although the diversionary actions along that coast were successful, the co-operation between the British squadron and the Spanish forces in the area reveal an important drawback: their improvised nature. In most cases, as Popham's correspondence shows, the combined attacks were not the result of a well-organised plan. This undoubtedly hindered their effectiveness in capturing the French-held ports on the Bay of Biscay. However, their success should be measured by their impact on Wellington's operations, in which these diversions played an important role. Hence, British newspapers regularly informed their readers about the

86 Carlos Rilova Jericó, 'Bilbao y la revolución de 1808 en el País Vasco a partir de la correspondencia de dos oficiales del ejército aliado (1812)', *Bidebarrieta* 20 (2009), p.155.
87 Popham, *A Damned Canning Fellow*, pp.208–209. Gurwood (ed.), *Dispatches*, Vol. 6, p.116, Wellington to Popham, 12 October 1812.
88 Rafael Palacio Ramos, *Santoña, plaza napoleónica* (Santoña: Ayuntamiento de Santoña, 2015), p.133.
89 Popham, *A Damned Cunning Fellow*, p.209. *The Morning Chronicle* (London), 1 January 1813, p.3; and, *The Morning Post* (London), 2 January 1813, p.3.
90 Gurwood (ed.), *Dispatches*,Vol. 6, p.122, Wellington to Melville and, also, to Bathurst, 26 December 1812.
91 Oman, *Peninsular War*, Vol. 6, pp.525, 257.

squadron's actions on the northern coast relaying mainly official reports. These periodicals did not make any reference though to the strategic importance of Santander, which was just described as the setting for those operations.

The relevance Wellington afforded to the Cantabrian port at that time seemed limited to it being the only place that, in his opinion, could guarantee those essential diversionary operations. Popham's presence in Santander though made Wellington aware of its advantageous qualities to receive and deliver supplies as well as communicate with England. The main flaws of this port were also unveiled: a severe lack of transportation assets, subsistence supplies and lodgings. Also, the enemy's proximity did not render it safe and, therefore, Santander was not turned into the official British logistics base in 1812. Nonetheless, the place emerged as a suitable hub for the forthcoming campaign.

Being Popham's logistics centre was not an easy burden to bear for Santander. The initial welcoming atmosphere in the city seemingly turned to coldness. The Anglo-Portuguese operations appeared to stall and there was a growing fear of a French return. Santander was also overwhelmed and lacked the most basic products, which contributed to the increasing uneasiness amongst locals towards British presence there. Provincial authorities were partly to blame for that strained situation. They avoided their duties and made Santander Council take full responsibility for the Anglo-Spanish relations. Despite that, local powers tried to do their best and coexistence was, in general, peaceful. However, Popham's life was not easy there, since he had to simultaneously deal with everything happening in the city, the diversionary operations eastwards and with Wellington's requests for supplies. All this tested the city, but also showed its potential as a British logistics centre for 1813 and 1814.

Bibliography

Manuscripts

The National Archives of the United Kingdom (TNA), War Office (WO): 1/261; 1/262; 1/263; 1/348; Foreign Office (FO): 72/99; 72/133

University of Southampton, Hartley Library, Wellington Papers (WP): 1/348/72, 74; 1/349/73; 1/350/4, 15, 46, 48, 69, 77, 78; 1/351/81

Archivo Municipal de Santander (AMS): *Libro de Actas de Sesiones del Ayuntamiento*, año 1812, Pleno 25 n.1; Leg. A-43; A-64; A-66; A-67; A-69; A-79

Archivo Histórico Provincial de Cantabria (AHPCan): Sautuola 11/55, 58; Real Consulado, 79/75/2A

Primary Source Books

Fullom, Stephen W., *The Life of General Sir Howard Douglas, BART., G.C.B., G.C.M.G., F.R.S., D.C.L., from his notes, conversations and correspondence* (London: John Murray, 1863)

Gurwood, John (ed.), *The Dispatches of Field Marshal the Duke of Wellington, K.G. during his various campaigns in India, Denmark, Portugal, Spain, the Low Countries, and France. From 1799 to 1818* (London: Parker, Furnivall and Parker, 1844)

Perrin, William G., and Christopher Lloyds (eds.), *The Keith Papers: Selected from the Papers of Admiral Viscount Keith* (London: Navy Records Society, 1927–55)

Stanier Clarke, James and John McArthur, *The Naval Chronicle for 1812: containing a General and Biographical History of the Royal Navy of the United Kingdom: with a variety of original papers on nautical subjects* (London: Joyce Gold and John Ralfe, 1812)

Newspapers and Periodicals

Aberdeen Press and Journal (1812)

Bury and Norwich Post (1812)
The Globe (1812)
Kentish Gazette (1812)
The London Gazette (1812)
The Morning Chronicle (1813)
The Morning Post (1813)
Nottingham Journal (1812)
Norfolk Chronicle (1812)
Oxford University and City Herald (1812)
Perthshire Courier (1812)
Public Ledger and Daily Advertiser (1812)
Salisbury and Winchester Journal (1812)
Star (1812)
Stamford Mercury (1812)

Secondary Sources

Barker, H. and Burrows, S., (eds), *Press, Politics and the Public Sphere in Europe and North America, 1760–1820* (Cambridge: Cambridge University Press, 2009)
Butrón, Gonzalo and Rújula, Pedro, (eds.), *Los sitios de la Guerra de la independencia: la lucha en las ciudades* (Madrid: Sílex and Universidad de Cádiz, 2012)
Esdaile, Charles, *The Duke of Wellington and the Command of the Spanish Army* (London: Macmillan, 1990)
Esdaile, Charles, *The Peninsular War: A New History* (Suffolk: Penguin Books, 2003)
Fortescue, John W., *A History of the British Army* (London: MacMillan and Co., 1917)
García Fuertes, Arsenio, *No sin nosotros: La Aportación Militar Española a la Victoria Aliada en las Campañas de 1811 y 1812 de la Guerra Peninsular* (Madrid: CSED, 2016)
Gómez Rodrigo, Carmen, 'Ayuda inglesa a Santander durante la Guerra de la independencia', in Institución Cultural de Cantabria (eds.), *XL Aniversario del Centro Estudios Montañeses* (Santander: Diputación Provincial, 1976)
Gregorio Sainz, Silvia, 'Relaciones hispanobritánicas durante la Guerra de la independencia (1808-1814). El caso de Cantabria: estudio y repertorio documental' (PhD thesis, University of Oviedo, 2017)
Laspra Rodríguez, Alicia, *Intervencionismo y Revolución. Asturias y Gran Bretaña durante la Guerra de la independencia (1808–1813)* (Oviedo: Real Instituto de Estudios Asturianos, 1982)
James, William, *The Naval History of Great Britain: From the Declaration of War by France in February 1793, to the Accession of George IV in January 1820* (London: Harding, Lepard and Co., 1826)
Moon, Joshua, *Wellington's Two Front War. The Peninsular Campaigns, at Home and Abroad, 1808–1814* (Oklahoma: University of Oklahoma Press, 2011)
Muir, Rory, *Wellington. The Path to Victory 1769–1814* (New Haven: Yale University Press, 2013)
Napier, William F. P., *History of the War in the Peninsula, and in the South of France, from the year 1807 to the year 1814* (London: John Murray, 1828)
Oman, Charles, *A History of the Peninsular War* (Oxford: Clarendon Press, 1914)
Palacio Ramos, Rafael, (coord.), *Monte Buciero 13. Cantabria durante la Guerra de la Independencia* (Santander: Ayuntamiento de Santoña, 2008)
Palacio Ramos, Rafael, *Santoña, plaza napoleónica* (Santoña: Ayuntamiento de Santoña, 2015)
Popham, Hugh, *A Damned Cunning Fellow. The eventful Life of Rear-Admiral Sir Home Popham KCB, KCH; KM, FRS. 1762–1820* (Cornwall: The Old Ferry Press, 1991)
Rilova Jericó, Carlos, 'Bilbao y la revolución de 1808 en el País Vasco a partir de la correspondencia de dos oficiales del ejército aliado (1812)', *Bidebarrieta* 20 (2009), pp.148–158
Santacara, Carlos, 'Bilbao visto por los británicos durante la francesada, 1808–1814', *Bidebarrieta*, No.14 (2003), pp.107–118
Santacara, Carlos, *La Guerra de la independencia vista por los británicos* (Madrid: Machado Libros, 2005)
Simón Cabarga, José, *Santander en la Guerra de la independencia* (Santander: José S. Cabarga, 1968)
Stucliffe, Robert K., *British Expeditionary Warfare and the Defeat of Napoleon, 1793–1815* (Suffolk: The Boydell Press, 2016)
White, Zack, 'From Cintra to Salamanca: Shifting Popular Perceptions of the War in the Iberian Peninsula, 1808–1812', *British Journal for Military History*, 1:3 (2015), pp.60–79

4

'Never was there in the annals of war a more decided case of annihilation:' The Sack of San Sebastian, the Customs of War and Restraint and Excess During the Age of Napoleon

Gavin Lewis

On 31 August 1813, at the height of the Peninsular War, the Spanish port of San Sebastian was stormed by an allied British and Portuguese force after a long and arduous siege. The French defenders retreated to the town's castle, but their situation was hopeless, and they were forced to surrender to the British Lieutenant General Sir Thomas Graham on 8 September.[1] A few weeks later, the Spanish newspaper *El Duende* published a report that strongly criticised the actions of allied troops in the aftermath of the town's capture. These charges were repeated in *The Times* on 30 October.[2] It was alleged that allied troops entered Spanish homes and 'contented themselves with stripping the inmates of everything valuable…fury seemed to have inspired the soldiers: outrages, assassination, and rape, were committed…neither infancy or age were respected…[3]

The sack of San Sebastian has been predominantly viewed by military historians as a shameful atrocity that stains the British Army's record on the Iberian Peninsula. William Napier wrote in his early history of the conflict that the storming of the town 'seemed to be the signal of hell for the perpetration of villainy which would have shamed the most ferocious barbarians of antiquity.'[4] Even very recently, Charles Esdaile has stated that during the assault on the town 'murder was common, and the sufferings of the populace severe in the extreme…what took place' he concludes, 'was quite simply a disgrace—a war crime, indeed.'[5]

---

1 R. Holmes, *Wellington: The Iron Duke* (St. Ives: Harper Collins, 2003), pp.188–190.
2 B. Collins, *Wellington and the Siege of San Sebastian 1813* (Barnsley: Pen and Sword, 2017), p.173.
3 *The Times,* (London), 30 October 1813, Issue 9053.
4 W.F.P. Napier, *English Battles and Sieges in the Peninsula* (London: John Murray, 1879), p.340.
5 C. Esdaile, *The Peninsular War: A New History* (London: Penguin, 2003), pp.482–485.

The extent to which British actions could be considered a 'war crime' or atrocity is highly debateable. These are 20th century terms, and they may have no place in describing the episodic incidences of violence that occurred during Napoleonic sieges. This chapter will argue that although such incidents are anathema to modern sensibilities, the fierce pillaging that accompanied the storming of San Sebastian was a well-established military practice and to an extent permitted by the prevailing customs of war. It will assert that allied behaviour was still heavily influenced by these old, dynamic conventions.

In order to demonstrate this notion, this chapter will first explain how the customs of war evolved in Europe during the Early Modern era. It will then review contemporary literature of the period, before determining the extent to which misconduct occurred within the walls of San Sebastian. Finally, it will consider whether such behaviour was permissible, and briefly analyse British reactions to this episode.

European customs of war were usually referred to as 'the ancient laws of war' in contemporary accounts. They were primarily derived from five different sources.[6] The first source was *jus gentium*, or the laws of nature and nations. This proposed the standards of behaviour that were expected from rational, moral Christians. It was based on the Bible, the *Summae* of St Thomas Aquinas, canon law, the works of St Augustine and roman law. John Childs has written that: '

> Sir James Turner's (1615–86) reference to the *jus gentium* in 1683 indicated that they had indeed become very firmly established: 'the Law of Nations is that which most nations agree in, either by a mutual, declared, or...tacit assent'. Secondly, *Pax Dei*, or the Peace of God movement, entrenched *inter alia*, the lasting principle that 'those who could do no harm should suffer none.[7]

Thirdly, military law created a legal anthology which armies used to maintain discipline. As early as 1621 Gustavus Adolphus introduced a Code of Military Law for his Swedish army which was copied throughout Europe.[8] The fourth source of the customs of war was the *jus armorum*, which were founded in the laws of chivalry, 'which had governed combat amongst the knightly and aristocratic classes.' The fifth source was reciprocity – 'do as you would be done by.' This principle originated from Christian values and the laws of nature.[9]

These laws and customs were particularly developed and tested during siege warfare. A defeated army could disperse and fight another day, whereas a besieged garrison had nowhere to go and were often at the mercy of the attacking force. They thus relied heavily upon the customs of war to protect them in the event of a capitulation, but this protection was not always forthcoming. Before 1650 defeated garrisons were often subjected to

6 G. Parker, 'The Etiquette of Atrocity: The Laws of War in Early Modern Europe,' in G. Parker, *War, Empire and Faith* (London: Penguin, 2002), pp.143–168.

7 J. Childs, 'Surrender and the Laws of War in Western Europe c. 1660–1783,' in H. Afflerbach and H. Strachan (eds.), *How Fighting Ends: A History of Surrender* (Oxford: Oxford University Press, 2012), p.154.

8 J.A. Lynn, *Women, Armies and Warfare in Early Modern Europe* (New York: Cambridge University Press, 2008), p.71.

9 Childs, 'Surrender and the Laws of War', p.154.

violence and towns were frequently sacked by poorly paid mercenary armies that jumped at an opportunity for plunder. In this environment, inhabitants trying to protect their belongings could easily become collateral damage.[10]

The Spanish theologian and moralist Francisco da Vitoria warned against such behaviour in his pioneering 1532 work *De jure belli Hispanorum in barbarous*, writing 'inasmuch as such authorization to sack results in many horrors and cruelties, enacted beyond all humane limits by a barbarous soldiery…it is undoubtedly unjust in the extreme to deliver up a city, especially a Christian city, to be sacked, without the greatest necessity and weightiest reason.' Paradoxically, some of his writing on the topic was also extremely bellicose, and in certain instances the sacking of a town and the killing of its inhabitants was encouraged. In da Vitoria's opinion, during 'the actual heat of battle, either in the storming or in the defence of a city, all who resist may be killed indiscriminately.'[11]

Dutch jurist Hugo Grotius, writing in the 17th century, went further than da Vitoria and stated that 'in the case of a city taken by assault, all those whose lives do not impede the execution of our rights shall be spared in so far as is possible.'[12] Childs has written how according to Grotius, 'men and property were synonymous and both became the legitimate chattels of the captor' who could deal with them as he pleased. Nevertheless, he maintained that 'the surrender of soldiers who sought 'fair terms' should be accepted, their lives spared, and the conditions of capitulation honoured.'[13]

The writings of da Vitoria and Grotius appear to have had some effect, but throughout the 16th and early 17th centuries towns continued to be sacked by besieging forces. The conventions of siege warfare relied upon the commander of the town being able to negotiate effectively with his attackers, but this was a complicated dynamic. Even if a commander negotiated a surrender, the attacking general could still lose control of his men.

Towns were most at risk if they put up a staunch defence. If a garrison tried to resist and the attacking force had to assault the town, soldiers and civilians could expect to be subjected to violence and pillage if they eventually stormed the settlement. This practise encouraged defenders to quickly capitulate. Occasionally, a garrison would try to hold out if they believed there was the chance an allied army could relieve them, but this was an extremely risky strategy. When the city of Magdeburg was besieged in 1631, for instance, at the height of the Thirty Years War, the German city desperately held out for two months in the hope that the Swedish king, Gustavus Adolphus, would come to its rescue. However, he never appeared, and Imperial troops breached Magdeburg's walls before the city council could surrender. What followed was truly horrendous. The city's inhabitants were subjected to rape, murder, plunder and torture.[14]

---

10 J.A. Lynn, 'Honourable Surrender in Early Modern European History 1500-1789,' in H. Afflerbach and H. Strachan (eds.) *How Fighting Ends: A History of Surrender* (Oxford: Oxford University Press, 2012), p.102.

11 F. da Vitoria, *De Jure Belli Hispanorum in Barbarous* (1532), article 45; 52.

12 H. Grotius, (ed.) G.L. Williams, *De Jure Praedae Commentarius* (Oxford: Clarendon Press, 1950), p.10.

13 Childs, 'Surrender and the Laws of War', p.156.

14 T. Helfferich, *The Thirty Years War: A Documentary History* (Indianapolis: Hackett Publishing Company, 2009) pp.107–113.

After 1650, and as professional standing armies gradually became more established, the sacking of towns in Europe became less common. Influential lawyer Emer de Vattel wrote in his 1758 seminal work *The Law of Nations:* 'in a siege, a garrison offering to capitulate are never to be refused their lives.' He questioned the wisdom in putting to death a garrison who had held out 'to the last extremity' because he believed it dishonourable to 'punish a brave man for having performed his duty.'[15] De Vattel also made the crucial distinction between a town's garrison and its inhabitants, writing 'women, children, feeble old men and sick persons come under the description of enemies' but 'these are enemies who make no resistance, and consequently we have no right to maltreat their persons or use any violence against them.'[16] He had a palpable influence, and during the late 17th and early 18th century European siege warfare became more limited, ordered and choreographed. Indeed, the sieges that were conducted by Louis XIV's engineer Vauban followed something of a script, and they were usually brought to a conclusion once the attackers had achieved a breach in the defender's walls. If the garrison had conducted their defence with honour, then they could surrender with their dignity intact and they were usually offered reasonable terms.[17]

Regularly paid and well supplied professional armies adhered more frequently to this custom and showed a degree of restraint when entering a captured fortification. Siege warfare remained a miserable and bloody pursuit for the inhabitants of an invested settlement, who could still be subjected to terrible hardship, however entire towns were less often devastated, and their populations were seldom slaughtered.

Gunther Rothenberg has postulated that throughout the French Revolutionary and Napoleonic Wars violence towards civilians once again increased and that 'the crucial distinction between combatants and non-combatants frequently disappeared completely.'[18] This was particularly the case on the Iberian Peninsula, one of the most violent theatres of the conflict. Here, Spanish, Portuguese, French and British soldiers were thrown into a tumultuous crucible of war. Alice Parker has demonstrated that the large French armies in Spain and Portugal had to live off the land, and 'they employed destruction, pillage and rapine as part of their means of occupation.' [19] This predictably provoked a negative reaction from the Spanish population, and they treated the French troops with hostility. Added to this combustible melting pot were bands of Spanish guerrillas who tormented enemy soldiers and subjected them to habitual incidences of cruelty and torture. Violence bred violence, and French troops frequently took out their frustration and anger on the Spanish populace.[20]

15 E. de Vattel, (trans. J. Chitty), *The Law of Nations; or, Principles of the Law of Nature Applied to the Conduct and Affairs of Nations and Sovereigns* (Philadelphia: T. & J. W. Johnson & Co., 1858[1758]), pp.348; 483.

16 Vattel, *Law of Nations*, p.351.

17 G. Daly, 'The sacking of a town is an abomination': Siege, Sack and Violence to Civilians in British Officers' Writings on the Peninsular War- The Case of Badajoz,' *Institute of Historical Research*, (March, 2018), pp.1–23, 5.

18 G. Rothenberg, 'The Age of Napoleon,' in M. Howard, G.J. Andreopoulos & M. Shulman (eds.), *The Laws of War: Constraints on Warfare in the Western World* (New Haven: Yale University Press, 1994), p.92.

19 A. Parker, '"Incorrigible Rouges": The Brutalisation of British Soldiers in the Peninsular War, 1808–1814,' *British Journal for Military History*, 1:3 (2015), pp.42–59, 51.

20 See, for example, Esdaile, *Peninsular War*, p.370.

The British also occasionally subjected Spanish civilians to acts of violence, and Parker has offered an explanation for such behaviour. She has described how the British army on the Peninsula went through a period of 'brutalisation' which was caused by 'the daily experience of campaigning...food was scarce, pay was sporadic, sickness was rife, and the men endured long marches with little shelter.' These hardships, combined with the 'physical and mental horrors of battle and sieges pushed men to extremes' and created 'behaviours lying outside the moral norms of the time'.[21]

Siege warfare could be particularly exhausting and mentally debilitating for the men concerned. Besieging troops would often spend weeks digging trenches in unsanitary conditions and exposed to enemy fire. If a breach was made in the wall of a fortified town, the soldiers, often led by a group of volunteers, would have to storm the breach while under heavy fire from muskets and artillery at close range. Those that made it through might subsequently abandon their normal inhibitions and take out the 'strain that accompanies close brushes with death' on the inhabitants of the town, be they soldiers or civilians.[22] Indeed, Bruce Collins has concluded that the 5th Division that assaulted and pillaged San Sebastian were partly motivated to do so because they sustained heavy casualties both in the build-up to the operation and while fighting their way through the breach that was made in the town walls.[23]

Unsurprisingly, some of the worst instances of violence from the Peninsular War occurred during and after the capture of enemy held settlements. The city of Tarragona, for instance, was sacked by the French in 1811 after a nearly two-month long siege. At least 2,000 inhabitants were killed.[24] However, Gavin Daly has pointed out that 'in every instance in which besieged cities were sacked during the Peninsular War, the garrisons refused to capitulate, fighting to the last extremity.'[25] When a stout defence was put up by the defenders, it was acknowledged by military commanders that the town would still, in all likelihood, be sacked. Wellington made this point explicitly clear in a letter to future prime minister Lord Canning in 1820, stating 'I believe that it has always been understood that the defenders of a fortress stormed have no claim to quarter, and the practice which prevailed during the last century of surrendering fortresses when a breach was opened, and the counterscarp blown in, was founded on this understanding.' In his view, by ignoring this convention, the French 'availed themselves of the humanity of modern war.'[26] Matters were further complicated during the Peninsular War because, for the most part, Spanish citizens residing in French-held towns were British allies. In these unusual circumstances, the prevailing customs of war could easily become strained, and they could not always guarantee protection to both garrisons and civilian populaces.

Wellington's British army was particularly prone to violent outbursts of brutality when they stormed Spanish towns. William Napier stated that at Ciudad Rodrigo there had been

21 Parker, 'Brutalisation', p.43.
22 Edward Coss, *All for the King's Shilling: The British Soldier Under Wellington, 1808–1814* (Norman: Oklahoma University Press, 2012), pp.217–218.
23 Collins, *Siege of San Sebastian*, pp.180–187.
24 Esdaile, *Peninsular War*, p.370.
25 Daly, 'Case of Badajoz', p.7.
26 C. Oman, *A History of the Peninsular War* (Oxford: Clarendon Press, 1914), Vol. V, p.260.

'intoxication and plunder,' at Badajoz 'lust and murder' and at San Sebastian 'the direst, most revolting cruelty.'[27] Given that such vehement language has been used to describe British actions, it is surprising that so few studies have analysed British behaviour in the aftermath of sieges during this period. Infamously, Wellington's army in the Peninsula sacked the Spanish towns of Badajoz and Ciudad Rodrigo, as well as San Sebastian, but these incidents have been somewhat overlooked in Napoleonic era historiography. Detailed studies of Peninsular War sieges have been carried out by scholars like Philip Haythornthwaite and Ian Fletcher, but these works have tended to focus on the strategic, operational and tactical aspects of individual operations, and have neglected their confusing aftermaths.[28]

Edward Coss has attempted to redress the balance and has written how, in his view, 'the behaviour of the British soldier after the successful siege assaults of 1812 and 1813 merits special attention,' because it helped shaped the popular perception 'of the redcoat as a drunken thug bent on rape and violence.' Coss suggests that having stormed a town, troops were motivated to plunder and cause havoc because they suddenly had immediate access to the things they 'desired most: drink, food, potential wealth, and, quite likely, women.' Incidences of 'gross misconduct,' as Coss terms it, should be seen as exceptional occurrences, and 'tied directly to the dynamics of siege assaults.'[29] Gavin Daly has contested this interpretation, and has argued that British troops regularly mistreated the Spanish population. However, he also admits that the worst excesses were committed during the sacking of the towns Ciudad Rodrigo, Badajoz and San Sebastian.[30]

The sacking of Badajoz is of particular interest to Daly, and he has analysed British officer's reactions to the episode. He has stated that most demonstrated a sense of revulsion towards the violence that occurred within the town and they condemned the army's loss of discipline.[31] He concludes that 'Badajoz was a stark reminder of what customary laws of war still permitted,' but the sacking of a town as a 'legitimate form of violence' was becoming morally unacceptable.[32] It is perhaps therefore significant that although Wellington was concerned for the welfare of civilians during assaults on fortified towns, he later wrote in a letter: 'I should have thought myself justified in putting [Ciudad Rodrigo and Badajoz] to the sword and if I had done so at the first, it is probable I should have saved 5,000 men at the second...the practice which refuses quarter to a garrison that stands an assault is not a useless effusion of blood.'[33] This cold but honest admission clearly demonstrates that for many officers, the slaughter of a resisting garrison remained a permissible military expedient. The practise may have been deemed morally objectionable, but for pragmatic officers

27 Napier, Sieges, p.340.

28 P. Haythornthwaite, 'Sieges in the Peninsular War,' in P. Griffith (ed.), *A History of the Peninsular War: Modern Studies in Spain and Portugal 1808–14* (London: Greenhill Books, 1999), pp.213–30; I. Fletcher, *In Hell Before Daylight: The Siege and Storming of the Fortress of Badajoz* (New York: Spellmount Publishers, 1984).

29 Coss, *King's Shilling*, p.234.

30 G. Daly, 'Plunder on the Peninsula: British Soldiers and Local Civilians During the Peninsular War, 1808–1813,' in E. Charters, E. Rosenhaft & H. Smith (eds.), *Civilians and War in Europe 1618–1815* (Liverpool: Liverpool University Press, 2012), pp.209–112.

31 Daly, 'Case of Badajoz', pp.20–23.

32 Daly, 'Case of Badajoz', pp.22–23.

33 Oman, *Peninsular War,* Vol. V, Wellington to Lord Canning, 1820, p.260.

like Wellington it clearly still had some utility. Indeed, had Wellington shown less leniency towards the French defenders after Ciudad Rodrigo and Badajoz had been captured, he may have met less resistance at San Sebastian, and a bloody assault could have been avoided.

What arose in the aftermath of the siege of San Sebastian is complex. It is difficult to unravel exactly what occurred within the town, but a close reading of the sources demonstrates a variety of contradictory behaviours and reactions. Although the town was sacked, many of the British troops that stormed San Sebastian showed a great deal of restraint. The town was still plundered; however, this was primarily because the prevailing conventions of siege warfare encouraged this practice, and British regulars felt entitled to a reward for penetrating the towns walls.

Wellington attacked San Sebastian in 1813 after its strategic importance was revived by the French. By holding on to the town, they planned to slow the allied advance and use it as a base for offensive operations if the allies were forced to retreat into Spain's interior. The commander of the garrison, *Général de brigade* Louis Emmanuel Rey, was ordered to defend the town 'with all means available.' Bruce Collins has stated that San Sebastian consequently became 'a symbol of French resolve' and that 'a siege was undertaken partly because the defenders sought to maintain national prestige and uphold French morale as much as they sought to retain a military asset.'[34] This may help to explain the fierce resistance that was put up by the town's defenders.

Lieutenant General Graham was put in charge of the operation.[35] After a heavy bombardment, a breach appeared in the town's walls, and an attempt to storm San Sebastian was made on 25 July. Unfortunately for the British and Portuguese, this assault was a costly failure, and after coming under heavy fire the attacking troops were beaten back to the trenches they had come from.[36]

Wellington blamed a lack of heavy artillery, and although the siege was momentarily halted, it was renewed on 6 August. Wellington was determined to avoid another failure, so additional ordnance and reinforcements were shipped to the theatre.[37] A heavy bombardment was directed against the French defences from 25 August, and volunteers led by Major General Sir James Leith assaulted the town's walls six days later.[38] The attacking force was met with fierce volleys of musketry and bombarded with grapeshot, but, after a long struggle, the allied troops fought their way into the interior of the town.[39] The French retreated to the town's castle so British artillery was brought into San Sebastian and quickly levelled against this last bastion of resistance. The castle was heavily bombarded, and Rey was forced seek terms eight days later.[40]

34 Collins, *Siege of San Sebastian*, pp.60–63.

35 J. Gurwood (ed.), *The Dispatches of Field Marshal the Duke of Wellington K.G., During his various Campaigns in India, Denmark, Portugal, Spain the Low Countries and France, 1799–1818* (London: John Murray, 1837), Vol. X, pp.512–513. Wellington to Graham, 4 July 1813.

36 J.T. Jones, *Journals of Sieges Carried on by the Army Under the Duke of Wellington in Spain between the years 1811 and 1814 with notes* (London: T. Egerton, 1827), Vol. II, pp.40–41.

37 Collins, *Siege of San Sebastian*, pp.100–103; 113; 121.

38 Collins, *Siege of San Sebastian*, pp.132–134.

39 J. Harley, ed. by Gareth Glover, *The Veteran or 40 Years' Service in the British Army, The Scurrilous Recollections of Paymaster John Harley 47th Foot- 1798–1838,* (Solihull: Helion, 2018), p.210.

40 Collins, *Siege of San Sebastian*, pp.164–165.

The town itself was sacked between 31 August and 1 September. On the second day, attempts were made to halt allied misbehaviour and sentries were placed at the doors of some houses as well as the entrances to the town.[41] Deputy Provost Marshal Edward Williams also erected gallows in the town to serve as a warning. No soldier was put to death, but he stated that he flogged every man he 'found plundering or committing excesses.'[42] It is impossible to know what impact this had, however pillaging would have soon been nearly impossible anyway as a fire that had broken out in San Sebastian intensified and spread.[43]

Wellington himself admitted that his men plundered the town, but he refuted the most virulent accusations of cruelty.[44] Indeed, there is plenty of evidence to suggest that the allies went on a pillaging spree, however allegations of rape and murder are much more difficult to determine.

Almost every officer and ranker who documented the storm of San Sebastian mentioned that the town was violently plundered. As the Scottish officer Andrew Leith Hay stated, 'no sooner had the town been secured to the allies than a scene of the most ferocious pillage commenced – the usual result of a successful storm, and one of the barbarisms of war.'[45] Soldiers of all ranks took part in the plundering. John Harley even witnessed the wives of officers enthusiastically dividing up their spoils while sat in a church.[46] As was often the case, the local populace flocked towards the town once it was taken and loot was enthusiastically bought, sold and traded between soldiers and civilians.[47]

In this environment some inhabitants of San Sebastian would undoubtedly have been exposed to acts of violence. This is partly because once allied troops got inside the walls of San Sebastian, the French continued to fiercely resist their opponents in the narrow streets of the town.[48] In this confusing urban setting, the distinction between combatants and non-combatants must have broken down. One British officer described how 'we forced a passage into the town, and before four o'clock the whole of it was in our possession…not however, till after' the French 'had made some …stands in the town, which was barricaded with great attention' and 'obstinately contested.'[49] George Gleig similarly noted that 'the French fought with desperate courage; they were literally driven from house to house and street to street.'[50] Urban warfare is notoriously difficult to manage, and it would be extremely surprising if no civilians were caught up in the fighting. In this respect, San Sebastian differs from the

41 Gurwood (ed.), *Dispatches*, Vol. XI, p.174, Wellington to Richard Wellesley, 9 October 1813.
42 University of Southampton, Hartley Library, Wellington Papers (WP): 12/1/8 (Folder 5), 'Undated statement by Edward Williams,' Hay to Wellington, 18 October 1813.
43 WP: 1/376 (Folder 6), Graham to Wellington, 3 September 1813.
44 Gurwood (ed.), *Dispatches*, Vol. XI, pp.171–174. Wellington to Wellesley, 9 October 1813.
45 A. Leith Hay, *Narrative of the Peninsular War* (London: Arkhose Press, 1831), Vol. II, p.257.
46 Harley, *40 Years' Service*, p.215.
47 Edward Sabine (ed.), *Letters of Colonel Sir Augustus Simon Frazer, K.C.B., Commanding the Royal Horse Artillery in the Army under the Duke of Wellington Written During the Peninsular and Waterloo Campaigns* (London: Longmans & Roberts, 1859), p.248.
48 Leith Hay, *Narrative*, p.252.
49 F.C. Carr-Gomm (ed.), *Letters and Journals of Field Marshal Sir William Maynard Gomm, G.C.B.* (London: John Murray, 1881), p.352.
50 G. Gleig, *Subaltern, or, Sketches of the Peninsular War from the Campaigns of 1813–15* (New York: G. & C. Carvill, 1825), p.42.

storms of Badajoz and Ciudad Rodrigo, where resistance quickly crumbled once soldiers had broken through the outer defences of both towns.

Significantly, there is strong evidence to suggest that not all the inhabitants who were subjected to acts of violence were simply caught up in street fighting. Some civilians tried to protect their property and get in the way of pillaging soldiers, but they were forcefully cast aside. Augustus Frazer stated that he even heard rumours that several inhabitants were shot and killed when opening their doors to 'our merciless soldiery.'[51] Such descriptions of cold-blooded murder are extremely rare, however some soldiers may well have omitted such instances from their accounts of the storm in order to protect their comrades. Also, there are no accurate records that document civilian casualties, so it is impossible to know the exact extent of the violence. A large-scale evacuation was made of Spanish women and children in between the first and second assaults on the town, but it is unclear just how many made it out safely.[52]

Generally, contemporary sources indicate that the soldiers were much more interested in plundering than they were inflicting violence upon San Sebastian's populace.[53] Gomm wrote that 'John Bull, while heartily fond of fighting, is not a man of blood, but he is a greedy fellow.'[54] Coss has determined that episodes of murder no doubt occurred, but these were probably carried out by a handful of individuals who already possessed a penchant for violent behaviour.[55]

Many soldiers that documented the sack of San Sebastian also indicate that some inhabitants were subjected to sexual, as well as physical, assaults. This was a depressingly common fate which befell female civilians when a town was stormed during the Napoleonic Wars. Indeed, Gleig wrote that 'as soon as the fighting began to wax faint, the horrors of…rapine succeeded. Fortunately, there were few females in the place; but the fate of the few which were there, I cannot even now think without a shudder.'[56] John Harley described a particularly harrowing incident. He wrote that a lieutenant in his regiment agreed to protect a young woman who called to him out of her window, and he fought off a British private who refused to leave the woman's house, throwing him down the stairs. At night, the lieutenant had to go back to the allied lines outside of the town, and when he returned the following day he discovered 'the young lady reclining on a sofa, with her…garments torn to pieces. She…begged' that the British officer 'would have compassion on her, and shoot her.' She told him that 'the soldier whom he had thrown down the stairs returned, with many others, and committed 'all the violence they could.' In Harley's opinion, this was only 'one instance out of many similar occurrences which took place after the storming of San Sebastian.'[57]

The impression given by men like Harley and Gleig is that this was one of the most shocking aspects of the sacking of the town. The story recounted above is particularly interesting as it reflects the class divide between officers and members of the rank and file.

51 Sabine, *Letters*, p.244.
52 Collins, *Siege of San Sebastian*, p.183.
53 Leith Hay, *Narrative*, p.257.
54 Carr-Gomm, *Letters and Journals*, p.247.
55 Coss, *King's Shilling*, pp.221–226.
56 Gleig, *Subaltern*, p.44.
57 Harley, *40 Years' Service*, pp.216–217.

Although one officer, no doubt motivated by ideals of gentlemanly honour, felt a duty of protection towards a Spanish female, another regular soldier felt that this woman was, to put no finer point on it, his chattel to do what he pleased with.

Notably, the allied infantry were not the sole cause of civilian woe. The bombardment of the town was noted for its ferocity and some civilians became victims of inaccurate artillery fire.[58] Furthermore, the fusillade contributed to the many fires that seem to have erupted in San Sebastian throughout the siege, which were also likely to have been a cause of casualties. One account describes how several women, trapped on top of their burning homes, had to leap from their roofs in order to escape the flames below.[59]

The conflagration was tremendously damaging, but there is little evidence that the allies set fire to the town purposefully. Wellington reported that several fires broke out on the afternoon of 31 August, but he put this down to the 'most severe contest in the streets of the town' and the exploding of 'traverses that were established' by the French garrison.[60] Several other accounts also suggest that the French were at least partly to blame. William Gomm, for instance, wrote that the French tried to set fire to the town to drive back the allied troops,[61] and Lieutenant Colonel John Burgoyne stated that a number of fires had been started by the French on the floors of houses.[62] British artillery fire no doubt contributed to the growing blaze, but this was an unintended ramification.

Although some isolated incidents of physical and sexual violence certainly occurred, and the ransacking of the town must have been a frightening experience, for the majority of inhabitants the most distressing impact of the allied siege must have been the demolition of their homes. Gomm stated that 'with the exception of ten or twelve fortunate buildings there is nothing left of San Sebastian but the walls of its houses, and these are falling every instant with a tremendous crash.'[63] In this respect, San Sebastian differs from Badajoz and Ciudad Rodrigo. The excesses committed by allied soldiers in these towns may well have exceeded what occurred in northernmost Spain, but neither were reduced to rubble.

Many accounts describe the suffering felt by the Spanish populace, but there is very little evidence that indicates the French garrison was treated anything other than equitably. The allied troops showed a great deal of restraint towards their wounded and captured opponents, which is surprising given that before the town was stormed Gleig noted how soldiers of the 5th Division:

> ...could not forgive the French garrison, which had now kept them during six weeks at bay, and they burned with anxiety to wipe off the disgrace of a former repulse; there was, therefore, little mention made of quarter, when the approaching assault chanced to be alluded to.[64]

---

58 Sabine, *Letters*, p.232.

59 George Hennell, (ed. Michael Glover), *A Gentleman Volunteer: The Letters of George Hennell from the Peninsular War, 1812–1813* (London, William Heinemann Ltd., 1979), p.130.

60 Gurwood (ed.), *Dispatches*, Vol. XI, pp.172–173, Wellington to Richard Wellesley, 9 October 1813.

61 Carr-Gomm, *Letters and Journals*, pp.319–320.

62 G. Wrottesley (ed.), *Life and Correspondence of Field Marshal Sir John Burgoyne* (London: Richard Bentley & Son, 1873), Vol. I, pp.280–281.

63 Carr-Gomm, *Letters and Journals*, p.319.

64 Gleig, *Subaltern*, p.39.

However, once allied soldiers had fought their way in, they did not remain in a perpetual, uncontrollable state of anger. Gomm described how because the fire quickly spread 'every effort' was made 'by all ranks and conditions to rescue some hundreds of wounded, French as well as English, from the flames.'[65] Major F.P. Robinson wrote, with more than a hint of jingoism, that 'although our people were destroyed by the Enemy in such numbers before they entered the town...all the Frenchmen they overtook were made Prisoners – hardly a man being killed – What other Troops in the whole World can act thus?'[66] This is not the behaviour of vengeful soldiers who made 'little mention of quarter.' Indeed, once the French defenders surrendered, many allied servicemen praised the bravery of the garrison. Leith Hay was gushing in his admiration, writing 'what praise is too great for the gallant garrison of San Sebastian? A more desperate defence has seldom been recorded, or one more calculated to uphold the military character of the nation to which the undaunted soldiers within its walls belonged.'[67] As this account shows, by the time of the Siege of San Sebastian a degree of mutual respect had developed between both armies.[68]

Conversely, historians like Gavin Daly have suggested that Spanish and Portuguese civilians, supposed allies, were viewed with a great deal of bitterness by British forces stationed on the Iberian Peninsula.[69] It could therefore be argued that although French combatants primarily made the lives of the 5th Division miserable during the siege, the allies took out their frustration on the inhabitants, with whom they had little sympathy.

Most British soldiers initially portrayed their allies in a negative light. When Private Wheeler first arrived on the Iberian Peninsula, he described the locals as being an 'ignorant, superstitious, priest-ridden, dirty, lousy set of poor Devils.'[70] For many British soldiers, daily interactions with war-weary civilians only helped to enforce these hostile attitudes. One sergeant wrote matter-of-factly, 'the ways of the inhabitants...very well agree with the manner of the country; for it is certain, they live in a very dirty, beastly way.'[71] Local inhabitants understandably became increasingly infuriated by the thousands of troops that roamed their country, and many became unobliging hosts. One young officer determined that the Spanish were jealous of the British and they would therefore avoid procuring supplies for his men.[72] This bred a great deal of resentment, which was exacerbated by the daily experience of campaigning.

Having been 'brutalised,' and with an already poor opinion of the Spanish, some soldiers undoubtedly released the strain caused by campaigning on San Sebastian's residents.

---

65 Carr-Gomm, *Letters and Journals*, p.320.

66 F.P. Robinson, (Ed. C.T. Atkinson) *A Peninsular Brigadier: Letters of Major General Sir F.P. Robinson, K.C.B.* (London: Army Historical Research, 1956), pp.167–168.

67 Leith Hay, *Narrative*, p.256.

68 See R. Muir, *Tactics and the Experience of Battle in the Age of Napoleon* (New Haven: Yale University Press, 1998), pp.252–255.

69 Daly, 'Case of Badajoz', p.12.

70 B.H. Liddell Hart (ed.) *The Letters of Private Wheeler, 1809–1828* (London: Michael Joseph, 1951), p.50.

71 J. Hale, *The Journal of James Hale, Late Sergeant in the Ninth Regiment of Foot*, (Cirencester: Longman & Co., 1826), p.99.

72 W.F.K. Thompson (ed.), *An Ensign in the Peninsular War, The Letters of John Aitchison* (London: Michael Joseph, 1994), p.72.

However, most individuals who documented the siege expressed nothing other than sympathy for the civilians of San Sebastian.[73] Overall, the actions of British soldiers cannot be considered to be unusual, given the circumstances, but that does not necessarily mean that they had strictly adhered to the prevailing conventions of the period.

Given their ambiguous nature, it is very difficult to ascertain the extent to which the British breached 19th century customs of war. As has already been established, these customs were influenced by the work of theorists like Grotius and de Vattel, but they were unwritten. There were no formal international treaties signed between European states that outlined acceptable and unacceptable conduct in wartime. Consequently, the conventions that governed battlefield etiquette were dynamic and depended upon the opponent and the situation. This may explain the leniency that was afforded to the French garrison at San Sebastian. The remaining French defenders were taken prisoner and sent to England, but they were first allowed to march out of the town's castle and lay down their arms. Their bravery afforded them, in the eyes of the British, an honourable capitulation.[74] Notably, the French were only allowed to safely leave the castle because Rey and Graham were able to successfully negotiate a surrender. Rey presented a white flag on the castle's ramparts and Graham understood this display of submission. The British commander was unwavering in his demands – he ordered that the French lay down their arms and become prisoners of war – but Rey reluctantly accepted these terms and it probably saved the lives of his men. Augustus Frazer, a normally deeply empathetic individual, admitted frankly that if the French commander refused and the British were forced to storm the castle, 'few would be spared.'[75] The French had already put up a fierce defence of the town, and Frazer appears to admit that any further resistance would have resulted in most of the garrison being put to the sword. This long-established convention of siege warfare and clearly not yet been totally abandoned.

A degree of cooperation was probably stimulated in the aftermath of San Sebastian's capture because of the mutual respect which had developed between British and French soldiers. Indeed, one French officer was widely commended by the allies as he had been seen helping allied wounded after the failed first assault, whilst another was given a tour of a British battery.[76] Graham was especially generous and asked Wellington whether several French officers could be permitted to return to France, rather than become prisoners in England. He received a stern reply from Wellington who 'was unwilling to allow any persons to return to France without exchange.'[77] Wellington did allow a French commissary, who was looking after his brother's widow and two daughters, to remain on the French-Spanish border until a British officer was found who could be exchanged for all three individuals.[78] Prisoner exchange in such circumstances was normal protocol, but the fact that Graham and Wellington were willing to show leniency towards their defeated opponents demonstrates that Enlightenment principles which demanded restraint and limitation in war appear to be

73 Sabine, *Letters,* p.231.
74 Carr-Gomm, *Letters and Journals*, p.319–321.
75 Sabine, *Letters,* p.263.
76 Sabine, *Letters,* p.265.
77 Gurwood (ed.), *Dispatches*, Vol. XI, p.111, Wellington to Graham, 15 September 1813.
78 Sabine, *Letters,* p.267.

ever present. There is very little evidence to suggest that the treatment of the French garrison violated customary laws of war.

It is more difficult to establish whether the plundering of San Sebastian could be considered an abuse of common conventions. Spanish property should have been left alone, and Wellington condemned the episode. However, he also suggested that it is impossible to stop troops acting in such a way once they have stormed a town, writing in a letter to his brother that 'every officer laments' the pillaging of a captured town 'on account of the evil thereby inflicted on the unfortunate inhabitants.'[79] The British articles of war, which defined British military law for much of the 19th century, explicitly outlawed the murder and plunder of civilians, but no mention was given to the specific circumstances of siege warfare.[80] After San Sebastian, Sir Thomas Graham alluded to this problem, telling Wellington that 'it would require a different military code from ours to stop men from being disorderly on such an occasion.'[81] Although allied actions were thus in violation of military law, and although the Spanish were British allies, the circumstance of a siege was viewed as a separate, distinct situation.

Andrew Leith Hay had little doubt that 'the prospect of individual enrichment' motivated British soldiers and that they continued to exert themselves during the assault of the town because there was a chance of 'obtaining plunder.' In his view, this was an 'immemorial privilege' for the attacking troops.[82] This sentiment was echoed by Wellington, who stated it was 'one of the evil consequences attending the necessity of storming a town.'[83] This may explain why Wellington failed to act decisively after the British sacked the towns of Ciudad Rodrigo and Badajoz. He realised that troops were more liable to undertake the extremely dangerous task of assaulting a breach if there would be afterwards access to loot, food and alcohol. British officers failed to adequately castigate and control their troops during the sieges of Badajoz and Ciudad Rodrigo, and rankers may have subsequently come to believe that in the specific circumstances of a siege a degree of plundering was acceptable.[84]

Soldiers that were caught plundering outside of this context were usually punished severely, as Wellington was often at pains to protect the civilian population from the ravages of war.[85] Troops still occasionally had to steal out of necessity, and on such occasions Wellington could turn a blind eye.[86] Even when this was the case, many soldiers saw the practice as immoral, and demonstrated empathy for the civilians from whom they were stealing. William Swabey, on one occasion, noted in his diary: 'marched to Villa Franca...I felt ashamed of showing my face there. We now have no bread, but such as we can press,

79 Gurwood (ed.), *Dispatches*, Vol. XI, p.173, Wellington to Richard Wellesley, 9 October 1813.

80 Anon., *Rules and Articles for the Better Government of All His Majesty's Forces, from the 24th Day of March, 1791* (London: Charles Eyre and Andrew Strahan, 1791).

81 A. Wellesley (ed.), *Supplementary Despatches, Correspondence and Memoranda of Field Marshal Arthur Duke of Wellington* (London, 1861), Vol. VIII, p.301, Graham to Wellington, October 1813.

82 Leith Hay, *Narrative*, p.257.

83 Gurwood, *Dispatches*, Vol. XI, p.173, Wellington to Richard Wellesley, 8 October 1813.

84 Z. White, 'The Curious Case of Badajoz: The Aftermath of British Sieges During the Peninsular War,' 7th Wellington Congress, University of Southampton, (April 2019).

85 C. Oman, *Wellington's Army, 1809–1814* (London: E. Arnold Publication, 1913), p.244.

86 A.L.F. Schaumann, (trans. A. M. Ludovici), *On the Road with Wellington: The Diary of a War Commissary in the Peninsular Campaigns* (London: W. Heinemann Ltd., 1924), p.395.

which is hard on the inhabitants…war and charity are two things truly incompatible with each other.'[87] William Surtees felt guilty for stealing cabbages from a nearby field for his battalion, and he reflected that in hindsight 'it is impossible to justify such an act, but the reader will be convinced, I trust, that sheer hunger alone urged me to the perpetration of this crime.'[88]

There is no indication that the troops that plundered San Sebastian were desperate for food or other basic supplies but, having spent the last four years campaigning in a foreign land fighting a tough and seasoned opponent, many must have felt entitled to a tangible reward for enduring such hardship. San Sebastian provided many soldiers and officers with the chance of enrichment, and they seized this opportunity with both hands. Although overt cruelty was probably carried out by a minority, many troops broke into theatres and churches, got drunk and became disobedient and unruly.[89]

Significantly, Graham and his subordinates did not stand by idly while their men plundered the town, and the British general tried to relieve the party that stormed the settlement. He told Wellington that 'General Hay and the staff officers of the division seem to be making every exertion to prevent excess.'[90] This behaviour was clearly becoming unacceptable in the eyes of many British officers, even if they felt they could not always prevent it. Only if the Spanish had aided the French garrison, and resisted the allied siege, would the sacking of the entire town would have been deemed admissible. This accusation was levelled at the Spanish by August Schaumann, who wrote 'the inhabitants had made common cause with the French in defending the town.' As Schaumann goes on to make clear, in such a circumstance, widespread plunder and violence could have been justified to a greater extent under the old customs of war.[91] However, there is very little evidence to suggest any collaboration was prevalent, and it may have been invented by Schaumann, an unreliable source at the best of times, in an attempt to justify allied misbehaviour.

Although plundering was definitely widespread, Wellington made it clear to his brother in London that any violence directed towards the inhabitants was likely to have been 'by accident, during the contest in the streets with the enemy.'[92] Whilst the looting of property was to a degree expected, the mindless killing of civilians was still understood to be deplorable behaviour and anathema to 19th century sensibilities. This point of view can be observed in the general orders Wellington issued before his army invaded France. The British general stated the allies were only at war with the French because Napoleon 'will not allow them to be at peace' and that to mistreat in any way 'the peaceable inhabitants of France would be unmanly and unworthy of the nations to whom the Commander of the Forces now addresses himself.'[93] Consequently, any purposeful harming of San Sebastian's inhabitants must be deemed to have been in violation of 19th century customs of war. The

87 Quoted in Daly, 'Plunder on the Peninsula', p.216.

88 W. Surtees, *Twenty-Five Years in the Rifle Brigade* (Edinburgh: William Blackwood & T. Cadell, 1833), pp.39; 90.

89 Harley, *40 Years' Service*, p.212.

90 Wellington, *Supplementary Despatches*, Vol. VIII p.217, Graham to Wellington, 1 September 1813.

91 Schaumann, *With Wellington*, p.389.

92 Gurwood (ed.), *Dispatches*, Vol. XI, pp.171–176, Wellington to Richard Wellesley, 9 October 1813.

93 Gurwood (ed.), *Dispatches*, Vol. XI, p.169, General Orders, 8 October 1813.

plundering of the town, on the other hand, was seen by many as an unavoidable, but regrettable, consequence of the assault. The behaviour of the allies was certainly deemed unacceptable by the Spanish government, and a formal complaint was made by the San Sebastian junta on 16 January 1814. However, it is perhaps significant that the focus of the complaint was on the plunder and destruction of the town. It claimed that around 36 of the towns 600 houses were left standing.[94] This calls into question the legality and morality of the artillery bombardment, which was described by Bruce Collins as the heaviest of the entire Peninsular War.[95]

It was not the first time that a British bombardment had caused controversy. In 1807, the British attacked Copenhagen and ship-to-shore artillery fire caused around 1,000 civilian casualties.[96] This action aroused serious debate in parliament and a motion was tabled to censure the engagement which was heavily defeated by the opposition.[97] Interestingly, such a discussion did not occur after San Sebastian was captured. In the House of Lords, Graham and Wellington were instead congratulated for taking a town which had shown such 'obstinate and protracted resistance.' The charge of 'setting fire to the town' was deemed 'utterly false,' and dismissed out of hand.[98] This should not discount the destructive impact of British ordnance, and Wellington, who was present during the siege of Copenhagen, wrestled with the consequences of a major bombardment in a letter to Graham on 23 August. He advised against the use of artillery for 'general annoyance' because in his view this 'answers no purpose whatsoever against...French troops' and instead harms 'the inhabitants of the place.' He also wrote that an inaccurate cannonade may set fire to the town, but despite this he 'authorised' Graham 'to use all the howitzers and mortars in any way you may think fit.'[99] In doing so Wellington demonstrated a cold pragmatism that was probably necessary for success.

It is likely that the town particularly suffered because, as John Aitchison wrote, 'the enemy have intersected the streets...with different defences.' The British had to thus target not only the walls of the town but also its interior.[100] As 19th century ordnance was extremely inaccurate by modern standards, the specific targeting of these defences would have been nearly impossible and attempts to limit the devastation were superfluous. Frazer noted this paradox, writing 'it is settled that we are to do the town as little damage as possible, but that little will, I dare say, extend to the destruction of half of it.'[101] In order to capture the town, artillery support was vital, and the unintended damage that was done by cannon balls and shells was an unfortunate ramification. With no international law regulating the attack of civilian positions, the bombardment cannot be considered illegal. Indeed, the international scholar Cornelius van Bynkershoek wrote in 1737 that the bombing of a town was acceptable

94 Jacques Vital Belmas, *Journaux des siéges faits ou soutenus par les français dans la peninsula, de 1807 á 1814* (Paris: Firmin-Didiot Frères, Fils, et Cie, 1837), Vol. IV, pp.731–733.
95 Collins, *Siege of San Sebastian*, pp.174–175.
96 A. Gillespie, *History of the Laws of War, Vol. II, The Customs and Laws of War with Regards to Civilians in Times of Conflict* (Oregon: Hart Publishing, 2011), pp.14–15.
97 W. Hinde, *George Canning* (London: Wiley-Blackwell, 1973), pp.187–189.
98 *House of Lords Debates,* 8 November 1813, Vol. 27, C. 46.
99 Gurwood (ed.), *Dispatches*, Vol. XI, pp.31–33, Wellington to Graham, 23 August 1813.
100 Thompson, *Ensign in the Peninsular War*, p.263.
101 Sabine, *Letters*, p.229.

because 'everything is legitimate against an enemy.'[102] Many soldiers saw the practise as a necessary military expedient, however many displayed a degree of dismay at the plight of the civilian population. Richard Henegan, for instance, wrote that 'the ravages of man' left 'the town in flames, the wretched inhabitants houseless and beggared.'[103]

Such evocative descriptions of San Sebastian's plight may well indicate a shifting in sensibilities. Yuval Harari has studied military memoirs of the period and has theorised that empathy towards civilian suffering is a common reoccurring theme. In his view, suffering was treated in a much more 'matter-of-fact' manner in earlier wartime accounts.[104] Margret Abruzzo has explained that this is because 'during the eighteenth and nineteenth centuries...Europeans recoiled from the infliction of pain with a depth of disgust unknown to their ancestors.' There was a 'transformation in moral thinking about the meaning of pain; the deliberate infliction of pain began to spark moral outrage.'[105]

This transformation is certainly visible in the memoirs of several soldiers who documented the storm of San Sebastian. Many eyewitnesses reflected very deeply upon the nature of their work and the ravages of war. Schaumann, for example, described the inhabitants as being 'wild and haggard from hunger, anxiety and sorrow.'[106] Furthermore, Frazer admitted that incessant campaigning had a debilitating effect on British troops, writing 'we who witness these horrid scenes do not feel them as we ought: the habit of continually seeing shocking sights takes away every finer feeling.'[107] As yet, no single study has been produced which analyses narratives of trauma during this epoch, though such a study would be a welcome addition to the historiography, and would help to shed further light upon British attitudes towards civilian casualties, death, suffering and restraint.

To conclude, the storming of San Sebastian was a bewildering and bloody experience for many of its participants, and desperate fighting occurred on both sides of the town walls. The confusing nature of urban warfare must have made it very difficult for soldiers to distinguish between combatants and non-combatants, and some civilians must have been caught up in the fighting. As soon as the French retreated into San Sebastian's castle, the British troops set about ransacking the town, and it appears that plundering was widespread and carried out by regulars and officers alike. Even the wives of officers appear to have taken part in illicit activity. Generally, theft was considered a serious misdemeanour and troops could be put to death for committing such a crime,[108] however Wellington implied that he was powerless to stop soldiers plundering once they had stormed a town, even if the town's inhabitants were British allies. Moreover, many senior officers were reluctant to take more stringent measures because the potential for plunder was a major motivating factor for the troops that volunteered to storm a practicable breach.

---

102 Gillespie, *History of the Laws of War*, p.13.

103 R. Henegan, *Seven Years Campaigning in the Peninsular and the Netherlands; From 1808 to 1815* (London: Henry Colburn Publishers, 1846), p.46.

104 Y.N. Harari, *The Ultimate Experience: Battlefield Experience and the Making of Modern War Culture, 1450-2000* (New York: Palgrave Macmillan, 2008), p.205.

105 M. Abruzzo, *Polemical Pain: Slavery, Cruelty and the Rise of Humanitarianism* (Baltimore: John Hopkins, 2011), pp.1–3.

106 Schaumann, *With Wellington*, p.396.

107 Sabine, *Letters*, p.198.

108 Oman, *Wellington's Army*, pp.244–245.

Undoubtedly, some allied soldiers committed acts of violence and sexual assault, but these were probably in the minority. Many troops appear to have been mostly concerned with plundering food, drink and valuables, rather than mistreating the Spanish inhabitants. It is probably very telling that the official complaint that was lodged by the San Sebastian *junta* focused on damage to property rather than the murder and rape of civilians. One would imagine that if the populace had been subjected to an orgy of violence it would have been mentioned in much greater detail by this governmental body.

Although a select few committed the most abhorrent acts, many still became drunk, lost their inhibitions and became unruly and undisciplined. The reasons for this misconduct are varied and multifaceted, and it would be specious to generalise the motivations for such behaviour. Indeed, suggestions that soldiers were 'pushed to the extremes' by their wartime experiences and therefore acted 'outside the moral norms of the time' are inadequately monocausal. Certain personalities perhaps did become 'brutalised' and act with callous disdain towards both Spanish civilians and French soldiers, however primary accounts suggest empathy was also shown towards the inhabitants of San Sebastian and that allied soldiers demonstrated a great deal of restraint towards the French garrison. The relationship that allied troops developed with both of these demographics was multidimensional and the way both parties treated one another depended on the individual and the situation.

Whilst it is difficult to establish whether allied actions were in breach of 19th century customs of war, this study has been able to highlight the dynamic nature of these conventions and the complicated relationship that evolved between attackers and defenders during siege warfare of this period. If the garrison at San Sebastian continued to put up a fierce, unrelenting defence, they would in all likelihood have been put to the sword. However, because terms were agreed, the remaining French troops were saved and allowed to march out of the town with their honour intact. The plundering of civilians was viewed by officers as an unfortunate consequence of the town's storming, but one which was still generally accepted under the customs of war. The outright murder of non-combatants, on the other hand, was deemed to be unacceptable, even if the towns garrison had resisted fiercely.

Not every garrison during the French Revolutionary and Napoleonic Wars was treated leniently, and several civilian populations were subjected to terrible violence on a scale that greatly exceeded the subject of this study. Nevertheless, the siege of San Sebastian makes for an interesting case study and sheds further light on the conduct of war and perceptions of conflict during this period, albeit from a distinctly British perspective.

Select Bibliography

Unpublished Primary Sources

The Wellington Papers (WP) at the Hartley Library, University of Southampton:

WP 12/1/8 (Folder 5), Undated statement by Edward Williams,' Hay to Wellington, 18 October 1813, WP 1/376 (Folder 6), Graham to Wellington, 3 September 1813

Edited Dispatches

Gurwood, John, (ed.) *The Dispatches of Field Marshal the Duke of Wellington K.G., During his various Campaigns in India, Denmark, Portugal, Spain the Low Countries and France, 1799-1818* (London: John Murray, 1834)

A. Wellesley (ed.), *Supplementary Despatches, Correspondence and Memoranda of Field Marshal Arthur Duke of Wellington* (London, 1861)

Published Memoirs

F.C. Carr-Gomm (ed.), *Letters and Journals of Field Marshal Sir William Maynard Gomm, G.C.B.* (London: John Murray, 1881)

Gleig, George, *Subaltern, or, Sketches of the Peninsular War from the Campaigns of 1813–14* (New York: G & C Carvill, 1825)

Harley, John, (ed.) G. Glover, *The Veteran or 40 Years' Service in the British Army, The Scurrilous Recollections of Paymaster John Harley 47th Foot, 1798–1838* (Solihull: Helion, 2018)

Henegan, Sir Richard, *Seven Years Campaigning in the Peninsular and the Netherlands; From 1808 to 1815* (London: Colburn Publishers, 1846)

Leith Hay, Andrew, *Narrative of the Peninsular War* (London: 1831)

Sabine, Edward, (ed.), *Letters of Colonel Sir Augustus Simon Frazer, K.C.B., Commanding the Royal Horse Artillery in the Army under the Duke of Wellington Written During the Peninsular and Waterloo Campaigns* (London: Longman & Roberts, 1859)

Schaumann, August, (trans. A. M. Ludovici), *On the Road with Wellington: The Diary of a War Commissary in the Peninsular Campaigns* (London: W. Heinemann Ltd., 1924)

Surtees, William, *Twenty-Five Years in the Rifle Brigade* (London: William Blackwood & T. Cadell, 1833)

Miscellaneous Printed Primary Sources

Anon., *Rules and Articles for the Better Government of All His Majesty's Forces, from the 24th Day of March, 1791* (London: Charles Eyre and Andrew Strahan, 1791)

da Vitoria, Francisco, *De Jure Belli Hispanorum in Barbarous,* (1532)

de Vattel, Emer, (trans. J. Chitty), *The Law of Nations; or, Principles of the Law of Nature Applied to the Conduct and Affairs of Nations and Sovereigns* (Philadelphia: T. & J. W. Johnson & Co., 1858)

Grotius, Hugo, (ed.) Williams, G.L., *De Jure Praedae Commentarius* (Oxford: Clarendon Press, 1950)

House of Lords Debates, 8 November 1813, Vol. 27 <https://api.parliament.uk/historic-hansard/lords/1813/nov/08/victories-of-the-pyrenees-capture-of-sr>

Secondary Sources

Afflerbach, H. and Strachan, H., (eds.), *How Fighting Ends: A History of Surrender* (Oxford: Oxford University Press, 2012)

Collins, Bruce, *Wellington and the Siege of San Sebastian 1813* (Barnsley: Pen and Sword, 2017)

Charters, E. Rosenhaft & Smith, H., (eds.), *Civilians and War in Europe 1618-1815* (Liverpool: Liverpool University Press, 2012)

Coss, Edward J., *All for the King's Shilling: The British Soldier Under Wellington, 1808–1814* (Oklahoma: Oklahoma University Press, 2012)

Daly, Gavin, 'The sacking of a town is an abomination': Siege, Sack and Violence to Civilians in British Officers' Writings on the Peninsular War – The Case of Badajoz,' *Institute of Historical Research,* (March, 2018), pp.1–23

Dwyer, Philip G., 'Violence and the Revolutionary and Napoleonic Wars: Massacre, conquest and the Imperial Enterprise,' *Journal of Genocide Research,* Vol. 15, (May, 2013), pp.117–131

Parker, Alice, '"Incorrigible Rouges": The Brutalisation of British Soldiers in the Peninsular War, 1808–1814,' *British Journal for Military History,* Vol. 1:3, (June, 2015), pp.42–59

Parker, Geoffrey, *War, Empire and Faith* (London, Penguin, 2002)

Napier, William Francis Patrick, *A History of the War in the Peninsular and the South of France from the year 1807 to the year 1814* (New York: D. and J. Sadler & Co 1850)

Napier, William Francis Patrick, *English Battles and Sieges in the Peninsula* (London: John Murray, 1879)

Oman, Charles, *A History of the Peninsular War* (Oxford: Clarendon Press, 1902–1928)

Oman, Charles, *Wellington's Army, 1809–1814,* (London: E. Arnold Publication, 1913)

5

Provisional Battalions Reconsidered: Wellington, York, and Manpower Management 1812–1814

Andrew Bamford

The genesis of this chapter, and of the paper from which it is developed, goes back to an argument that was first ventured over a decade ago as part of a doctoral thesis and subsequently developed in print when that thesis was adapted for publication.[1] That argument was intended as a challenge to the conventional historiography, which may very broadly be summed up as two interlinked points. Firstly, that Wellington, in seeking to retain numerically weak battalions of experienced and acclimatised infantry in the Peninsula after the conclusion of the 1812 campaign, was acting entirely correctly; secondly, and following on from that premise, that the efforts of Field Marshal HRH the Duke of York to return these battalions to the home station were based on a mistaken premise. Wellington, after all, had managed to overcome the fact that the units that he wished to keep were so low in numbers by pairing them to form Provisional Battalions, sending home the ineffective manpower along with the cadres of six of each battalion's 10 companies so as to facilitate recruitment and the speedy rebuilding of the units concerned. So drawn-out were the arguments over which units should be retained in the Peninsula and which sent home, that most of those which Wellington sought to retain were still with him at the end of the war. There seems to be little appreciation of the fact that Wellington's scheme, inventive and practical though it was, worked directly against the systems of manpower management and unit rotation by which York sought to meet the British Army's commitments not only in the Peninsula but across the globe.[2] This conflict of interests was all the more significant because of the fact

---

1 Andrew Bamford, *Sickness, Suffering, and the Sword: the British Regiment on Campaign 1808–1815* (Norman: University of Oklahoma Press, 2013).

2 The standard view can be traced back, at least, to Sir Charles Oman, *A History of the Peninsular War* (Oxford, Oxford University Press, 1902–1930), Vol.VI, pp.231–235 which presents an essentially neutral narrative but with a tone that is decidedly favourable to Wellington's viewpoint. Jac Weller, *Wellington in the Peninsula* (London: Nicholas Vane, 1967), p.248 and Robert Burnham, 'Filling the Ranks: How Wellington kept his Units up to Strength', p.219 in Muir et al, *Inside Wellington's Peninsular Army 1808–1814* (Barnsley: Pen and Sword, 2006), respectively praise Wellington's stubbornness and obstinacy in defying York. Rory Muir, in the online commentary to his two-volume

that by the time that the fighting in Europe came to an end in April 1814, there could be little doubt but that the British Army was on the point of running out of effective manpower.[3] One might argue, of course, that the solution was to recruit a greater portion of the population, but the reality is that this would have been impossible without some form of conscription (beyond that already inherent in the Militia ballot) and this opens up an entirely different debate that takes us from the military sphere to the political: for the purposes of this chapter, the focus is on what the Army could most usefully do with the men it had.

The intention, therefore, is firstly to revisit Wellington's scheme and examine its origins and the manner in which it was implemented, as well as looking at the arguments and counter-arguments between York and Wellington, which also drew in a third participant in the shape of Henry, 3rd Earl Bathurst, Secretary of State for War and the Colonies. Secondly, however, use of the Army's monthly returns, showing the strength and location of all infantry battalions and cavalry regiments, allows the consideration of a historical counterfactual against which the effectiveness, or otherwise, of Wellington's scheme can be measured. The author's expectation, in commencing that exercise, was to be able to thereby demonstrate that Wellington's retention of units in the Peninsula through the Provisional Battalion scheme directly contributed to the near-collapse of the manpower system during the closing months of the war. In fact, as this chapter reveals, the actual situation can be seen as being rather more complex, with underlying institutional failings tending towards a situation where no manner of clever management could prevent an eventual breakdown of the system.

In order to understand the various measures that were proposed, and on occasion enacted, to tweak the regular systems of manpower management, it is first necessary to understand how the regimental system was supposed to work. An infantry regiment was ideally to be constituted on the basis of a two-battalion structure, but, unlike the situation found in continental armies, these battalions did not serve together and the regiment did not function as a tactical unit. In the British system, the first battalion would be prioritised for active service: kept up to full establishment strength (or as near to it as possible) and held in readiness at home as part of the disposable force from which expeditions overseas might be put together. Once sent overseas, the first battalion would be reinforced as required by drafts of men from the second battalion, which would typically then function in a role combining

---

biography of Wellington, having previously asserted in his *Britain and the Defeat of Napoleon* (New Haven: Yale University Press, 1996), p.276 that York was correct only 'in theory' in wanting to bring the battalions home, and 'should have been more flexible', allows that there were 'good arguments on both sides' but believes that Wellington 'got the best of the resulting compromise'; see Rory Muir, 'Commentary for Volume 1, Chapter 31: Vitoria (Dec 1812–June 1813)' at <https://www.lifeofwellington.co.uk/commentary/chapter-31-vitoria-dec-1812-june-1813> acessed 10 April 2020, under the heading 'Quarrel with Horse Guards over recall of weak second battalions'. An exception to this trend is Joshua Moon, *Wellington's Two-Front War. The Peninsular Campaigns at Home and Abroad, 1808–1814* (Norman: University of Oklahoma Press, 2011), pp.154–158, who takes a rather more balanced view and recognises the fact that York and Wellington had different perspectives and priorities, but fails to present any real critique of either stance.

3 Robert Burnham, 'The British Army in the Napoleonic Wars: Manpower Stretched to the Limits?' *The Napoleon Series*, at <https://www.napoleon-series.org/military-info/organization/c_casualties.html> accessed 10 April 2020.

home defence, garrison, and/or policing duties with that of a depot unit. A further nuance of the system was that the most senior officers in a given rank belonged to the first battalion, and the more junior to the second; thus, in theory, a senior lieutenant in the first battalion who had obtained his captaincy would revert to the second battalion in his new rank and have the opportunity to learn his new duties on a less demanding station. The qualification 'in theory' should be particularly noted here; what was more common was for the first battalion to retain a full complement of officers, leaving the second shorthanded.

Only very rarely were both battalions of a regiment sufficiently strong that both could be deployed overseas, and rarer still was it the case that such a deployment could continue for any length of time – most often, as both battalions shrank, the effective men of the second battalion would be discharged into the first, and the rump of the second sent home to recruit. It is important to appreciate the distinction here that whereas this sort of manpower transfer between different battalions of the same regiment was an accepted, indeed essential, part of the system, transfer of men between regiments was anathema to be avoided at all costs due to the disastrous consequences that could ensue insofar as morale and discipline were concerned. In the eighteenth century, when regiments almost always mustered only a single battalion, 'drafting' was a common practice, whereby a regiment at home might give up much of its manpower to reinforce those going overseas, or else a weakened unit on campaign might give up its remaining manpower to other regiments in the same theatre with the officers and NCOs going home to recruit. However, opposition to this had become so strong by the 1790s, to the extent that fears of drafting to regiments in the West Indies even led to mutiny, that the idea fell out of favour and was ultimately rendered unnecessary, at least in theory, by the institution of the two-battalion regimental model.[4] Voluntary manpower transfer was possible – for example, men desirous of remaining in India when their regiment went elsewhere were often encouraged to transfer to regiments remaining behind – but enforced transfer was a different matter.

The few regiments that were able to maintain multiple battalions overseas for any length of time were generally those where the overseas posting was to a healthy and inactive garrison, or those that were able to benefit from an establishment running in excess of the standard model. Leaving aside special cases like the Foot Guards and the rifle regiments, only the 1st and 27th Foot fielded 'extra' battalions during the era covered by this study – four and three respectively – although the 14th and 56th Foot would both gain third battalions at the very end of the period under circumstances which will be returned to later. Conversely, a number of regiments had either lost their second battalion by 1812 or had never been able to raise one, and thus whilst it was entirely within the norms of the system for such single-battalion regiments to be selected for overseas service, battalions thus deployed could rely on only a

4 For a case-study of the 1790s experience, see T.H. McGuffie, 'The Short Life and Sudden Death of an English Regiment of Foot: An Account of the Raising, Recruiting, Mutiny and Disbandment of the 113th regiment of Foot or "Royal Birmingham Volunteers" (April, 1794, to September, 1795)', *Journal of the Society for Army Historical Research*, Vol.33, No.133 (Spring 1955), pp.16–25, and No.134 (Summer 1955), pp.48–56.

company-strength depot to supply their manpower needs and thus typically shrank more quickly in comparison to first battalions that had a second battalion back at home.[5]

Up until 1808, the system had largely worked as intended. At the beginning of 1809, however, the bulk of the British contingent in the Peninsula was evacuated from Corunna at the end of Sir John Moore's epic winter campaign. Since the various contingents that had gone to Portugal in 1808 came from Britain's disposable force, and since Moore had taken the pick of that force with him into Spain, the troops sailing back from Corunna represented a large proportion of the active first battalions. Having been built back up to strength, the bulk of these battalions were earmarked for the expedition to Walcheren, which was to be Britain's main military effort for 1809. However, it was also necessary to reinforce the British contingent in Portugal, which would in due course form the nucleus of Wellington's Peninsular army. Until late 1810, when the first ex-Walcheren battalions began to reach Portugal, only a small number of first battalions could be spared – most of them redeployed from overseas garrisons, although a brigade apiece of Foot Guards and light infantry went out from home. The greater proportion of the reinforcements sent to Wellington in 1809 and 1810, however, were second battalions or single-battalion regiments.[6] As these units began to shrink under the rigors of campaigning, so began to develop the problem that Wellington would seek to address with his Provisional Battalions scheme.

Wellington first formed a Provisional Battalion – unnumbered, since there was only the one – in the aftermath of Albuera out of the cut-up 29th, 2/31st, and 2/66th. The first of these was ultimately so weakened that it was recalled home, but the remaining pair functioned as a single combined unit throughout the rest of 1811 and all through 1812. This first experiment was not quite the model for the enlarged Provisional Battalions scheme of 1812: no men were sent home and the field and staff officers from both battalions remained in the field. For command purposes the combined unit came under the officer commanding the 2/31st – first Lieutenant Colonel Guy l'Estrange and then Lieutenant Colonel Alexander Leith – but Lieutenant Colonel Charles Nicol of the 2/66th was still present with the battalion as late as early 1813, albeit that his function was restricted to maintaining order and discipline in that portion of the combined unit that came from his own regiment.[7]

At the same time as his army was absorbing the heavy losses at Albuera that had led to the measures just outlined, Wellington was speculating on the need to build up his forces for offensive operations in Spain now that Portugal was secure. He made it clear to Lord Liverpool, then still Secretary of State for War and the Colonies, that this would mean retaining units in the Peninsula that might otherwise have gone home. In order to do this,

5 The system is summarised in Philip J. Haythornthwaite, *The Armies of Wellington* (London: Arms and Armour, 1994), pp.76–79. For a case study of the system in practice, see Carole Divall, *Redcoats Against Napoleon. The 30th Regiment During the Revolutionary and Napoleonic Wars* (Barnsley: Pen and Sword, 2009): this study has particular relevance to the topic of this chapter since the 2/30th was briefly part of the Provisional Battalions scheme under discussion.

6 The movements of battalions to and from the Peninsula are tracked in Steve Brown, 'Bound For Mondego Bay: British Infantry Regiment Movements To and From the Peninsula, 1808 to 1814', *The Napoleon Series*, at <www.napoleon-series.org/military-info/battles/1808/Peninsula/BritishArmy/c_MondegoBay.html>, accessed 10 April 2020; see also C.T. Atkinson's appendix to Sir Charles Oman, *Wellington's Army* (London: Edward Arnold, 1913), pp.343–373.

7 TNA: WO17/117, Inspection Report of 12 May 1813.

Wellington proposed that he 'form into six companies the 2nd battalions of the 24th, 31st, 38th, 42nd, 58th, and 66th, and to send home to recruit, or to form the recruits, the Officers and non-commissioned officers of the four companies drafted'.[8] The proposal does not make it clear whether or not the resulting cut-down battalions would have been paired or not (although this would seem likely and, indeed, the 2/31st and 2/66th already had been); the main point here was the sending home of companies to recruit. Nevertheless, as early as 1811 it can be seen that the two main tenets of the Provisional Battalions concept as enacted 18 months later were already established in Wellington's mind.

Wellington at this stage was also conscious that he had only so much political leverage to employ in changing the system, and accepted that some of his weakest units would have to go home; at this date, at least, with ex-Walcheren battalions still being sent out from home, he knew that these would replace any losses. Nevertheless, he went on to try and obtain Liverpool's blessing for an expansion of his proposals with regards to the battalions that he wished to keep, sugaring the pill with a suggestion that his schemes would also lead to financial economies:

> According to this plan we should reduce in some degree our expense in this country. We should keep here Officers inured to the climate and accustomed to the service; at the same time that we should send to England Officers and non-commissioned officers to raise and train recruits. Indeed, it would be desirable if I were authorised from time to time to incorporate the ten companies of a regiment into eight or six companies, according to their numbers, and to send home to recruit, or to train recruits, the Officers and non-commissioned officers of the drafted companies.[9]

Unsurprisingly, not least since blessing for it was in the gift of the Commander-in-Chief, not the Secretary of State, nothing came of Wellington's 1811 proposal. As time went on, the 2/38th and 2/42nd were absorbed into their respective first battalions when those joined the Peninsular field army in 1812, which was exactly how the system was supposed to work. Indeed, the same process also took place in the 5th Foot at this time. In a variant, but still very much within the spirit of the system, the second battalion of the 4th Foot came up from Gibraltar, where it had been in garrison, served briefly alongside the first battalion, and then handed over its effective manpower and returned home. In all of these cases, the experienced and acclimatised men of the second battalions were able to remain in the theatre of war, whilst the sick could go home to recover, and the officer and NCO cadre could set about recruitment and training. Even if the battalions themselves were unable to return – and, indeed, none of these four did – they could at least serve as feeder units for their respective first battalions. On the utility of these arrangements, there can be little doubt but that Wellington as field commander and York as Commander-in-Chief were of a like mind.

Nevertheless, such a neat and by-the-book solution to the problem of understrength second battalions in the Peninsula could only be achieved if the matching first battalion was

8 J. Gurwood (ed.), *The Dispatches of Field Marshal the Duke of Wellington, During his Various Campaigns in India, Denmark, Portugal, Spain, The Low Countries, and France* (London: John Murray, 1837–1839), Vol. VII, pp.521–525, Wellington to Liverpool, 7 May 1811.

9 Gurwood (ed.), *Dispatches*, Vol. VII, pp.521–525, Wellington to Liverpool, 7 May 1811.

available to come out and take the place of its junior regimental partner. At the end of the 1812 campaign, however, with his army back on the Portuguese frontier, the remaining four second battalions that had featured in Wellington's 1811 proposal had shrunk even further and were scarcely creditable as independent units. Furthermore, four additional battalions had now been reduced to similar straits, for a total of eight. The units now at risk of being sent home were the single-battalion 2nd, and the second battalions of the 24th, 30th, 31st, 44th, 53rd, 58th, and 66th. None of these units had any appreciable hope of receiving replacement manpower, relying solely on their home depot for recruiting and training replacement manpower. Worse, with the powers-that-be at Horse Guards still working the system by the book, the seven second battalions all had to play second fiddle to the first battalions of their various regiments, which had first call on any available manpower notwithstanding that the majority of them were in less active postings (1/31st, 1/44th, and 1/58th stationed around in the Mediterranean, the rest in India). Accordingly, as of 6 December 1812, Wellington ordered six of these battalions to implement a similar organisation to that already employed for the 2/31st and 2/66th, forming one strong unit out of two weak ones.[10] This time, he did not seek permission but presented his military and political masters at home with a fait acompli.

Incorporating the ideas that he had proposed in 1811, Wellington required that these battalions draft their effectives into four companies of equal strength, sending the unfit men home with the officer and NCO cadres of the six remaining companies. The intention was that these companies would recruit up to strength and then return, allowing the battalions to resume their original independent identities. The units formed were the 2nd Provisional Battalion from the 2nd and 2/53rd, with the staff (that is to say, commanding officer, field officers, adjutant, and so forth) of the latter; the 3rd Provisional Battalion from the 2/24th and 2/58th, with the staff of the former; and 4th Provisional Battalion from the 2/30th and 2/44th, with the staff of the former.[11] Taking the entire staff from one battalion or the other enabled Wellington to keep the commanding officers that he felt most useful. With the 3rd and 4th Provisional Battalion, the contributing units had already served alongside each other; indeed, the units comprising the latter had a lengthy history of shared service.[12] The previously-un-numbered battalion formed out of the 2/31st and 2/66th became the 1st Provisional Battalion, but no men were sent home and both regimental staffs were retained. The case of the 2/30th exemplifies the manner in which units were split. Retained in Portugal were 19 officers, three staff serjeants, 31 serjeants, 10 drummers, and 438 rank and file (of whom, however, only 189 were present for duty); sent home were 12 officers, six serjeants, three drummers, and 66 rank and file.[13]

Wellington's logic was that the men thereby retained in Spain were experienced soldiers who, perhaps more importantly, were acclimatised to the Iberian weather and diet. New battalions that might be sent out from home would be trained soldiers, but lacking in

10 J. Gurwood, (ed.), *The General Orders of Field Marshal the Duke of Wellington KG* (London: T. Egerton, 1838), Vol. IV, pp.229–235, GO of 6 December 1812.
11 Robert Burnham, 'Filling the Ranks', pp.216–219.
12 Carole Divall, *Inside the Regiment. The Officers and Men of the 30th Regiment During the Revolutionary and Napoleonic Wars* (Barnsley: Pen and Sword, 2011), p.14.
13 Divall, *Redcoats*, pp.124–125.

experience and likely to fall sick in large numbers until they became used to serving in the theatre. For Wellington, his decision was justified by their subsequent effectiveness.

Table 5.1: Peninsular Provisional Battalions

	1st Prov. Bn.	2nd Prov. Bn.	3rd Prov. Bn.	Average, Prov. Bns.	Average, all Infantry
Effectives as % of strength	75.5	70.4	63.0	69.9	66.1
Sick as % of strength	18.9	26.0	32.3	25.4	28.8
Deaths per 1000 Men	9.9	12.4	14.6	12.2	18.8
Desertions per 1000 Men	0.6	0.4	1.2	0.7	1.5

Notes: Computed from Monthly Returns, December 1812–April 1814, TNA: WO17/2470–2476. These returns list the numbers of men present, detached ('on command') and sick in all units serving under Wellington, along with the numbers of deaths and desertions in the month prior to the return being made out; entering this data into a spreadsheet facilitates easy comparison between units, or of a unit against the overage for the army as a whole. Figures used here are for rank-and-file only, excluding officers, NCOs, and drummers. The short-lived 4th Provisional Battalion has not been included in the table, so as not to skew the averages.

The figures given in Table 5.1 under the heading 'Regular Infantry' are an average of the rest of the British infantry under Wellington's command. Naturally, it therefore includes data from strong, experienced battalions on the one hand, and weak, sickly, units on the other; nevertheless, direct like-for-like comparison with other units does demonstrate that the Provisional Battalions were a good bargain for Wellington. For example, to take a sample of long-serving regular battalions then with Wellington, the 1/7th maintained an average effective strength of 62 percent of its total manpower over the same period that the Provisional Battalions were in existence, whilst the 1/11th averaged 65 percent, the 1/45th 64 percent, and the 1/71st 68 percent. All these figures fall in the same region as those for the Provisional Battalions. Indeed, the average for the Provisional Battalions would be better still were the figures not skewed by the heavy casualties incurred by the 3rd Provisional Battalion at Orthez, the monthly returns allowing no distinction between sick and wounded. Nor was Orthez the only occasion that these units stood up well in action: after Vitoria Wellington would inform Lord Bathurst, who had replaced Liverpool as Secretary of State when the latter became Prime Minister in June 1812, that it was 'impossible for any troops to behave better' than had the 2nd and 3rd Provisional Battalions.[14]

It will be noted that the table does not mention the 4th Provisional Battalion. It was the weakest of the four, and Wellington found himself given no choice by Horse Guards but to break it up and send it home. In order to prevent a similar occurrence, his plans to create a 5th Provisional Battalion out of the 51st and 68th were quietly shelved and these two units remained in the theatre. Otherwise, York acquiesced for the moment to Wellington's scheme. Indeed, so far as the effectiveness of the units in the field was concerned, the Commander-in-Chief had no convincing counterargument. However, he had a wider point. Acknowledging his receipt of Wellington's notification that the Provisional Battalions had been created against his wishes, York conceded that he would be:

14 Gurwood (ed.), *Dispatches*, Vol. VI, pp.674–675, Wellington to Bathurst, 11 August 1813.

> [E]xtremely sorry to withhold my concurrence from an arrangement which your Lordship has already carried into effect, particularly where an immediate objection would tend to reduce your effective force in the field. But when I state the grounds upon which I consider this formation detrimental to the well being of the regiments included in it, I trust your Lordship will see, that while I have every disposition to support and agree to any arrangement of yours, I could not possibly concur in the expediency of the present measure consistently with the opinion I entertain of what is essential to secure the continued efficiency of the army in general; and that you will not be surprised that I should strongly urge the recall of the detachments forming these provisional battalions, when I have the means of proposing an adequate reinforcement for their relief.

York then went on to explain what the knock-on effects of such a policy would be, noting that:

> Experience has shown that in every instance wherein a battalion has been brought home a skeleton, composed of its officers, non-commissioned officers, and a certain foundation of the old and experienced soldiers, the greatest success has attended its re-formation for any service within a short period; and this is fully exemplified in the case of the 29th regiment, which is now complete in numbers and ready for foreign service; but if a corps reduced in numbers be broken up by the division of its establishment, it is quite impossible but that such an interruption must be occasioned in its interior economy and esprit de corps as a regiment as would effectually prevent that speedy completion of numbers and reorganization which I look to as the only means of providing for the demands for foreign service.[15]

The commander-in-chief concluded his reply by seeking to convince Wellington that a minor local advantage in the short term would not be worth the wider long-term problems, believing that Wellington gained only a 'comparatively trifling advantage' which was not worth the 'sacrifice the only foundation upon which we can look to the eventual efficiency of the army'.

Because of this, York believed that Wellington would have to give up the bulk of the battalions that he had sought to retain, keeping only the 2/31st and that only until the 1/31st might be transferred from Sicily to replace it. He instead sought to demonstrate that the established regimental system, as it stood, could solve the perceived manpower shortfall in the Peninsula and that by sending home weak second battalions the ongoing rotation of manpower that was part of the established regimental system would see strong first battalions sent out in their stead.

York's main, and most valid, point was that Wellington's scheme blocked the effective rebuilding of weak units, in which York's choice of the 29th as example was apt. As we have seen, that battalion had to be recalled from the Peninsula in mid-1811 as too weak to

15 2nd Duke of Wellington (ed.), *Supplementary Despatches, Correspondence, and Memoranda, of Field Marshal Arthur, Duke of Wellington* (London: John Murray, 1858–1862), Vol. VII, pp.524–525, York to Wellington, 13 January 1813.

function after its heavy losses at Albuera, but after 18 months at home it was again available for service. True, it was not immediately fit to take the field, but posting it to Cadiz freed the more seasoned 2/59th to leave that station and join Wellington. York was trying to make Wellington see that by hanging on to weak but experienced battalions in the short term, he was hazarding the availability of reinforcements being available in the future. Furthermore, Wellington's unilateral decision to suspend the Army's systems of manpower rotation had the potential to do harm well beyond the confines of the Peninsula, since by cutting off the stream of attenuated battalions going home to be rebuilt it further limited the already small pool of battalions available for deployment from the home station to other theatres.

Notwithstanding that he had a strong argument behind him, York nevertheless hesitated rather than seeking to force the issue. Although he achieved an early success in obtaining the return of the 2/30th and 2/44th, it was not until January 1814 that he gave a direct order to break up the remaining Provisional Battalions. Even then, a caveat meant that Wellington need not do so until it could be achieved 'without inconvenience to your present operations', with the additional proviso that men from these battalions could remain in the Peninsula if they could be persuaded to volunteer into other regiments (even now, it will be noted that forcible drafting of men to other regiments was not considered).[16] With this loophole, Wellington was able to retain the Provisional Battalions until the end of the war. York, meanwhile, was obliged to institute a series of increasingly desperate measures to find additional manpower for Britain's commitments elsewhere in the world; most notably North America, where the War of 1812 rumbled on and the initially-laughable US Army grew ever more proficient, and Northern Europe where the need to find troops for Sir Thomas Graham's little army in the Low Countries stretched the system practically to breaking point.

York's January 1814 order in fact only required the recall of four of the six component units of the 1st–3rd Provisional Battalions. Wellington was to be permitted to retain the 2/53rd, since a draft had been assembled at the regiment's depot large enough to enable the battalion to again take the field as an independent entity (the 1/53rd, away in India, would evidently have to manage without its yearly reinforcement). Tellingly, however, this could not be managed for any of the other five battalions that Wellington had held on to, although York's order also permitted his retention of the rank and file of the 2/58th, who were to be drafted off into the 1/58th once it could be reassigned from duty with the British contingent serving on the east coast of Spain. No reinforcements were available for any of the other four units involved in the Provisional Battalion project, and, since the 2/31st and 2/66th had been awaiting such augmentation for two-and-a-half years, they were unlikely to be forthcoming. Prioritisation of the first battalions certainly did not help – although the 2nd, as a single battalion regiment, could hardly use this excuse – but the cadres sent home by Wellington were for the most part too weak to recruit effectively, if the tiny contingent sent home by the 2/30th, or the mere 71 all-ranks sent home from the 2/58th, are any sort of example.[17] Conversely, once the 2/30th was reunited back at home it was quickly able

16 Wellington (ed.), *Supplementary Despatches*, Vol. VIII, pp.495–496, York to Wellington, 10 January 1814.

17 Bamford, *Sickness, Suffering, and the Sword*, p.147; on the 2/30th, see Divall, *Redcoats*, pp.124–125 and see also above. This highlights the main flaw of delegating recruitment to the regimental level, wherein success bred success while numerically-weak units struggled to rebuild themselves.

to increase its numbers, as was the 2/44th. Indeed, when York ordered the break-up of the three remaining Provisional Battalions the constituent units of the erstwhile 4th Provisional Battalion, although by no means at full strength, were again fit for further employment with the 2/44th already on active duty with Graham in the Netherlands and the 2/30th about to embark on the same service.

With this in mind, it is hard to escape the conclusion that York's rejection of the Provisional Battalion concept was correct, and that the dislocation to the regimental system as a whole more than outweighed the small advantage gained for Wellington's field army. Having written extensively on the British operations in the Low Countries from December 1813 to April 1814, the present author may be showing an element of bias in focusing on this minor campaign but doing so does beg the question: how much more effective Graham's operations could have been, had he been able to call upon, if not a greater number of troops, at least a greater proportion of veterans? Likewise, would the removal of three battalions – veterans, certainly, but totalling 1,931 out of an army of 81,276 at the commencement of the Vitoria campaign, or 5.5 percent of the 35,018 effective British infantry – have truly affected the course of the Peninsular War?[18] Indeed, had Wellington been prepared to toe the Horse Guards line from the outset and send the Provisional Battalions home in early 1813, might other reinforcements have been more readily forthcoming to take their place? The second half of this chapter, therefore, will consider an administrative counter-factual. Let us assume that York ordered the break-up of all four provisional battalions at the beginning of 1813, rather than just recalling the 2/30th and 2/44th. What might then have been done to replace them and what would the longer-term consequences have been?

York's response to Wellington had already suggested that the 2/31st could be retained and the 1/31st sent to Wellington from Sicily. In that the latter battalion was still 713-strong in early 1814,[19] it can safely be assumed to have been at least that strong a year previously. Adding in the effective manpower of the 2/31st would have created a battalion in excess of 800-strong; a more than viable unit. Alternatively – or, indeed, additionally – the 2/58th might also have been retained in the Peninsula with a view to incorporating its manpower into the 1/58th which was then part of the force that had been sent from the Sicilian garrison to operate on the east coast of Spain. This would probably have speeded up the redeployment of the 1/58th to the Peninsular field army, whereas in reality that battalion was still on the east coast when the war ended (albeit by that stage as part of a force earmarked to reinforce Wellington). The 1/58th had 660 effective rank and file in May 1813, which, if added to the 242 effectives of that portion of the 2/58th still in the Peninsula, produces a powerful battalion of 902 rank and file – making up in itself nearly half of the shortfall created by removing the Provisional Battalions from the Anglo-Portuguese order of battle.[20] Furthermore, the 1/58th having been on the east coast since June 1812, and on Sicily

18 Provisional Battalion effective strength figures, and British infantry totals, computed from Monthly Return for 25 May 1813 in TNA: WO17/2472; army total marching strength, including cavalry, artillery, and Portuguese units integrated with Wellington's field army, from Oman, *Peninsular War*, Vol. VI, p.752.

19 Hon. J.W. Fortescue, *A History of the British Army* (London: Macmillan, 1899–1930), Vol. 10, p.60.

20 Strength figures from Monthly Returns for 25 May 1813 in TNA: WO17/2478 (East Coast Spain) and WO17/2472 (Peninsular field army).

prior to that since 1805, it can be safely assumed that these were troops well acclimatised to the Mediterranean climate and diet; exactly the sort of men that Wellington wanted in his army and sought to retain through the Provisional Battalion scheme.[21] Sending the 1/58th to Wellington could have been counterbalanced by retaining the 6th KGL Line Battalion on the east coast, which historically went back to Sicily in mid-1813. In terms of minimising troop movements, therefore, it could be argued that if only one battalion could be spared from the Mediterranean command then the 1/58th would have been a more readily-available option than would the 1/31st.

Speculating on the 1/58th, indeed, rather begs the question of whether Wellington's manpower shortfall might best have been resolved simply by bringing more troops across from the British contingent serving on the east coast and leaving that theatre to the Spanish. Under those circumstances, the 1/44th, which started the year split between Sicily and Malta but went to eastern Spain in the spring, might conceivably have also gone straight to Wellington and absorbed the 2/44th. We now know that the British contingent made a lacklustre showing – albeit at the fault of the commander, Sir John Murray, rather than the units concerned – during the Tarragona expedition of May-June 1813, and subsequently sank into relative inactivity. With hindsight, thereafter, abandoning operations in Catalonia in the spring of 1813 and using the troops employed there to reinforce Wellington seems like an ideal solution to the Peninsular manpower shortage but it is unlikely that it was perceived as such in the first months of 1813. At that stage, with the main Anglo-Portuguese army still possessing barely a toehold in Spain, Murray's 9,410 men had a vital role to play in tying down Suchet's *Armée d'Aragon*, over which, indeed, Murray was even able to obtain a minor victory at Castalla on 13 April 1813.[22] Wellington was fully appreciative of the theoretical contribution that this force made to his plans to evict the French from north-central Spain, and does not appear to have proposed drawing men from Murray's command to reinforce his own.[23] This perhaps predicates against the idea of the 1/58th being shifted to the main Peninsular field army in addition to the 1/31st, let alone the 1/44th as well.

If we assume, though, that one battalion could be spared from the Mediterranean then this still leaves five weak battalions that historically stayed on in Spain as part of the Provisional Battalion scheme but which would under this counterfactual instead go home in their entirety, as, indeed, would the cadre of whichever of the 2/31st or 2/58th was united with its corresponding first battalion. We know that the 2/30th and 2/44th, which really did sail home in May 1813, were historically built up to be fit to go on service again by the end of the year. The improved manpower situation at the depot of the 53rd, that would have historically permitted the 2/53rd to stay in the Peninsula after January 1814, suggests that it too would certainly have been rebuilt by then as well. Whether the same could be said for the others is less certain. The 2nd was a regiment beset by numerous internal problems, having suffered under a succession of bad commanding officers, and had not fielded

21 Oman, *Peninsular War*, Vol. V, p.608; Richard Partridge and Michael Oliver, *Napoleonic Army Handbook* (London: Constable, 1999), Vol. I, p.72

22 Strength figures from Oman, *Peninsular War*, Vol. VI, p.748; Spanish troops operating alongside Murray's Anglo-Italian force took the total to 18,716 for the Castalla campaign.

23 Nick Lipscombe, *Wellington's Eastern Front. The Campaigns on the East Coast of Spain 1810–1814* (Barnsley: Pen and Sword, 2016), pp.100–103; Oman, *Peninsular War*, Vol. VI, pp.308–313.

a second battalion since 1796. It possibly would not have been ready to go overseas again before the war's end; likewise, whichever regiment had had its first battalion transferred from the Mediterranean to join Wellington would, as part of that arrangement, have seen the second battalion default to its role as feeder unit for the first. On the other hand, it is fair to assume that the remaining units would have been sent to the Netherlands towards the end of the war – at the very least, they could not have been in a worse shape than some of the units that historically were sent out to form and then reinforce Graham's force.

The effects of this would have been twofold. Firstly, Graham would have had far more experienced infantry than he actually fielded. This probably would have made no difference at the siege of Antwerp, where the failure of the operation was down to lack of a decent battering-train combined with an uncooperative ally. However, such a reinforcement might well have been enough to swing the balance during the attack on Bergen-op-Zoom which, historically, ended with collapse and a surrender, caused, at least in part, by failings of inexperienced officers and men (although, from a military point of view, the outcome of this operation was utterly inconsequential insofar as the success of the Sixth Coalition was concerned, and its failure did not appreciably dent Britain's efforts to stake a claim in the post-war future of the area).[24] Secondly, Graham's command formed the nucleus of the force that Wellington led at Waterloo 18 months later. Because they had gone home in 1813 and then to the Netherlands, the 2/30th and 2/44th were at Quatre Bras and Waterloo where they played a vital role, as Carole Divall's study of the 30th makes plain.[25] Ironically, then, one unexpected long-term benefit of this counterfactual from Wellington's point of view is that it would have given him a further four or five experienced battalions in 1815, when he surely needed them far more than in the closing Peninsular battles – not, of course, that anyone could have known or planned for this back in the winter of 1812–1813.

Self-evidently, if these battalions had been recalled from the Peninsula in 1813, something would have had to replace them. The limited options for redistribution of manpower already overseas has already been discussed with reference to the case of the 31st and 58th. Barring the unlikely option of the first battalions of both of these regiments being transferred to Wellington's command, any further augmentation would therefore have had to have come from the home station. Reviewing the monthly returns for January 1813, as the Commander-in-Chief and his staff would have been obliged to do in order to make a first survey of likely battalions (a final decision would necessarily have also required consulting the most up-to-date reports from the bi-annual unit inspections) a number of likely contenders present themselves, as tabulated below. This list ignores a number of relatively strong second battalions stationed in the Channel Islands, which were combining depot and garrison functions and as such were not available for overseas employment (although by the year's end this had changed and the 2/35th and 2/81st were drawn on to go to the Low Countries). Nor would there have been any point deploying second battalions of regiments whose first battalions were with Wellington, since the second battalion could better function at home as a feeder unit and still send manpower drafts to the Peninsula. The 85th Light Infantry, then at Hythe, is also omitted; although it would go to the Peninsula later in the

24 Andrew Bamford, *A Bold and Ambitious Enterprise. The British Army in the Low Countries 1813–1814* (Barnsley: Frontline, 2013), pp.177–234.

25 Divall, *Redcoats*, pp.143–178.

year, it was in the process of having its officer corps replaced en masse due to disciplinary problems and was, therefore, self-evidently not an immediate candidate for deployment.[26]

Table 5.2: Potential Extra Reinforcements from Home, January 1813

Battalion	Effective R&F	Total R&F	Station	Next Actual Deployment
4/1st	998	1,294	Musselburgh	Baltic, August 1813
16th	431	570	Sunderland	North America, May 1814 (via Ireland)
2/21st	334	434	Inverness	Netherlands, January 1814
29th	669	887	Windsor	Cadiz, April 1813
33rd	428	525	Windsor	Baltic, August 1813
46th	341	420	Jersey	New South Wales, August 1813
54th	475	608	Woodbridge	Baltic, August 1813
7/60th	350	650	Isle of Wight	See Notes
2/69th	335	431	Ipswich	Netherlands, December 1813
70th	401	501	Montrose	North America, November 1813 (via Ireland)
2/73rd	375	435	Tower of London	Baltic, August 1813
2/78th	392	479	Aberdeen	Netherlands, January 1814
97th	431	533	Jersey	North America, May 1814 (via Ireland)

Notes: Compiled from Monthly Returns for 1813, TNA, WO17/259–276. The 7/60th was still raising; by the end of the year it had 544 effectives out of 561 total and had moved to Guernsey, from where it deployed to North America in 1814. As a unit formed from foreign prisoners of war, it would have been an unlikely candidate for Peninsular deployment but is included for completeness' sake; it might at the very least have gone to Cadiz or Gibraltar to free up a better battalion for the field army.

Indicative of the fact that the manpower situation grew increasingly desperate as 1813 went on, the following units, not included in Table 5.2, had in fact also gone overseas by the year's end (strengths as of January 1813 given as effective/total): 2/25th (237/297), to Baltic August 1813; 2/52nd (257/446), to Netherlands December 1813; 55th (256/483, but with elements still returning from Jamaica), to Netherlands December 1813; 2/91st (491/611, but not included above as 1/91st in Peninsula), to Baltic August 1813. Other line battalions sent out with Graham did not even exist at this point. The 2/37th and 3/56th were not raised until June, along with the 3/14th: the two first-named were on service before the end of the year.[27]

It will be observed, in addition to the omission of the 85th already noted, that the above table does not include any of the battalions that were in reality sent out from home to the Peninsular army during 1813–1814: the 2/62nd, 76th, and 2/84th. These three units were then in Ireland, from where returns have not survived; nevertheless, the fact that they were on that station suggests that they were already being held in readiness to go overseas, with the possibility of topping up their manpower from the Irish Militia at the same time. The same process can be seen with the 16th and 97th in the above table, which each spent the

26 Haythornthwaite, *Armies of Wellington*, p.36.

27 For Graham's order of battle, see Bamford, *Bold and Ambitious Enterprise*, pp.267–271, 276–277 also sent out were detachments from the second battalions of all three of the Foot Guards regiments, a composite battalion drawn from the depot of the 95th Rifles, and the 1st Royal Veteran Battalion.

best part of a year in Ireland before crossing the Atlantic, and even the 70th was detained a couple of months at Cork. The 70th was the final battalion sent as a reinforcement from Europe to North America until after the conclusion of the war in Europe in April 1814, suggesting an increasing focus on the settlement of affairs in Europe and a concentration of all available manpower into the struggle against Napoleon. Indeed, it is remarkable just how few battalions were sent to North America as reinforcements after the outbreak of hostilities there – three in 1812 and a further five (plus a cavalry regiment) in 1813, with three of those being redeployments from elsewhere in the Americas – whereas 1813 saw six battalions sent to North Germany for garrison duty at the Baltic ports, even before the more significant deployment to the Low Countries at the end of that year.[28]

Looking again at Table 5.2, there is, therefore, not a great deal by way of likely prospects for an immediate counterfactual reinforcement of Wellington to replace the Provisional Battalions. Assuming the transfer of one battalion from either Sicily or the east coast of Spain, in the region of a thousand additional effective rank and file would be required to make up the remaining shortfall. This would mean the dispatch of at least three of the listed units. In the event that two battalions joined Wellington from the Mediterranean then perhaps only one extra would have been needed to go out from home to the Peninsula, but in that case it is possible that another might have been sent to Sicily. Of the units potentially available, the 29th was the strongest of the lot but must be discounted for the reasons outlined in York's letter above; as it was, sending this battalion to Cadiz permitted the more seasoned 2/59th to join Wellington. Assigning the 29th as a direct reinforcement would, therefore, have an ultimately negative effect. The most likely contenders, therefore, would be the battalions that historically went to America – 16th, 70th, and 97th, with the latter having the advantage of prior Peninsular service – or the best of the home-station regiments that ultimately went to the Baltic and then on to Graham. In the latter category, the 33rd and/or 54th would seem the likeliest possibilities. The 4/1st, though stronger than any of them, was already serving as a source of drafts for the regiment's three senior battalions – one of which was already with Wellington in any case – such that when it did go overseas it was forced to leave a substantial proportion of its manpower behind as a depot. As such, it seems an unlikely battalion for York to have chosen for service at this juncture although with so many men on strength it is perhaps surprising that some of this manpower was not employed to provide a reinforcing draft to the 3/1st in the Peninsula.

By no stretch of the imagination would any of these troops have been the equivalent, man-for-man, of those that York was asking Wellington to give up. With the possible exception of a few veterans in the 97th, they would not have been at all acclimatised to active service, let alone to active service in the climate of the Iberian Peninsula. Yet as we can see from the circumstances of the reinforcing battalions that did go out to the Peninsula in 1813 and 1814, Wellington was able to put systems in place to easily integrate raw units into the army. As well as the four battalions sent out from the British Isles during 1813, Wellington also brought the 77th up from Lisbon to join his field army, to which was added the 1/37th from Gibraltar in early 1814.[29] It is possible, of course, that in our counterfactual the latter move

28 Ron McGuigan, 'The British Army Stationed in British North America 1812–1815', *Napoleon Series*, at <https://www.napoleon-series.org/military-info/battles/bna/c_bna1.html>, accessed 14 April 2020.

29 Oman, *Wellington's Army*, pp.368, 371, 373.

might have taken place earlier, with one of the hypothetical early-1813 reinforcements from home going to Gibraltar to release the 1/37th rather than going directly to the field army, Indeed, in reality, it was at one time intended that the 2/84th would do exactly that.[30] In all likelihood, too, the battalions that historically went out in mid-late 1813 would have instead sailed earlier in the year, with those identified above as extra reinforcements following on. Either way, we most likely need to imagine a further three new battalions joining the field army in the course of 1813, over and above the historical six.

In order to make the best use of the fresh battalions that did join the Peninsular Army in the last year of its existence, they were formed into a special brigade under Major General Lord Aylmer, which was specifically intended to 'nurse' – Wellington's own word – these new units until they became more acclimatised, the battalions being kept 'as a kind of reserve for some time, before they are put into one of the divisions'.[31] In the case of the 2/84th, this process was completed before the end of the war and the battalion moved to a regular posting in the 5th Division. The 85th also seems to have swiftly become an effective unit under its new officers, but appears to have been retained with Aylmer as it was a light infantry battalion and there was a shortage of such troops with the Left Wing of the army where Aylmer's Brigade was posted. 85th aside, though, these battalions whilst being 'nursed' were used in secondary roles, blockading fortresses, rather than in active operations. The earlier creation of such a brigade as a holding formation for new battalions thus seems a likely possibility. Accommodating it outside of the divisional system would have required a certain amount of flexibility within the army's order of battle, perhaps taking a battalion from some of the strongest brigades in order to make up to strength those which in reality contained one of the Provisional Battalions. The potential for disruption as a result of such a reorganisation, spread over so strong a force, would surely have been negligible.

The purpose of this counterfactual analysis is to seek to demonstrate that Wellington's response was not necessarily the best one, and certainly not the only one, to a manpower shortfall that was affecting the British Army as a whole by 1813 and not just the Peninsular army on which Wellington was naturally focused. However, pursuing this approach also helps make it clear that Wellington's decision to circumvent the British Army's regimental manpower management systems in his own interest did not, of itself, cause the effective collapse of the system that was facing Britain by the first quarter of 1814 and which has been analysed by the present author elsewhere.[32]

The alternative deployments discussed above present what can be argued to be a better distribution of the available manpower so as to meet both Wellington's need of reinforcements in his role as commander of Britain's most important army in the field and York's need for units to come home to be rebuilt in order to keep the system going, so as to have men available for future operations. To make it work, however, it is still necessary to rob Peter to pay Paul. In order for the component units of all four of the erstwhile Provisional Battalions to come home in time to have some chance of being rebuilt for service by the winter of 1813-1814, we need to 'steal', for service in the Peninsula, units that historically

30 Wellington (ed.), *Supplementary Despatches*, Vol. VIII, p.60, Bathurst to Wellington, 5 July 1813.

31 Gurwood (ed.), *Dispatches*, Vol. XI, p.203, Wellington to Lieutenant General Sir John Hope, 18 October 1813.

32 See, in particular, Bamford, *Sickness, Suffering, and the Sword*, pp.160–176, 286–302.

went to North America or the Baltic. They in turn need to be replaced in those postings, probably by some of the units that historically deployed with Graham in December 1813, and these in turn need to be replaced either with the last handful of units that went out to Graham in early 1814 or, hopefully, by the rebuilt battalions recalled from the Peninsula a year previously. At best, then, Graham is left a little better off qualitatively if not quantitatively, but still lacking anything like a truly effective force with which to represent Britain's commitment to the war in Northern Europe. Depending on whether one battalion or two is taken from the Mediterranean garrisons, the options for offensive operations in that theatre are correspondingly constrained.

All of which brings us back to the point that no amount of shuffling of manpower – a battalion here, a battalion there – could really have avoided the fact that by 1814 the British Army, hamstrung by a regimental system better suited to short campaigns and imperial garrison duty, and unable for political reasons to move any closer to the continental conscript model, was running out of men. York would still have been obliged, in the closing months of the war, to authorise some of the more desperate expedients that were forced upon him: sending new battalions like the 2/37th and 3/56th overseas within months of their formation, calling upon the Militia to volunteer for overseas service, and, ultimately, forming Detachment Battalions out of the fit men from depots and second battalions in England.[33] The fault was with a system that was stretched to accommodate the long-term deployment of a major field army, bent further when a second front opened in North America, but finally pushed to breaking point when political concerns necessitated the opening of a third front in Northern Europe.

It is a measure of the man's sense of his own importance that by 1813 Wellington felt that he was right to challenge the way in which the British Army managed its manpower, and, perhaps, a measure of correctness in that self-assessment that York largely let him get away with it. Equally, it is hard to see York as being anything other than correct in preferring to run the regimental system in the way that the multi-battalion system was indented to function. The personal nature of the argument should also not be neglected. York had spent the best part of two decades rebuilding the British Army from its nadir in the mid-1790s, and any suggestion that Britain's leading field commander knew better was hardly going to sit well. Wellington, for his part, had built up a great reputation over years of successful campaigning, but if that reputation was to translate into further advancement in the post-war world it could not now be hazarded. After the shock of the retreat from Burgos and the loss of much that had been gained in his campaigns of 1812, strident demands for manpower priority would, if fulfilled, prevent the recurrence of such a setback, or, if ignored, provide a convenient justification for any future retreats.

If this chapter's diversion into counterfactual manpower management has achieved anything, then it has hopefully demonstrated that a by-the-book approach would have caused fewer problems for the British Army as a whole than Wellington's attempt to rewrite the rules did. Equally, it would not have been sufficient, on its own, to solve Britain's

33 For the Militia, see Burnham, 'Filling the Ranks', pp.221–223; for York's Detachment Battalions, see Andrew Bamford, 'Battalions of Detachments in 1814 – the Duke of York Responds to Britain's Manpower Shortfall', *Napoleon Series*, at <www.napoleon-series.org/military-info/battles/1814/c_BritishDetachments1814.html>, accessed 15 April 2020.

manpower problems. By looking at York's problems as well as Wellington's, it is possible to see that each man was right by his own standards but wrong by the other's. Whether that makes either man entirely 'right' is hard to say, but it remains this author's contention that Wellington's uncompromising stance created more problems than it solved, for only a limited short-term Peninsular manpower gain, and hindered rather than helped the Army's resolution of a manpower crisis the effects of which were still being felt as late as Waterloo.

Select Bibliography

The numerical data underpinning much of this study is taken from the monthly unit strength returns in the WO17 series at The National Archives, Kew; further insight into the state of specific units can be obtained from the inspection returns and reports in the WO27 series. In addition, the following published sources were of particular use in developing the arguments presented above:

Printed Primary Sources

Gurwood, J. (ed.), *The Dispatches of Field Marshal the Duke of Wellington, During his Various Campaigns in India, Denmark, Portugal, Spain, The Low Countries, and France* (London: John Murray, 1837–1839)

Gurwood, J. (ed.), *The General Orders of Field Marshal the Duke of Wellington KG* (London: T. Egerton, 1838)

Wellington, 2nd Duke of (ed.), *Supplementary Despatches, Correspondence, and Memoranda, of Field Marshal Arthur, Duke of Wellington* (London: John Murray, 1858–1862)

Secondary Sources

Bamford, Andrew, *A Bold and Ambitious Enterprise. The British Army in the Low Countries 1813–1814* (Barnsley: Frontline, 2013)

Bamford, Andrew, *Sickness, Suffering, and the Sword: the British Regiment on Campaign 1808–1815* (Norman: University of Oklahoma Press, 2013)

Divall, Carole, *Inside the Regiment. The Officers and Men of the 30th Regiment During the Revolutionary and Napoleonic Wars* (Barnsley: Pen and Sword, 2011)

Divall, Carole, *Redcoats Against Napoleon. The 30th Regiment During the Revolutionary and Napoleonic Wars* (Barnsley: Pen and Sword, 2009)

Fortescue, Hon. J.W., *A History of the British Army* (London: Macmillan, 1899–1930)

Haythornthwaite, Philip J., *The Armies of Wellington* (London: Arms and Armour, 1994)

Lipscombe, Nick, *Wellington's Eastern Front. The Campaigns on the East Coast of Spain 1810–1814* (Barnsley: Pen and Sword, 2016)

Moon, Joshua, *Wellington's Two-Front War. The Peninsular Campaigns at Home and Abroad, 1808–1814* (Norman: University of Oklahoma Press, 2011)

Muir, Rory, *Britain and the Defeat of Napoleon* (New Haven: Yale University Press, 1996)

Muir, Rory, et al, *Inside Wellington's Peninsular Army 1808–1814* (Barnsley: Pen and Sword, 2006)

Oman, Sir Charles, *A History of the Peninsular War* (Oxford, Oxford University Press, 1902–1930)

Oman, Sir Charles, *Wellington's Army* (London: Edward Arnold, 1913)

Online Resources

Bamford, Andrew, 'Battalions of Detachments in 1814 – the Duke of York Responds to Britain's Manpower Shortfall', *Napoleon Series*, at <www.napoleon-series.org/military-info/battles/1814/c_BritishDetachments1814.html>

Brown, Steve, 'Bound For Mondego Bay: British Infantry Regiment Movements To and From the Peninsula, 1808 to 1814', *The Napoleon Series*, at <www.napoleon-series.org/military-info/battles/1808/Peninsula/BritishArmy/c_MondegoBay.html>

Burnham, Robert, 'The British Army in the Napoleonic Wars: Manpower Stretched to the Limits?' *The Napoleon Series*, at <https://www.napoleon-series.org/military-info/organization/c_casualties.html>

McGuigan, Ron, 'The British Army Stationed in British North America 1812-1815', *Napoleon Series*, at <https://www.napoleon-series.org/military-info/battles/bna/c_bna1.html>

6

It is Not Just About Desertion: Foreign Soldiers and the British Army during the Napoleonic Wars

Alistair Nichols

When Sir Charles Oman, in his 1913 book *Wellington's Army*, described the foreign corps under Wellington's command in the Peninsular War he began with the King's German Legion which had been formed in 1803, following the French invasion of Hanover, describing its soldiers as:

> ... the legitimate representatives of the old Electoral army of Hanover ... All through 1804 new units were being rapidly created, mainly from Hanoverians, but not entirely, for other recruits of German nationality were accepted. But all the officers, nearly all the sergeants, and the large majority of the rank and file came from the old Electoral army.[1]

Later he moved on to the condition of the legion from 1811:

> It had now become impossible to keep the ranks of the Legion filled with the genuine Hanoverians who had been its original nucleus. Communication with the electorate was completely cut off, and German recruits of any kind had to be accepted ... Matters became still worse when, later in the war, German recruits of any sort became so hard to obtain that Poles, Illyrians, and miscellaneous foreigners of any sort were drafted out to fill the shrinking ranks.[2]

Oman then turned to the Brunswick Oëls infantry, the quality of which had also apparently declined:

1 Charles Oman, *Wellington's Army, 1809–1814* (London: Edward Arnold, 1913), p.221.
2 Oman, *Wellington's Army*, pp.223–224.

> ... [the] men had all the vices of the mercenary, though in time of battle they displayed many of the virtues. Their officers had a hard task to keep them together, and they could never be trusted at the outposts. But the regiment was full of good shots and bold adventurers, and furnished several of the detached rifle companies with which Wellington strengthened the light infantry of his brigades.[3]

Oman did not explain the apparent incompatibility between the statements that the Brunswick Oëls infantry 'could never be trusted at the outposts' but, nevertheless, 'furnished several of the detached rifle companies.' He then continued with his survey, by describing another unit:

> There was, however, one foreign regiment which was even more tiresome to manage than the Black Brunswickers. This was the Chasseurs Britanniques, a corps formed early in the Revolutionary War from French royalists, and taken into the British service in 1801. It was recruited entirely from deserters of all sorts when it came out to Portugal in the spring of 1811. At absconding it was far worse than the Brunswickers ... The unenviable task of keeping together this body of deserters and adventurers fell to a body of officers who were almost without exception furious French royalists ... They kept the miscellaneous horde committed to their charge under an iron discipline, and used the lash freely. All that their personal courage could accomplish was done, to make the Chasseurs an efficient fighting force. But they could not stop desertion, nor frequent misconduct ... The regiment melted away whenever it came near the French lines, and Wellington had a standing order that it must never be trusted with the outposts. Yet as a fighting body it had no bad record – as witness Fuentes de Oñoro and many other fields. This was the work of the zealous service of the officers – and was indeed a wonderful tour de force. The material with which they had to work was detestable.[4]

Oman's comments are important in this context as they set the tone for historians who followed. Even the considered Philip Haythornthwaite when providing a summary of the foreign units in another book entitled *Wellington's Army*, published in 2002, described the Chasseurs Britanniques, since its creation in 1801, as having been: '... diluted in quality by the enlistment of ex-prisoners-of-war and other nationalities, including Italians and eastern Europeans. It served with some distinction in the Peninsular War – notably at Fuentes de Oñoro – but its desertion record was such that it was not trusted with "outpost" duty.'[5]

It has become inevitable that when foreign troops in the British Army in the era of the French Revolutionary and Napoleonic Wars are considered the issue of desertion is given undue prominence, often in juxtaposition to their fighting record if the latter was good. This stems from the predominance of the Peninsular War in British military history for this era. Battlefield performance and desertion are, undeniably, significant considerations

3 Oman, *Wellington's Army*, p.225.
4 Oman, *Wellington's Army*, pp.225–227.
5 Philip J. Haythornthwaite, *Wellington's Army, The Uniforms of the British Soldier, 1812-1815* (London: Greenhill Books, 2002), p.25.

in assessing the contribution of units, and individual soldiers. However, a preoccupation with these two issues has created a distorted view of the role of foreign troops in the British Army during the Napoleonic Wars. Their role was multifaceted and so other aspects need to be included for an accurate assessment. Without pretending that it is a comprehensive review or, indeed, critique of the approach illustrated above, the following chapter seeks to introduce some of these other aspects to assist in developing such an assessment.

Probably the most important contribution of the foreign units was to put 'boots on the ground' for an army which consistently struggled to match the number of effective troops it had available against its losses, let alone the demands it faced. Regular units were needed in Britain, Ireland and the Channel Islands for defence against foreign invasion and internal strife. During the Napoleonic Wars, with the exception of some from the King's German Legion, foreign units rarely served in home stations at a time when the British Army faced increased demands abroad, not only for active, but also garrison, duties. These demands had emerged during the latter part of the 18th Century, even before France declared war in February 1793. In 1785 the British Army had 13,878 troops (rank and file) serving abroad and already in 1792 this number had grown to 23,476; demands multiplied rapidly during the French Revolutionary Wars and at their close, in 1802, 64,292 were deployed abroad.[6] They continued throughout the Napoleonic Wars: in 1809 85,171 men were committed to garrisons and other static forces abroad, that is 38.7 percent of the total force, with a further 4,223 on passage and only 22,623 in the force in Portugal.[7] Even in 1814, when such commitments had been considerably reduced, the authorised establishments of overseas garrisons took up almost 30 percent of the total available force.[8] Almost always serving overseas, the foreign units provided a significant proportion of these troops, especially in the Mediterranean and, alongside the West India regiments, in the West Indies.

To give accurate numbers for the foreigners serving Britain at any given time is problematic. One particular issue is that of the data sets used in contemporary returns: the units counted as foreign were not consistent across different submissions and, indeed, the categories used were often not defined. The table for the years 1804 to 1813 provided by Fortescue, which has often been used by subsequent historians, has the benefit of including those in the Ordnance branches, the artillery and engineers, alongside those in the infantry and cavalry which fell under the authority of the War Office. However, this table divides units into the undefined categories of 'British Corps' and 'Foreign and Colonial Corps'.[9]

Tables prepared by the War Office, in reports dealing with its manpower requirements, used similar categories, but, in this case, the units were listed. This permits the units raised for local service, such as the Ceylon Regiments and the fencibles in North America, along with the West India regiments, to be separated from those which were regarded as foreign, so giving a more accurate number for soldiers in such units. The calculation shows that

6 The National Archives (TNA): WO 25/3225, Account of the Amount and Distribution of the Forces on the British Establishment dated 13 February 1815.

7 J W Fortescue, *The County Lieutenancies and the Army 1803–1814* (London: Macmillan, 1909), p.305, dated 25 May 1809, there were a further 107,857 men in Britain and Ireland.

8 Robert Burnham and Ron McGuigan, *The British Army Against Napoleon Facts, Lists and Trivia 1805–1815* (Barnsley: Frontline, 2010) p.4–5.

9 Fortescue, *British Army*, p.293.

the numbers of rank and file in the foreign units (including the 60th Foot) were 24,938 in September 1810, 29,718 in September 1811 and 39,130 November 1812; when the total number in the Army (in the following January, shown by Fortescue) was 234,594 in 1810, 243,885 in 1811, and 255,876 in 1812. Thus forming 10.6, 12.2 and 15.3 percent respectively.

Table 6.1 – Effective strength of the Foreign and Provincial Corps in 1810, 1811 and 1812.[10]

	25 Sep 1810	25 Sep 1811	25 Nov 1811	25 Nov 1812
King's German Legion Cavalry	2,902	3,015	3,314	3,734
King's German Legion – Infantry	7,114	8,303	8,103	1,0021
Duke of Brunswick's Corps – Cavalry	511	555	530	524
Duke of Brunswick's Corps – Infantry	1,049	1,095	1,168	1,092
Ceylonese – Cavalry	30	27	27	27
Ceylonese – Infantry	2,383	2,444	2,444	2,619
Foreign Troop of Cavalry	83	93	91	91
West India Regiments	6,802	6,547	6,505	6,416
60th Regiment – 6 Battalions	5,195	4,378	4,952	6,272
Meuron	797	1,014	1,031	1,064
Roll	1,503	1,489	1,469	1,469
Watteville	1,072	1,444	1,510	1,468
Chasseurs Britanniques	1,023	1,529	1,603	1,439
Dillon	807	1,218	1,245	1,318
Corsican Rangers [sic]	725	1,365	1,438	1,596
York Light Infantry Volunteers	1,063	1610	1,660	1,680
Royal Regiment of Malta	138	Disb.	-	-
Maltese Provincials	212	254	259	251
Cape Corps	550	542	541	515
Sicilian Regiment	956	1,179	1,195	1,325
Black Pioneers, Jamaica etc. [sic]	354	340	328	348
Greek Light Infantry	-	1,000	1,033	821
Unattached Foreign Recruits at Cadiz	-	431	420	452
American Fencibles (* below)	1,482	1,615	*	*
Nova Scotia Fencibles	*	*	502	505
Newfoundland Fencibles	*	*	468	483
Canadian Fencibles	*	*	612	666
Glengarry Fencibles	-	-	-	435
Canadian Voltigeurs	-	-	-	240
Bourbon Corps	-	-	-	626
1st Foreign Independent Company	-	-	-	150
Italian Volunteers – 1st Battalion	-	-	-	1,097
Italian Volunteers – 2nd Battalion	-	-	-	1,277
Calabrian Corps	-	-	-	1,466
Ionian Greek Infantry	-	-	-	308
Unattached Recruits – Lymington	-	-	153	460
TOTAL	36,751	41,487	42621	52,255

10 TNA: WO 25/3224 (table dated 29 November 1811) and 3225 (table dated 31 December 1812).

The estimates presented to Parliament for expenditure on the foreign units provide supporting information about the strength of the different foreign corps for the extent of the Napoleonic Wars, as they show the sanctioned and projected numbers for specific units (excluding the 60th Foot). In the second half of 1802 (25 May to 24 December) the ten existing foreign units had 7,808 rank and file. In addition, the Dutch Brigade, formed around officers loyal to the House of Orange after the attempted British and Russian invasion of the Netherlands in 1799, had 6,092, providing, in all, 13,900 rank and file in foreign units. With the disbanding and repatriation of the Dutch Brigade, as well as the wholescale reduction of the British Army after the Peace of Amiens, only six foreign regiments, and the Foreign Invalids, remained in 1803 and were to have 5,168 rank and file.

The estimates show how the size and number of the foreign units grew steadily from 1804 until the peace of 1814, with the King's German Legion (KGL) providing a significant element throughout.

Table 6.2 – Numbers (rank and file) to be in foreign units in line with estimates of expenditure.[11]

Year	KGL	Other units	TOTAL
1804	12,559	7,309	19,868
1805	10,644	6,742	17,386
1806	13,715	9,274	22,989
1807	12,588	8,885	21,473
1808	13,243	8,882	22,125
1809	13,207	9,771	22,978
1810	12,395	11,558	23,953
1811	12,345	12,644	24,989
1812	15,632	15,109	30,741
1813	15,907	17,418	33,325
1814	15,958	16,258	32,216
1815	11,758	9,556	21,314

As the demands on the British Army increased, national recruiting could not keep up, so recruitment for the foreign units, from deserters from the French army and prisoners of war, not only grew in importance but came to be relied upon. A review of the manpower requirements of the army and recruiting, dated 20 October 1813, considered the inflow of recruits to the foreign units as having been at a healthy level over the previous years and 'allowing the same degree of success to continue, which may fairly be looked to hereafter' should continue to provide an average of 4,660 men a year.[12] The other sources of manpower were domestic recruitment, which was expected to provide 13,630 annually, and volunteers from the British and Irish militia. This last source, since the spring of 1811, was meant to produce 10,000 men a year, but the number of such volunteers had consistently failed to

11 TNA: WO 25/3213, Estimates for Foreign Corps.
12 TNA: WO 25/3225.

reach this number and so the overall shortfall had grown incrementally to 9,855 men by the time of the report.[13]

Individual foreigners were recruited into British regiments, in particular if they had specific skills or trades, notably as musicians. In late 1812 at the Foreign Depot which was on the south coast of England, at Lymington in Hampshire, Franz Netscher, from Mainz in Germany, and then Joseph Schmidt, from Geneva, Switzerland, were recruited for the 1st (Royal Scots) Foot. Both were musicians, the latter also a 'master of the band.'[14] This was on the specific request of the Duke of Kent, the regiment's colonel, who had requested that the staff at the depot look out for talented musicians.[15] Another example of the recruitment of foreign soldier musicians was that of three such men who joined the 1/40th (2nd Somersetshire) Foot in 1814 from the Chasseurs Britanniques after it had been disbanded; all three received the Waterloo Medal for their service with the 40th in 1815.[16] Lewis Foghell, enlisted again in 1827 with the 66th Foot later transferring to the 1/60th Foot with which he served until 1842; Louis Guerin served with the 40th until 1836 and Joseph Reichenberg, who has a place in the early history of Australian music, did so as regimental bandmaster until 1829.[17]

There were also examples of individual as well as larger-scale recruitment of foreigners into British regiments. In May 1802, 135 men from foreign regiments stationed in Egypt volunteered to go to India to be drafted into British regiments on the sub-continent. Six men who had come from the Watteville Regiment served long enough to receive pensions: one had joined the 80th Foot, later serving in the 53rd Foot from 1816 to 1819, while another joined the Light Dragoons – the 19th, 22nd and then, for his last six years, the 13th – to be discharged in 1825.[18] Four went to the 1/84th Foot and one of them, the Austrian Francois Missley, after being discharged in England in 1811, joined the 2/73rd in London; he was recorded as serving at Waterloo as a corporal in the regiment, only to be discharged in 1817, as he was considered unfit for service in India.[19]

In January 1806, within a week of the surrender of the Cape Colony to British forces, about 300 men from the garrison, soldiers of the 5th Waldeck Battalion, a German unit in the pay of the Batavian Republic, were recruited into the British Army. Almost all were immediately taken into regiments present with the British expeditionary force: 140 became Highlanders, joining the 71st and 72nd Regiments, and 120 went to the 38th and 83rd Foot. Amongst the others, thirty-two went to the 20th Light Dragoons, in which another German was already serving, Sergeant Norbert Landsheit who had joined the regiment in 1803 after

13 TNA: WO 25/3225.
14 TNA: WO 25/674 and 675, enlistment books.
15 TNA: WO 7/88, Foreign Depot correspondence.
16 The first two, at least, also received the Military General Service Medal, TNA: MINT 16/112, medal recipients.
17 TNA: 97/562, 565 and 729, service documents, Royal Hospital Chelsea. Reichenberg performed, composed and taught music in Sydney and then Hobart as bandmaster and then a civilian. In 1825 he advertised the 'first set of Quadrilles for Australia' he had composed, Graeme Skinner, 'Joseph Reichenberg and family' *Australharmony* <https://www.sydney.edu.au/paradisec/australharmony/reichenberg-joseph.php>, accessed 12 May 2020.
18 TNA: WO 97/41 and 662, Chelsea service documents.
19 TNA: WO 97/951 and 937; 121/123 and 251 – Chelsea service documents; 12/8062, pay list.

his previous unit, the York Hussars, had been disbanded. It is remarkable that only six of the Waldeckers were recruited for the 60th, the regiment for which all of them had originally been intended and which would have been a more obvious destination.[20]

Other instances include local recruitment into British regiments serving in Europe, perhaps the earliest example was when twelve infantry battalions were authorised to recruit Sicilians when serving on the island in early 1807. This was at a time when a specific unit, the Sicilian Volunteers, was also being recruited.[21] Some of these regiments recruited more actively than others. When a hundred or so men were drafted into the Sicilian unit from the British battalions prior to their leaving the island, later that year, 23 came from the 21st and 25 from the 27th Foot.[22] The following year, when the regiments had reached Britain, more Sicilians were likewise drafted permitting the Sicilian Regiment to expand from six to 10 companies; the 113 men of the 10th Company all coming from the 20th and 52nd Foot.[23] Later, in 1812, Wellington resorted to the same expedient, authorising the recruitment of Spaniards into British battalions, but this initiative appears to have been less fruitful.[24]

Despite the last example, this form of recruiting seems to have diminished over time. A survey of British infantry regiments inspected in 1812 shows that most battalions had between two and 10 foreigners in their ranks, especially those battalions serving abroad while many at home, second battalions in particular, had none. There are examples of battalions with larger numbers of foreigners, including 2nd Battalion Coldstream Guards with a sergeant and 13 guardsmen; 1/1st (Royal Scots) with a corporal, a drummer and 54 privates; 1/3rd (Buffs) with two corporals, a drummer and 24 privates; 86th with a corporal, six drummers and 31 privates and the 104th Foot with five sergeants, two corporals and 44 privates. The 97th Foot, formerly the Minorca and then Queen's German Regiment but from 1810 no longer considered a foreign unit, still had a large number of foreigners in its ranks: 26 (out of 45) sergeants, 13 corporals, nine drummers and 160 (out of 491) privates.[25]

Later in the war this recourse to foreign recruits was adopted in some instances again, when there was a shortage of suitable men at home. One example is the former New South Wales Corps that had been brought back from Australia and re-constituted as the 102nd Foot with recruits from Ireland. However, when it was committed to the war in America it was still significantly understrength, so the Foreign Depot supplied it with 202 men in March 1813. Almost two thirds of these men had been recruited from amongst prisoners of war at Portsmouth and Gosport, and the rest from among the foreign deserters held at Gibraltar. This additional element, if anything, improved the regiment so that when it was

20 John D Grainger, *British Campaigns in the South Atlantic 1805–1807* (Barnsley: Pen and Sword, 2015), p.34; Ben Hughes, *The British Invasion of the River Plate 1806–7* (Barnsley: Pen and Sword, 2013), p.18; George Gleig (and Landsheit, Norbert), *The Hussar: a German Cavalryman in British Service throughout the Napoleonic Wars* (Driffield: Leonaur, 2008), pp.79–86.

21 TNA: WO 1/304, report. The battalions were from 20th, 21st, 27th (1st and 2nd Battalions), 31st, 35th (1st and 2nd Battalions), 52nd, 58th, 61st 62nd and 81st Foot.

22 TNA: WO 12/12002, pay list.

23 TNA: WO 12/12003, pay list.

24 Andrew Bamford, *Sickness, Suffering and the Sword: The British Regiment on Campaign, 1808–1815* (Norman: University of Oklahoma Press, 2013) p.167.

25 TNA: WO 27/106,107, 108 and 113, inspection reports. It was seen that around two to four foreigners served in the English militia battalions, with London units appearing to have more.

inspected in 1814, the foreigners, forming just over a quarter of the men, were described as 'the best conducted men in the Battalion.'[26] Similarly foreign recruits sent to serve in the Royal York Rangers and Royal West India Rangers, both regarded as 'disciplinary' units which were stationed in the West Indies, made up about a third of their strength. Although these foreigners had, perhaps, been considered unsuitable for units serving in Europe they were still regarded as superior to the units' other, British or Irish, recruits.[27]

It is, perhaps, worthwhile recognising that foreigners also contributed, willingly or otherwise, to other aspects of the British war effort. At the Battle of Trafalgar HMS *Victory* had a crew of 820 men, at least 73 of whom were of foreign birth, coming from, among other places, the United States of America, Italy, the Netherlands, Sweden, France, the West Indies and India. One of the petty officers killed in the battle was the Yeoman of the Sheets, called Andrew Sack, from Geneva, who was one of two men in the crew from Switzerland. There are likely to have been more foreigners in the crew as a further 48 men were shown as being of unknown origin.[28]

The army's foreign recruits came from across Europe; the variety of their national backgrounds widening as the wars continued and there was greater reliance on men who had previously served in units of the army of France or her allies. However even before this time, the British Army did not restrict itself to men from particular nations. As Oman observed, the King's German Legion was founded after the French invasion and occupation of the Electorate of Brunswick-Lüneburg (generally known as Hanover) which took place immediately after Britain's declaration of war in 1803. The British government needed to rapidly expand the Army and, with the personal interest of members of the Royal family, the disbanded officers and soldiers of the Hanoverian Army, who had traditionally served alongside the British, were regarded as a source of reliable and experienced men.

It is generally accepted that, in its early years, the King's German Legion can be considered as a homogenous corps, however the recruiting effort was never envisaged to be restricted to Hanoverians, or even Germans, alone. Recruitment began with two officers, Johann Friedrich von der Decken and Colin Halkett, being warranted to raise foreign troops for British service. Their efforts were assisted by an address from the Duke of Cambridge, dated 10 August 1803, inviting, 'All foreigners, but preferably all gallant Germans ... to take service in this corps.' As recruitment progressed it was decided to raise an all-arms legion, combining the recruits collected by Halkett and Decken. Article III of the Patent, of 19 December 1803, authorising the Duke of Cambridge to raise the corps, dealt with recruitment:

26 TNA: WO 25/673 and 27/127, inspection reports.

27 TNA: WO 27/108, inspection reports: 1812, Royal York Rangers: 17 sergeants, 18 corporals, 7 drummers and 263 (of 911) privates; Royal West India Rangers: 9 sergeants, 18 corporals, 3 drummers and 341 (of 1,000) privates.

28 'Nelson, Trafalgar, and those who served ...' *The National Archives* <http://www.nationalarchives.gov.uk/trafalgarancestors>, accessed 5 August 2019 and 'HMS Victory and her crew at the Battle of Trafalgar' *HMS Victory: The National Museum of the Royal Navy* <https://www.hms-victory.com/restoration-log/hms-victory-and-her-crew-battle-trafalgar>, accessed 5 August 2019.

> Natives of France, Italy and Spain are not to be accepted under any circumstances, but your Royal Highness may take men of other European States, also Polish, Hungarians, Danes, Russians and Germans who reside in this country. No British subjects may be accepted. Your Royal Highness may accept Dutch nationals from the prison ships provided they fulfil the conditions [regarding age, height and physical fitness] stated in Article II.[29]

Thus, from the very beginning not only could a range of European nationalities be recruited but also prisoners-of-war – Dutchmen on the prison hulks – and also others who, in circumstances that were not specified, were resident in Britain. However, such recruiting was not significant in the early years of the King's German Legion, as good progress was made through 1804 and 1805 in forming its composite units from large numbers of Hanoverians arriving in England. This process was given a significant boost when the legion took part in the expedition that landed in Hanover late in 1805. Recruitment depots were established at Hanover and Stade, on the Elbe, which brought many more recruits to the legion, despite significant desertions when the expedition departed, so that by April 1806 7,876 men had been recruited. The legion was to reach the peak of numbers in the ranks, 14,175 men, on 15 June 1812.[30]

In most cases the King's German Legion carried out its own recruitment. A depot was maintained on Germany's Baltic coast at Stralsund, then controlled by Sweden, until the summer of 1806 and, when the legion took part in the 1807 expedition to Denmark, 'about 1,000 Danes, Swedes, Poles, and men of various German nationalities, many of them deserters from the Danish army, were enrolled.'[31] Its agents were also active amongst the prisoners-of-war and deserters held in Britain as well as in the Mediterranean theatre. It did not rely on the Foreign Depot for the supply of men so from 1806 to 1809 only 509 recruits came from this source. However, as the aforementioned restrictions on recruitment came into effect the supply from the Foreign Depot became more important, with 2,860 men joining the legion, including its cavalry, from Lymington in the next three years. When, in the last years of the wars, northern Europe became accessible to recruiters once more, the Foreign Depot's contribution again dipped, only supplying 417 men in 1813 and 1814.

29 R. North, 'The Raising and Organizing of the King's German Legion', *Journal of the Society for Army Historical Research*, 39:160 (1961), pp.168–171.

30 North, 'Raising and Organizing', pp.175, 183.

31 Daniel Savage Gray, '"Prisoners, Wanderers and Deserters": Recruiting for the King's German Legion, 1803–1805', *Journal of the Society for Army Historical Research*, 53:215 (1975), pp.152–153.

Nevertheless, the origins of the recruits from Lymington provide a glimpse of the changing backgrounds of the King's German Legion's recruits.

Table 6.3 – Origin of men recruited at the Foreign Depot for the King's German Legion.[32]

Origin	1806	1807	1808	1809	1810	1811	1812	1813	1814
Hanover	134	118	6	150	82	35	21	31	11
Germany (other)	5	3	50	-	268	491	582	115	124
Austria				1	14	34	20	4	-
Bohemia	-	-	-	1	10	11	6	-	-
Brabant	-	-	1	-	96	65	60	7	1
Ceylon	-	-	-	-	-	1	-	-	-
Denmark	-	-	-	-	-	-	1	-	-
Egypt	-	-	1	-	1	-	1	-	-
Flanders	-	-	14	-	57	91	62	16	3
France (Alsace)	-	-	-	-	9	70	68	7	8
France (Lorraine)	-	-	-	-	-	-	7	-	2
France (other)	-	-	-	-	-	-		-	4
Guyana (?)	-	-	-	-	1	-	-	-	-
Holland	-	1	12	-	40	87	42	35	2
Hungary	-	-	-	2	8	46	46	11	2
Italy	-	-	-	-	6	-	1	-	1
Latvia	-	-	-	-	-	-	1	1	1
Liege	-	-	-	-	-	-	4	-	-
Luxembourg	-	-	3	-	-	2	15	7	4
Moldova	-	-	-	-	-	-	1	-	-
Moravia	-	-	-	-	1	4	4	-	-
Poland	-	-	3	-	50	153	131	16	2
Portugal	-	-	1	-	1	1	-	-	-
Russia	-	-	-	1	6	7	10	2	-
Scotland	-	-	1	-	-	-	-	-	-
Sweden	-	-	-	-	3	2	2	-	-
Switzerland	-	-	1	-	1	21	-	-	-
TOTAL	139	122	93	155	654	1,121	1,085	252	165

Notes: Those from Tyrol have been combined with Austria and those from 'German Lorraine' or 'Lotheringen' have been counted as from Germany (other).

So, when the 21-year old Englishman Edmund Wheatley joined the 5th Line Battalion of the King's German Legion as an ensign, in August 1813, he described the legion as 'a compound of Saxons, Poles, Swedes, Hungarians, Prussians, Russians, French and Dutch. There is scarce a soldier but speaks two or three languages …'[33]

32 TNA: WO 25/669–676, recruitment books.

33 Christopher Hibbert (ed.), *The Wheatley Diary* (Moreton-in-Marsh: Windrush Press, 1997), p.8.

Despite Oman's assertion, the officers were not all 'from the old Electoral army.' Wheatley is an example of a number of British and Irish men who obtained commissions in the legion from 1812 onwards, commissions in the foreign units being attractive as that they were not 'for purchase.'[34] However, even from the start there were non-Hanoverian officers. One of these was none other than Colin Halkett himself, who had been born in the Netherlands, the eldest son of Frederick Godar Halkett and from a long line, including his father, of officers in the Scotch Brigade in the service of the United Provinces. In 1782, with a breach between the Dutch and Britain, the brigade's regiments lost their distinctions and were to be treated henceforth as Dutch national units; the officers had to swear undivided allegiance to United Provinces or be discharged. Frederick Halkett took the latter option and went to Scotland, but when the Dutch faced French invasion he was recalled as an advisor. He declined a commission for himself but obtained one for Colin who served in the Dutch Foot Guards from 1792 until the United Provinces were invaded, and dissolved, in 1795. Having left the Netherlands, Colin obtained a British commission in 1799, as ensign in the 3rd Foot but never joined the regiment as in the same year he was appointed captain in the 2nd Light Battalion of the Dutch Brigade, serving until the brigade was disbanded in 1802. His role in the formation of the King's German Legion led to him being appointed lieutenant colonel in command of its 2nd Light Battalion and he was joined in this battalion by four officers who had not only previously served in the Dutch Brigade but also the army of the United Provinces before that.[35]

Over time others, who had formerly served with the Dutch Brigade, joined the King's German Legion, on the staff of its various units, while one of the legion's brigade majors, Pieter or Pierre de Salve de Bruneton, had been a junior officer in the Dutch Hesse-Cassel dragoons from 1789 to 1795 before entering British service, firstly in the York Rangers and then the York Hussars. One paymaster had had a very different and perhaps even more varied career. Matthew O'Toole, who served with the 1st Light Dragoons (Hussars), King's German Legion, from 1804 until his death in 1807, had begun his military career in the Brigade Irlandaise of the French royal army. He emigrated during the Revolution and served, with other officers of the Régiment de Berwick, as a volunteer in the Princes' émigré army and then in the Dutch army from 1792 to 1794. He obtained, in 1795, a lieutenancy in the 4th (O'Connell) Regiment of the Irish Catholic Brigade – an attempt by the British Government to resurrect the former French organisation and often referred to as Pitt's Irish Brigade. However, he left the next year to serve in different foreign cavalry regiments in British pay, successively, the Hompesch, Guernsey and York Hussars, before being placed

34 The published Army List of 1813 shows that King's German Legion with at least 37 subalterns with British or Irish names – some, of course, could have been of other nationalities.

35 The officers were James Mackenzie, Pierre Arnaut Twent, Ludwig Hausdorff and Colin Pringle; for details of the Dutch Brigade officers see Alistair Nichols, 'Officers and Organisation of the Dutch Brigade 1802' *The Napoleon Series* <http://www.napoleon-series.org/military/organization/Britain/Foreign/BritishDutchBrigade1802.pdf>, accessed 12 May 2020. Also appointed senior captain, and so soon major, in the battalion was Colin's younger brother Hugh who had been born in Scotland in 1783. Hugh was commissioned ensign in the second battalion (which was commanded by his father) of the re-formed Scotch Brigade (later 94th Foot) in 1794 and promoted lieutenant in 1795; he appears to have been present with the regiment between 1798 and 1803.

on half pay, as captain, in 1803.[36] These men were, it must be recognised, exceptions and the bulk of the officers of the King's German Legion were indeed Hanoverians most of whom had served, or came from families with a tradition of service, in the Electoral army.

The officer cadre of the Chasseurs Britanniques was, as Oman stated, firmly based on French émigrés. When the regiment was formed the more senior officers had served in their country's army under the *ancien régime* and they were joined by others who had gained their experience in the émigré army of the Prince de Condé and, later, by the sons born to families that had emigrated. The Prince's army had been created in 1792 and developed with two elements, the 'noble' units of French aristocracy, former officers and gentry and 'paid' regiments made up of soldiers, from a variety of sources, commanded by former French army officers. Britain's contribution to the Second Coalition's (1798–1802) war effort in Europe against France had been financial support for the allies as well as paying for auxiliary forces which fought alongside the Austrians, including the Swiss Corps and the Armée de Condé. When Austria, the last of the Coalition fighting in Europe, was finally defeated and sued for peace, the auxiliary units that Britain paid for were concentrated in Slovenia. At this point, Britain not only remained at war but also urgently needed to reinforce its small expeditionary force in Egypt. So, it was decided to try to recruit soldiers from Condé's 'paid' regiments as well as the Swiss Corps, with the requisite number of their officers, under a new engagement and send them to Egypt. In the end two new regiments were formed, the Chasseurs Britanniques from men of the Armée de Condé and the Watteville Regiment, from the Swiss Corps along with the equivalent of a company from Condé's Régiment de Durand.

As they were from Condé's 'paid' regiments the soldiers of the Chasseurs Britanniques were from a variety of countries: of the 733 other ranks in the first formation the nationality of 111 was recorded as 41 French; 33 Germans; 17 Polish; eight Italians; three Austrians; three Swiss and one from each of Belgium, Hungary, the Netherlands, Romania, Russia and Spain. The Condéan noble units not only contributed several officers to the Chasseurs Britanniques, including the lieutenant colonel, the Chevalier Thomas Le Forestier, but also a number of volunteers who served in the ranks adding to the number of Frenchmen in the above list. As more comprehensive records survive for the Watteville Regiment, a better picture of the men who joined it from the Régiment de Durand is provided and there is no reason to consider that they were not representative of the other 'paid' regiments the Armée de Condé and thus of the Chasseurs Britanniques. The origins of 53 of the 91 other ranks have been identified: 24 Germans, eight Polish, seven French (including three from Alsace), four Swiss, three Italians, two Belgians, two Austrians and one each from the Netherlands, Russia and Bohemia.[37]

So, from the start both these regiments were made up of soldiers from a wide range of nationalities. The cadres of officers, although becoming more diverse, retained strong core identities: French émigrés in the Chasseurs Britanniques and in the Watteville Regiment, Swiss, particularly from Bern who either had previously served in the Swiss regiments in

36 North Ludlow Beamish, *History of the King's German Legion* (London: Boone, 1837) Vol. II, p.620.

37 Alistair Nichols, 'Soldiers of the Armée de Condé who joined the British Army in 1801' Parts 1 and 2 *La Sabretache* <http://lasabretache.fr/?lang=en>, accessed 10 December 2019.

the army of the United Provinces or had strong family links to this service.[38] Similarly the other Swiss regiments of the British Army, despite undergoing similar changes over time, also maintained, amongst their officers, core identities. Those of the Roll Regiment had strong links to French service and the Meuron Regiment to the principality, now canton, of Neuchâtel. This last unit was particularly successful in maintaining a strong Swiss identity with a high proportion of Swiss soldiers; of the officers, as late as 1812, twelve were from Neuchâtel (these included the colonel, a major and two captains who were of the Meuron family) and only five were not from Switzerland: three Germans, one Alsatian from Altkirch (only 32 kilometres from Basel) and one from England (whose father although naturalised had come from Geneva).[39]

This regimental identity along strong, but not exclusive, national lines can be seen across Britain's foreign regiments in this era. The exceptions being the York Light Infantry Volunteers which although initially formed from Dutch colonial troops soon became a multi-national unit commanded by mainly British officers and Froberg's Regiment that mutinied on Malta even before it was formed and so was disbanded in 1807. The other regiment without a specific designation, Edward Dillon's, was almost exclusively composed of Italian soldiers (the Foreign Depot provided 359 recruits to the regiment between 1807 and 1813 of which all bar eleven were Italian) commanded by officers who were mainly French émigrés. Edward Dillon, or the Comte Edouard de Dillon, (1751–1839) courtier, diplomat and, before the Revolution, *colonel* of the Régiment de Provence, had raised his regiment in 1795. In August 1814, when King Louis XVIII had been restored to the French throne, Dillon explained to his monarch that, although the Chasseurs Britanniques and his regiment were comparable, unlike his own the former, 'is commanded by an English general who can have nothing in common with the service of France.'[40]

These identities provided the officers, who were often commanding men from different backgrounds, with cohesion and esprit de corps. Evidence that this was recognised at the time by the army was only stated subtly. When, during the winter of 1812/1813, the Chasseurs Britanniques were inspected the previous, British, commanding officer had returned to England on leave a month before, to be replaced by one of the original French émigrés who had served in the Armée de Condé and the report stated:

> The present Commanding Officer, Major du Hautoy, appears to have the Confidence and assistance of the Officers, and the Regiment has improved under his command, and have made progress in their discipline and Field exercise. ... The Captains ... are fully competent to the Command of them [their companies] on every occasion,

38 Of the 40 officers actually present with the regiment on formation (thus excluding the colonel, a lieutenant and an ensign) 17 were Bernese, 14 came from other Swiss cantons and territories, five were German, two were French and two were from Piedmont; at least 10 of those from Bern had served in the Netherlands (including the three field officers and four captains) and several more were young men whose families traditionally served there.

39 TNA: WO 65/62, Army List 1812; Guy de Meuron, *Le Régiment de Meuron 1781–1816* (Lausanne: Forum Historique, 1982), Annexe VI.

40 Robert de Grouvel, *Les corps de troupes de l'émigration française (1789–1815)* Vol. I (Paris: La Sabretache, 1957) p.160.

> as may be expected from old Officers, who have derived the advantage of serving under the Prince of Condé.[41]

However, a lack of cohesion, when found, was clearly commented upon. In the summer of 1813 Major General Sir Thomas Saumarez took the 1st and 2nd Independent Companies of Foreigners under his immediate command at Halifax, Nova Scotia, after they had been sent from Chesapeake Bay where they had been grossly ill-disciplined and had, apparently, committed serious crimes.[42] He made a thorough inspection of them and concluded that:

> ... [the soldiers] would behave as well as Men of other Corps in the Service if they were equally well commanded ... but I am concerned to state ... that I have already observed a great Want of Unanimity and good Understanding between Captain Smith the senior Officer of the two Companies and some of his Officers ... good Order and Discipline cannot be expected from Non Commissioned Officers and Soldiers under the existing circumstances, and that it is necessary they should be newly organized as soon as possible, in order to establish proper Discipline among them, and to prevent those Crimes which the improper Conduct and Example of their Officers may lead them to commit.[43]

Another aspect of the foreign regiments, and especially their officer cadres, was that they provided an alternative perspective, and even a challenge, to Napoleonic hegemony in Europe. Taking Switzerland as an example, young men who wished to pursue a family tradition of military service abroad did not have only the option to be part of the French Imperial army, an alternative path was open to them. The employment of foreign troops, and especially officers, with a geo-political agenda was neither unique to the British Army nor even to this era. Indeed, France provides many examples of this policy providing similar 'alternatives' including the Brigade Irlandaise of the old royal army and also Napoleon's Régiment Irlandais.

41 TNA: WO 25/113, inspection report by Major General Henry de Bernewitz. Alexis du Hautoy (1766–1838) had attended the artillery school at Metz, receiving instruction in all arms, from 12 years-old before being appointed *sous-lieutenant* in the Régiment de Noailles (dragoons) in 1782. When on 4 June 1815 a large number of field officers, and their Royal Navy counterparts, were appointed Companions of the Order of the Bath, other than those from the KGL, he, as lieutenant colonel, was the only officer from a foreign unit to be so rewarded (apparently the only other foreign officers were John Galiffe, Swiss, and George Henry Zühleke, German, both of the 5/60th and, in the latter's case, the Portuguese army), *The London Gazette* No. 17061 16 September 1815. As an aside, the same report indicates that Oman's observation that the officer's used 'the lash freely' was incorrect. Since 25 March 1812, so nine months, 29 cases had been brought to a regimental court martial with 21 floggings as a result (averaging 190 lashes), for the following offences: losing/selling equipment – eight, theft – six, insubordination – four, drunkenness – two and 'absent without leave' – one. This does not appear to be an excessive number of cases or, for the time and service, unduly harsh punishments.

42 See Alistair Nichols, *They Turned Out So Ill! The Independent Companies of Foreigners 1812–1814* (Peterborough: FastPrint Publishing, 2018).

43 TNA: WO 27/118.

Those that chose British military service did not take an easy option, paying the price in isolation and sanction by authorities at home. Even the journey to join a regiment was hazardous. Returning to the example of Switzerland, Auguste de Loriol made such a journey from Bern in 1812 to join the Meuron Regiment, which was then stationed on Malta, his companion was Lieutenant Charles Manuel of the same unit who had been on leave. The latter had taken four months to reach his family home in Bern, having been shipwrecked, robbed, imprisoned, placed in quarantine and sick on his journey; after only ten days at home he was warned to either immediately go or quit British service. On 22 April the two took a coach to Schaffhausen, from where they travelled to Ulm to take a boat down the Danube to Vienna. After being delayed waiting for passports, they then went on to Slavonski Brod (Croatia), on the frontier with the Ottoman Empire, where they eventually joined a caravan and travelled for almost a month through the Balkans, via Sarajevo, to Thessaloniki, in Greece. From there they sailed to Malta where after a voyage of three weeks they were placed in quarantine. Loriol was commissioned ensign some months later on 29 October.[44]

The cohesion between the officers was, for several, cemented further by family links. For example, one branch of the May family from Bern provided two British army officers, in the Roll and Watteville Regiments, while six more were cousins, despite another being *colonel* of the 3e Suisse in Napoleon's French army, a throw-back to the former Swiss practice of brothers seeking their fortunes in the service of different countries (see family tree below).

The provision of an alternative to a career under Napoleon could filter from the military to other spheres, in a manner that may be referred to as 'soft power' today. In 1806 Johann Ludwig Burckhardt, from a prominent Basel family, after studying at university in Germany, travelled to Britain with the intention of entering the civil service. Unsuccessful, he obtained employment with the African Association to explore Timbuktu and the Niger River. In preparation for the journey, which he would have to make incognito, he first studied at Cambridge University and then went to Syria and Egypt to immerse himself in the language, culture and religion. He made expeditions throughout the Near and Middle East, writing extensively of his experiences, was the first European to visit Petra in modern times and also had an important role in the acquisition of the bust of Ramesses II by the British Museum. With no apparent connection to the country, Burckhardt's decision to seek his future in Britain, given France's place in contemporary Europe, may seem strange. The answer seems to lie with the experiences of his father, Johann Rudolf, who had been an officer in the Basel militia as well as a successful businessman and a sponsor of the arts. He had been fundamentally opposed to the French Revolutionary government that had continually meddled in the affairs of the city and its dependencies. Accused of assisting the Austrians when they attacked the French stronghold of Huningue, immediately adjacent to Basel, in 1796, he was imprisoned and then, two years later, exiled. He then entered British

44 T. de Meuron, 'Charles-Daniel de Meuron' *Musée Neuchatelois* (1884), pp.215–216; also Guy de Meuron, *Le Régiment de Meuron*, p.204. The article states that Loriol's travelling companion was Lieutenant May, however both officers of that name were captains (from 1807 and 1810) and the 1812 Malta Returns (TNA: WO 17/2126) show that it was Manuel who returned from leave in Switzerland in the summer of 1812.

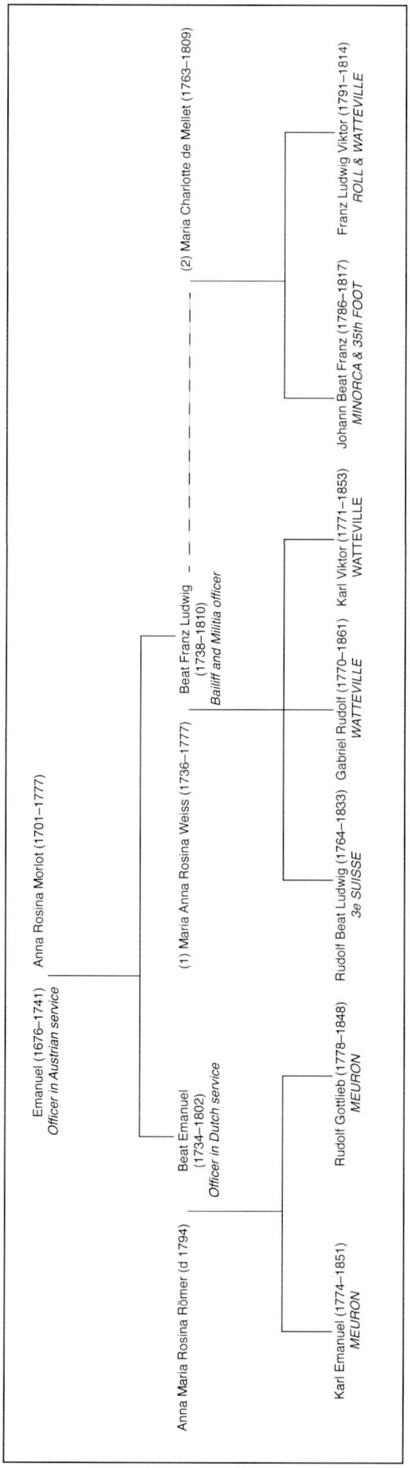

The family relationships of officers from a branch of the May family from Bern, Switzerland.

service, appointed colonel on the staff of the Swiss Corps and served in this capacity until being placed on half pay in 1800.[45]

The effect of this challenge to the contemporary status quo in Europe is hard to quantify, however it is noteworthy that Napoleon was concerned enough to demand, on a number of occasions, that steps be taken to counter it. He pressed for sanctions to be taken against officers serving in Britain's foreign regiments by, for instance, the seizure of their property. One man who succumbed to such a threat was the Dutchman, Lieutenant Colonel Hendrik de Perponcher Sedlnitsky, who retired from British service in 1810, the same year that his homeland was subsumed into France; he was later to make a significant contribution in the Waterloo campaign as commander of the 2nd Netherlands Division. On 29 June 1811, frustrated by what he saw as a reluctance by the Swiss authorities to act as he wished in this matter, Napoleon berated a deputation from the country, stating that Britain's Swiss regiments were 'veritable agencies of desertion.' Stung into a response, the Diet decreed that the Swiss in British service had to return by the end of the year and that those who refused to obey the recall 'would lose their civic rights, their nationality and their property' and that it would use 'all the means of persuasion or authority' at its disposal to get them to comply.[46] Nevertheless it was for the individual cantons to enforce these measures and some seem to have been more compliant than others, it was thus that Lieutenant Manuel was forewarned by the Bern authorities that they were, apparently, under pressure from the French embassy to act against him.

It should not be thought that ordinary soldiers were completely untouched by such considerations. Although soldiers' desertion from Napoleon's armies and enlistment in Britain's foreign regiments are normally assigned base motives, it seems that this was not the case for all. Although it can only by drawn from his actions rather than any words, it seems that one soldier, who joined the Chasseurs Britanniques, was fundamentally opposed to serving in the French army. Born on 13 September 1779 and baptised Wilhelmus Vossen, he was the seventh child in a family living on a small farm in the village of Leveroy, near Weert, which is now in the Netherlands. In the late 18th Century, the area, including Leveroy, was part of the Austrian Netherlands which, was annexed by France in 1795. In 1798 the French introduced a new law for military conscription, leading to a revolt in the region that had to be suppressed by the army. In the first year, Year VII of the French Revolutionary calendar, the conscripts from Leveroy, Weert and the surrounding area avoided being drafted into the French army by simply crossing the nearby frontier into Holland. Vossen took the same route into Holland when he was selected as a recruit the following year.

Despite the French authorities tightening their grip and taking severe counter-measures against the families of the draft evaders, Vossen did not return. However, his situation changed when Napoleon installed his brother, Louis, on the throne of the new Kingdom of Holland in 1806. Vossen was arrested there, handed over to the French authorities and subsequently sent to the depot for refractory conscripts in the huge fortress and barracks at Givet in Northern France. There, under strict surveillance, his time was filled with normal military training and working on the fortifications; as a further punishment, and to deter

45 Historical Dictionary of the Swiss (DHS), <https://hls-dhs-dss.ch/fr/>, accessed 27 September 2016 – Johann Ludwig (1784–1817) and Johann Rudolf Burkhardt (1750–1813); TNA: AO 3/64, pay list.

46 Edouard Guillon, *Napoléon et la Suisse 1803–1815* (Paris and Lausanne: Plon, 1910), pp.333–334.

escape, every week his head was clipped or shaved. Over time he was considered sufficiently disciplined to be transferred to a military unit which was sent to Spain. Unfortunately, when this happened and in which unit is not known. Nevertheless, there is circumstantial evidence to suggest that he may have been sent to one of the Légions de Reserve originally intended for internal second-line duties, but when sent to the Peninsula, formed part of Dupont's army that surrendered at Bailén.

What is clear is that on 25 February 1809 he was attested as a recruit in the British Army at the Foreign Depot, under the name of Wilhelm Voss, and joined the Chasseurs Britanniques. Later that year, he sailed from Portsmouth to join his regiment which was then in Sicily. He served with it, including in Portugal and Spain, until his discharge in France on 24 June 1814. Throughout this time, far from being 'detestable,' he appears to have been a good soldier, only being recorded as absent at the monthly musters on four occasions, once when he was sick in the general hospital in June 1811 and, for three months in 1813, when he did duty as 'Staff Servant.' After his discharge he returned home and, as was common for men who could not read or write, he deposited his discharge certificate at the local mayor's office for safe keeping.[47]

Foreign soldiers who joined the British Army, from whatever source, should not necessarily be regarded as having motives that are somehow less worthy than British or Irish recruits. Of course, many of them enlisted to escape the prospect of detention as a prisoner of war or as a result of their desertion, just as men in Britain and Ireland did so to escape poverty or the disruption of traditional ways of life as the Industrial Revolution evolved.

Foreign recruitment enabled Britain to make use of the services of not only experienced officers but also seasoned men who were, generally, more able to sustain military service, on campaign or in garrison, than raw recruits. It was recognised that some had more aptitude for soldiering and most were superior at living in the field than British soldiers. There are many testaments to this in the histories and memoirs of the period. In 1824 the foreign soldiers in the 1st Battalion, 60th Foot, were discharged in preparation for it to be recruited as a standard British regiment and it was observed: '... it ought to be recorded in justice to the German soldiers that they were a most quiet and orderly set of men, attentive to their duty and always particular in having their necessaries complete and everything in good order so that Captains of Companies had very little or no trouble with them.'[48]

When the Watteville Regiment served in Canada during the War of 1812, most of its soldiers were former prisoners of war and deserters and a high proportion of the men were Polish. A medical officer who served alongside observed:

> The [regular soldiers of the] line might nearly as well have slept in the open air... De Watteville's regiment ... consisted of all the nations of Europe, but all of them had served in the armies of Napoleon, and all of them had there learned how to make the best of a bad bargain. These, though they had not the skill in the axe inherent

47 Correspondence with Joost Welten regarding *In dienst voor Napoleons Europese droom: de verstoring van de plattelandssamenleving in Weert* (Leuven: Davidsfonds, 2007); TNA: WO 12/11639–11641, pay lists, and 25/669, recruitment book.

48 Quoted in Lewis Butler, *The Annals of the King's Royal Rifle Corps* (London: Murray, 1923), Vol. II, p.311.

> in their brethren of the Militia, took down hemlock boughs … and cutting off the tails of them, made thatched wigwams, perfectly weatherproof; and though they could not equal the Canadian Militia in *woodcraft*, they greatly excelled them in gastronomic lore; and thus, while our fellows had no better shift than to frizzle their rations of salt provisions on the ends of their ramrods, these being practical botanists, sent out one soldier from each mess, who gathered a haversack full of wild pot herbs, with which and a little flour their ration was converted into a capital kettle of soup.[49]

Any assessment of the worth of the foreign troops in the British Army during the Napoleonic Wars needs to have many more and broader factors taken into consideration than simply that of desertion. These include clearly quantifiable ones, such as steady recruiting figures, but also more qualitative and subtle factors. The Chasseurs Britanniques, for example, had high rates of desertion as compared with the rest of the Peninsular army an issue Wellington was particularly concerned about, but it is an indication that he saw other value in foreign corps when he retained the regiment's services as he sent other, British, regiments he was displeased with home or to secondary stations.[50]

Bibliography

Printed Sources

The National Archives, WO 65, Army Lists

Bamford, Andrew, *Sickness, Suffering and the Sword: The British Regiment on Campaign, 1808–1815* (Norman: University of Oklahoma Press, 2013)

Beamish, North Ludlow, *History of the King's German Legion* (London: Thomas and William Boone, 1837)

Burnham, Robert, and McGuigan, Ron, *The British Army Against Napoleon Facts, Lists and Trivia 1805–1815* (Barnsley: Frontline Books, 2010)

Butler, Lewis, *The Annals of the King's Royal Rifle Corps* Volume II (London: J Murray, 1923)

Dempsey, Guy C, *Napoleon's Mercenaries: Foreign Units in the French Army under the Consulate and Empire, 1799–1814* (London: Greenhill Books, 2002)

Dunlop, William, *Recollections of the American War 1812–14* (Toronto: Historical Publishing, 1905)

Fortescue, J W, *The County Lieutenancies and the Army 1803–1814* (London: Macmillan, 1909)

Gleig, George R, (and Landsheit, Norbert), *The Hussar: a German Cavalryman in British Service throughout the Napoleonic Wars* (Driffield: Leonaur, 2008)

Grainger, John D, *British Campaigns in the South Atlantic 1805–1807* (Barnsley: Pen and Sword, 2015)

Gray, Daniel Savage, "Prisoners, Wanderers and Deserters": Recruiting for the King's German Legion, 1803–1805, *Journal of the Society for Army Historical Research* 53:215 (1975)

Griffith, Robert, 'A Serious Inconvenience? Foreign Prisoners of War and Deserters in Wellington's Peninsular Army 1808–1814' in A. Bamford (ed.), *Life in the Redcoat: The British Soldier 1721-1815* (Warwick: Helion & Co, 2020)

Grouvel, Robert de, *Les corps de troupes de l'émigration française (1789–1815)* Tome I (Paris: La Sabretache, 1957)

Guillon, Edouard, *Napoléon et la Suisse 1803–1815* (Paris and Lausanne: Plon et Payot, 1910)

Gurwood J. (ed.), *The Dispatches of Field Marshal the Duke of Wellington, During his Various Campaigns in India, Denmark, Portugal, Spain, the Low Countries and France* (London: John Murray, 1837)

49 William Dunlop, *Recollections of the American War 1812–14* (Toronto: Historical Publishing, 1905), p.61. Several examples from the Peninsular War were given by Robert Griffith in his paper, *A Serious Inconvenience?* presented at Helion's 'From Reason to Revolution Conference' conference in Spring 2019.

50 For a review of desertion, especially from Wellington's army see Bamford, pp.245–259.

Haythornthwaite, Philip J, *Wellington's Army: The Uniforms of the British Soldier, 1812–1815* (London: Greenhill Books, 2002)

Hibbert (ed.), Christopher, *The Wheatley Diary* first published 1964 (reprint Moreton-in-Marsh: Windrush Press, 1997)

Hughes, Ben, *The British Invasion of the River Plate 1806–7* (Barnsley: Pen and Sword, 2013)

The London Gazette No. 17061 16 September 1815

Meuron, Guy de, *Le Régiment de Meuron 1781–1816* (Lausanne: Forum Historique, 1982)

Meuron, T. de, 'Charles-Daniel de Meuron', in Sociéte d'Histoire du canton de Neuchâtel (ed.), *Musée Neuchatelois* (Neuchatel: La Société Typographique, 1884)

Nichols, Alistair, *They Turned Out So Ill! The Independent Companies of Foreigners 1812–1814* (Peterborough: FastPrint Publishing, 2018)

North, R. E. F. G., The Raising and Organizing of the King's German Legion, *Journal of the Society for Army Historical Research* 39:160 (1961)

Oman, Sir Charles, *Wellington's Army, 1809–1814* (London: Edward Arnold, 1913)

Welten, Joost, *In dienst voor Napoleons Europese droom: de verstoring van de plattelandssamenleving in Weert* (Leuven: Davidsfonds, 2007)

Online sources

HMS Victory and her crew at the Battle of Trafalgar, *HMS Victory: The National Museum of the Royal Navy*: <https://www.hms-victory.com/restoration-log/hms-victory-and-her-crew-battle-trafalgar>

Nelson, Trafalgar, and those who served, *The National Archives* <http://www.nationalarchives.gov.uk/trafalgarancestors>.

Historical Dictionary of the Swiss (DHS): <https://hls-dhs-dss.ch/fr>

Nichols, Alistair, 'Officers and Organisation of the Dutch Brigade 1802', *The Napoleon Series* <http://www.napoleon-series.org/military/organization/Britain/Foreign/BritishDutchBrigade1802.>.

Nichols, Alistair 'Soldiers of the Armée de Condé who joined the British Army in 1801' Parts 1 and 2 *La Sabretache* <http://lasabretache.fr/>

Skinner, Graeme 'Joseph Reichenberg and family' *Australharmony* <https://www.sydney.edu.au/paradisec/australharmony/reichenberg-joseph>

7

'A Metaphysical Distinction': British Policy and the Prussian Occupation of Hanover in 1801

Hailey Stewart

In February 1801, in the midst of the conflict with the Second Armed Neutrality, Baron Franz von Reden, the envoy for Hanover at Berlin, attempted to learn if Russia viewed Hanover as an extension of Britain and the magnitude of the Prussian threat to Hanover.[1] He shared the Hanoverian Regency's communications with the British diplomat at Berlin, John Proby, Earl of Carysfort, and confirmed Prussia's intentions to invade Hanover. Christian von Haugwitz, the Prussian Foreign Minister admitted to Reden that the Armed Neutrality and the ongoing war against France made Prussian defence of Hanover challenging, particularly since 'Denmark and Russia and France would seek their enemy wherever they could reach him.' Reden argued that Hanover remained separate from the British Empire, a difference advantageous to Prussia. Haugwitz dismissed Reden's points and claimed 'it was a metaphysical distinction, which the Frenchmen would not understand.' Aside from foreign pressure, he named British attacks on Prussian commerce as detrimental and demanded restitution for damages. Reden emphasised the consequences to the entirety of North German commerce as a result of breaking with England.[2]

Hanover, in periods of war, emerged as a British imperial target for belligerent powers. France adopted the position that Hanover was a British possession open to attack, a strategy that developed from the Anglo-Hanoverian relationship and repetitive Anglo-French hostilities. While France viewed Hanover as an extension of Britain, the language and interactions between other continental powers and Britain embraced a similar posture when it proved beneficial. British policy resisted and denied any accusation of Hanover's attachment to Britain, avoiding any impression that Hanover was an imperial province. Regardless, the perception of Britain's empire and the actions of other European powers mattered in relation to British policy as much as Britain's efforts to send a non-imperial message. As such,

1 Niedersächsisches Hauptstaatsarchiv (NHstA): Cal. Br. 24/1003, pp.33–39, Franz von Reden to the King, 12 February 1801.

2 The National Archives (TNA): FO 64/60, pp.280–282, Lord Carysfort to Lord Grenville, 13 February 1801; NHstA: Cal. Br. 24/1003, pp.46–49, Reden to the King, 14 February 1801.

the Anglo-Hanoverian connection prompted fierce parliamentary debate during periods of war against France.[3] Britain's official policy narrative, that Hanover remained detached from Britain, and the position that Hanover entangled Britain in continental matters and drained resources, persisted, but the discourse fails to fully capture the relationship.

Conceptions of the British Empire rarely include Hanover, the German territory that belonged to the British royal family from 1714 to 1837, as an imperial possession but rather as a 'composite state,' meaning that Britain and Hanover were separate political entities that shared one sovereign.[4] Ideological assessments of 'Hanover' and 'empire' have centred on British perceptions of empire and Hanover. Nick Harding's intellectual study stresses the imperial discourse between Britain and Hanover, demonstrating Hanover's role in British imperial thought toward Europe.[5] Scholarly interpretation of the conflict of British and Hanoverian policy during the French Revolutionary and Napoleonic Wars has evolved only slowly. Guy Stanton Ford's analysis emphasises British apathy toward Hanover and Hanover's national security, while scholars such as Brendan Simms, Philip Dwyer, and Torsten Riotte have contributed to advancing a better understanding of the Anglo-Hanoverian relationship. Simms stresses the importance of Hanover to Prussian neutrality and French policy, which made it a point of conflict, and like Dwyer, notes that, in 1801, Britain proved unenthusiastic regarding Hanover and only cared after the Armed Neutrality dissolved.[6] In addition, Dwyer remarks that British diplomats showed concern for the Electorate.[7] Riotte's study, which does the most to reassess the political relationship between Britain and Hanover, argues that George III managed British and Hanoverian

3 Jeremy Black, *Continental Commitment: Britain, Hanover and Interventionism, 1714–1793* (London: Routledge, 2005); Jeremy Black, 'Hanover and British Foreign Policy, 1714–60', *The English Historical Review,* 120:486 (2005), pp.303-339; T. C. W. Blanning, '"That Horrid Electorate" or "Ma Patrie germanique"? George III, Hanover, and the Fürstenbund of 1785', *Historical Journal,* 20:2 (1977): pp.311–344; Uriel Dann, *Hanover and Great Britain, 1740–1760: Diplomacy and Survival* (Leicester: Leicester University Press, 1991); Ragnhild Hatton, *George I: Elector and King* (Cambridge: Harvard University Press, 1978); *The Anglo-Hanoverian Connection, 1714–1760* (London, 1982); Brendan Simms and Torsten Riotte (eds.), *The Hanoverian Dimension in British History, 1714-1837* (Cambridge: Cambridge University Press, 2007); Torsten Riotte, *Hannover in der Britischen Politik(1792–1815): Dynastische Verbindung als Element außenpolitischer Entscheidungsprozesse* (Münster: Lit Verlag, 2005).

4 Nick Harding, *Hanover and the British Empire, 1700–1837* (Woodbridge: The Boydell Press, 2007), p.5; H. G. Koenigsberger, 'Composite States, Representative Institutions and the American Revolution', *Historical Research,* 62:148 (1989), pp.135–153; J. H. Elliott, 'A Europe of Composite Monarchies', *Past and Present,* 137:1 (1992), pp.48–71.

5 Harding, *Hanover,* pp.6–14; Marie Peters, 'Early Hanoverian Consciousness: Empire or Europe?', *The English Historical Review,* 22:497 (2007): pp.632–668; Stephen Conway, 'Continental Connections: Britain and Europe in the Eighteenth Century', *History,* 90:299 (2005): pp.353–374.

6 Guy Stanton Ford, *Hanover and Prussia, 1795–1803: A Study in Neutrality* (New York: Columbia University Press, 1903), p.218; Brendan Simms, *The Impact of Napoleon: Prussian High Politics, Foreign Policy and the Crisis of the Executive, 1797-1806* (Cambridge: Cambridge University Press, 1997), pp.83–85; '"An Odd Question Enough". Charles James Fox, The Crown and British Policy During the Hanoverian Crisis of 1806', *The Historical Journal,* 38:3 (1995): p.573.

7 Philip G. Dwyer, 'Prussia and the Armed Neutrality: The Invasion of Hanover in 1801', *The International History Review,* 15:4 (1993): pp.682–683.

policies separately, that war forced these policies to conflict prompting the involvement of Britain, and that Britain focused on securing Hanover through peace negotiations.[8]

Building on the work of scholars who have challenged previous assumptions and changed the historical understanding of the Anglo-Hanoverian connection, this chapter reassesses the events of 1801 and Britain's policy toward Hanover within the context of empire and as part of the larger North German system. Britain employed economic and indirect methods such as diplomacy to maintain influence in North Germany. Within this, Hanover's importance to both Britain and Prussia provided Britain with a justification for any involvement they deemed necessary. Austria, the major land force waging war against France in Europe, sued for peace at the end of 1800, and in February 1801, signed the Treaty of Lunéville ending their involvement in the war against France. Austria's withdrawal from the conflict left Britain to wage war with France from sea. Maritime rights in the North Sea and the Baltic as well as trade with the Baltic powers and North Germany was a crucial component to Britain's commercial empire.[9] Prussia exported naval stores and grain to Britain, so any disruption that disconnected Britain from continental trade had ramifications.[10] Within the British policy that emphasised the North German and Baltic markets and British access to those markets, Hanover represented a secondary level of importance to British policy. Nevertheless, Britain's enemies centred Hanover as part of Britain, which made the Electorate relevant. Britain preferred to manage Hanover diplomatically as opposed to militarily. British and Hanoverian envoys demonstrated the indirect methods of cooperation that proved essential in acquiring information, in negotiations, and communications when threats to the Electorate emerged. In situations when British and Hanoverian policy conflicted or intersected, the values of the connection to Hanover arose and Britain did not abandon the opportunity to leverage the relationship to influence politics to Britain's advantage. Britain wanted to benefit from the Hanoverian relationship while avoiding any risk associated with it.

During the War of the Second Coalition, Britain, Russia, and Austria shared different interests and strategies, which weakened the alliance. Russian disagreements with Austria led to Russian withdrawal from the coalition in spring 1800. Britain supported Austria in the dispute with Russia due to Austria's inability to disengage from the war with France without difficulty. Similarly, Prussia remained territorially neutral, which meant Britain needed Austria to persist in the fight with the French. Britain's choice angered Tsar Paul I, and Anglo-Russian relations deteriorated, most notably when Paul dismissed Charles Whitworth, the British envoy in St. Petersburg in April 1800, expressed outrage with British attacks on neutral shipping, and in September 1800, disputed British authority in Malta.[11]

8 Torsten Riotte, 'George III and Hanover', in Brendan Simms and Torsten Riotte (eds.), *The Hanoverian Dimension in British History, 1714–1837* (Cambridge: Cambridge University Press, 2007), pp.58–85; *Hannover in der Britischen Politik*, pp.95–96, 98–100.

9 Dwyer, 'Armed Neutrality', pp.663, 667.

10 Philip G. Dwyer, 'Prussia and the Second Armed Neutrality, 1800–1801' (PhD Dissertation, University of Western Australia, 1992), pp.28–29; Joshua Jepson Oddy, *European Commerce, shewing new and secure channels of trade with the continent of Europe* (London: W. J. and J. Richardson, 1805).

11 Hugh Ragsdale, 'A Continental System in 1801: Paul and Bonaparte', *The Journal of Modern History*, 42:1 (1970), pp.71–72; 'Russia, Prussia, and Europe in the Policy of Paul I', *Jahrbücher für Geschichte Osteuropas*, 31 (1983), pp.81-118; Ole Feldbaek, 'The Foreign Policy of Tsar Paul I, 1800–1801: An

In response to the disintegration of the alliance, Paul I pursued more amicable connections with the neutral northern powers. He appealed to Denmark, Sweden, and Prussia who all shared complaints about the British Navy's attacks on neutral maritime rights, a repetitive conflict regarding the freedom of the sea.[12] Prussia claimed that the Royal Navy's seizure of Prussian ships in search of goods intended for French aid harmed Prussian trade. Sweden encountered trouble with the capture of Swedish ships in British blockaded ports in the Mediterranean, and Denmark too, endured assaults on their neutral vessels. The British government remained firm that they held the right to inspect neutral vessels for contraband and any challenge to this position made one hostile to Britain.

The *Freya* affair motivated the northern powers to enter discussions to form the Armed Neutrality.[13] On 25 July 1800, a British frigate attempted to confiscate a Danish frigate, the *Freya*. On orders to stand against British violations of maritime neutrality, the Danish commander resisted Britain's attack resulting in British and Danish causalities. In reaction to the *Freya* episode, Paul I announced an embargo on British ships in Russian ports and appealed to Denmark, Sweden, and Prussia to join in reviving the Armed Neutrality of 1780.[14] Initially, the northern powers wavered in accepting Paul's proposal since Britain and Denmark had reached an agreement related to the *Freya* incident deescalating tensions. Once news of the agreement between Denmark and Britain reached Russia, Paul I lifted the embargo against Britain, which lasted approximately a week.[15]

The Armed Neutrality upset British continental policy. As a result, Russia courted Prussia, who remained territorially neutral, to respond to the altered situation in northern Europe.[16] Prussian withdrawal from the first coalition, and the 1795 Treaty of Basel with France, established a neutral North Germany. Hanover was included in the line of demarcation and maintained neutrality while fighting continued between Britain, the Holy Roman Empire, and France. Britain, isolated and without allies, worried about Russian influence on Prussian policy and aimed to strengthen relations with Prussia. Prussian incentives for joining the Armed Neutrality differed from the other northern powers since they depended less on commerce. Haugwitz supported Prussian participation and attempted to assuage

Interpretation', *Jahrbücher für Geschichte Osteuropas,* 30 (1982), pp.16–36; Memoranda by Lord Whitworth, in *Report on the Manuscripts of J. B. Fortescue, Esq., Preserved at Dropmore,* J. B. Fortescue (ed.), 10 vols., (London: Historical Manuscripts Commission, 1892-1927), VI, pp.286–287.

12 Leos Müller, *Neutrality in World History* (London: Routledge, 2019), pp.2–3, 8–10, 42, 47–48; David Armitage, *The Ideological Origins of the British Empire* (Cambridge: Cambridge University Press, 2000), pp.102–104.

13 Dwyer, 'Armed Neutrality', pp.662-3; 'Second Armed Neutrality', pp.54–57; Ragsdale, 'Policy of Paul I', p.110; 'Continental System in 1801', p.77–78; Ole Feldbaek, *Denmark and the Armed Neutrality, 1800–1801: Small Power Policy in a World War* (Copenhagen: Akademisk Forlag, 1980), pp.48–66; *The Battle of Copenhagen 1801: Nelson and the Danes* (South Yorkshire: Leo Cooper, 2002,) pp.22–23; 'The Anglo-Danish Convoy Conflict of 1800. A Study of Small Power Policy and Neutrality', *Scandinavian Journal of History* 2 (1977) pp.161–182.

14 James Brown Scott, (ed.), *The Armed Neutralities of 1780 and 1800* (New York: Oxford University Press, 1918), pp.489–492.

15 Grenville to George III, 26 August 1800, in A. Aspinall (ed.), *The Later Correspondence of George III* (Cambridge: Cambridge University Press, 1967), III, pp.402–403; Grenville to George III, 5 September 1800, *Later Correspondence,* III, p.407; Dwyer, 'Second Armed Neutrality', pp.56–7, 96.

16 Dwyer, 'Armed Neutrality', pp.666–668.

relations with Paul I and Bonaparte to Prussia's advantage. This policy forced him to maintain Prussian neutrality while appeasing France and Russia.[17]

Policies antagonistic to Britain, notably, the formation of the Armed Neutrality, Franco-Austrian peace negotiations, and French and Russian attempts to influence Prussia to act against Britain, converged on Hanover in North Germany. In December, Russia, Denmark, and Sweden agreed to contribute ships to the maritime coalition. Prussian acquiescence to the Armed Neutrality prompted discussion on Prussia's contribution to a naval agreement as a land power and stipulated that Prussia act against those who attacked neutral ships, the power in question meant Britain with Hanover as the target.[18] Instead of offering a subsidy, Haugwitz proposed that Prussia block Britain's access to the major rivers in North Germany to hurt British commerce. Prussian control of its own major rivers, along with the Weser and Elbe through the occupation of Hanover, disconnected Britain from North German trade. British trade with North Germany provided materials such as grain and naval stores and a place to export imperial goods. Approximately half of British grain imports came from Prussia, which influenced Britain's efforts to sustain friendly relations with Prussia to prevent losing access to markets.[19] Within the uncertain state of continental affairs, British policy emphasised preserving a positive relationship with Prussia. A consistent thread in Anglo-Prussian policy, based on appearances rather than reality, stressed the familiar and long-standing affiliation between the two courts, of which Hanover was central.

In the summer of 1800, Lord Carysfort received the appointment as envoy to Prussia with the objective of gathering information on Russia's plan to unite the northern powers to defend neutral maritime rights. In August, he informed William, Lord Grenville, the Secretary of State for Foreign Affairs that Haugwitz denied Prussian involvement with Russian efforts to create a maritime league. Carysfort expressed confidence that Russia's endeavours to form the Armed Neutrality remained a lesser concern in the face of the French threat.[20] Despite Carysfort's prioritisation of France over Russia, Paul I's dismissal of Whitworth elevated the importance of acquiring intelligence. Grenville told Carysfort to relay any news involving Russia and continue his conversations with Paul Krüdener, Russian envoy to Prussia.[21]

As Anglo-Russian tensions escalated, Carysfort directed his focus towards Russian actions, and Prussian involvement, to impede British violations of maritime neutrality. Grenville argued that the confiscation of neutral shipping was crucial to British security and Britain planned to resist any attempts to suppress their naval supremacy. He situated British security in direct opposition to France in his assertion that any reduction in British

17 Dwyer, 'Armed Neutrality', pp.664–665; 'Second Armed Neutrality', pp.21–22, 46–50.

18 G. Martens, *Recueil des principaux traités ... conclus par les puissances de l'Europe* (Göttingen: Dieterich, 1817–1835), Vol. VII, pp.172–196; Ragsdale, 'Continental System in 1801', p.79; Dwyer, 'Armed Neutrality', p.666.

19 Dwyer, 'Armed Neutrality', pp.663, 667; John Stevenson, 'Popular Radicalism and Popular Protest, 1789–1815', in H. T. Dickinson (ed.), *Britain and the French Revolution, 1789–1815* (London: Macmillan, 1989), pp.61-81; W. Freeman Galpin, *The Grain Supply of England during the Napoleonic Period* (New York: Macmillan, 1925), pp.123–134.

20 TNA: FO 64/58, pp.41–49, Carysfort to Grenville, 13 August 1800; FO 64/58, pp.55–56, Carysfort to Grenville, 19 August 1800.

21 TNA: FO 64/58, pp.59, 61, Grenville to Carysfort, 22 August 1800; Grenville to Carysfort, 26 September 1800, *Dropmore Papers*, Vol. VI, p.311.

naval power only strengthened France and allowed for Bonaparte to dominate land and sea.[22] In September, Britain captured Malta, further deteriorating Anglo-Russian relations and prompting Paul I to sever communications with Britain. Grenville urged Carysfort to adopt an apathetic approach to Russian matters as opposed to adulation. He further advised against any efforts to restore Britain's relationship with Russia. Malta and Paul I's attempts to secure a league of neutral powers against Britain increased the potential for hostilities for Britain in the Baltic.[23]

Britain approached Prussian relations with scepticism and a refusal to comply with demands. Grenville viewed Haugwitz's insistence that Britain would win the conflict with Russia as disingenuous. Since he believed the disagreement about maritime neutrality a fleeting disruption and Prussia as hostile to British naval supremacy, he ordered Carysfort to project indifference. Aware of Britain's precarious position, Grenville ascertained fear as Prussia's primary motivation and dismissed persuasion and flattery as effective methods to gain support for Britain. He argued 'that the only mode to obtain their friendship is to convince them that we do not want it.'[24] More broadly, he depicted the powers hostile to Britain's maritime policy as envious and foolish and portrayed Britain as the protector of Europe from French hegemony. Grenville refused to acquiesce or compromise with the demands of the other European powers.

Anglo-Prussian commercial tensions intensified Britain's suspicion of Prussia's engagement with the Armed Neutrality. In early November, Grenville informed Carysfort that the British captured a Prussian ship intended for the Netherlands, an enemy port, in the Ems and transferred it to Cuxhaven.[25] British actions against Prussian vessels forced a Prussian response that alleged a violation of the line of demarcation. Rumours circulated that Charles, Duke of Brunswick, had received orders to ready troops to militarily control Cuxhaven, which Frederick William III justified as necessary for the defence of North German territorial neutrality. Grenville, who suspected Russian influence on Prussia's reaction to the Cuxhaven incident, ordered Carysfort to inquire to Prussia's motivations. Carysfort's meeting with Haugwitz resulted in the foreign minister's assurance that protecting neutrality was the sole reason for Prussian behaviour. He stressed that Cuxhaven did not alter the Anglo-Prussian friendship, denied Prussian involvement in forming a maritime league against Britain, and offered to mediate an end to hostilities with the Baltic powers.[26]

22 TNA: FO 64/58, pp.66-67, Grenville to Carysfort, 22 August 1800; Carysfort to Grenville, 30 September 1800, *Dropmore Papers,* Vol. VI, pp.334–335; Reports from Sandoz-Rollin from Paris, 4 September 1800, in Paul Bailleu (ed.) *Preussen und Frankreich von 1795 bis 1807: Diplomatische Correspondenzen* (Leipzig: S. Hirzel, 1881), Vol. I, pp.390–391; TNA: FO 64/58, pp.210–215, Carysfort to Grenville, 27 September 1800.

23 Grenville to Carysfort, 9 October 1800, *Dropmore Papers,* Vol. VI, pp.345–346; 7 November 1800, *Dropmore Papers,* Vol. VI: p.373; TNA: FO 64/58, pp.266–268, Grenville to Carysfort, 10 October 1800.

24 Grenville to Carysfort, 9 October 1800, *Dropmore Papers,* Vol. VI, pp.345–346.

25 Grenville to Carysfort, 7 November 1800, *Dropmore Papers,* Vol. VI, pp.373–374; TNA: FO 64/59, pp.35–36, Grenville to Carysfort, 7 November 1800; Dwyer, 'Second Armed Neutrality', pp.97–98.

26 Grenville to Carysfort, 7 November 1800, *Dropmore Papers,* Vol. VI, pp.374; TNA: FO 64/59, pp.77–86, Carysfort to Grenville, 13 November 1800; Dwyer, 'Second Armed Neutrality', pp.100–101.

Accounts of Prussian orders to occupy Cuxhaven signified a foundering of the beneficial rapport established between Britain and Prussia, a vulnerability Britain anticipated Russia and France to exploit. While Carysfort received notice that Prussia intended to halt troops advancing towards Cuxhaven, he was hesitant to believe Prussian promises. A noted shift in his opinion of Prussia occurred in November. Prior to mid-November, he had remained steadfast in his belief of the absence of Prussian participation in the Armed Neutrality. Afterward, Carysfort remarked 'that the occupation of Cuxhaven was premeditated, and is connected to the plan of the Neutral Maritime League.' He believed that Prussia had long planned to occupy the city, and Russia represented the most obvious co-conspirator. He suggested to Grenville that providing protection for Prussian commerce undermined the antagonistic endeavours of 'Paul I and Haugwitz,' who he specifically identified as the opposition.[27] On 18 November, Carysfort, in official correspondence to Haugwitz, insisted that Frederick William cease any plan to inhabit Cuxhaven. He argued that Prussia's decision aided Britain's enemies.[28] Haugwitz's reply defended the choice to occupy Cuxhaven and argued that British actions disregarded North German neutrality despite Britain's restoration of the seized Prussian ship. In an attempt to ensure Carysfort of Prussia's pure intentions, he guaranteed the continuation of trade at the Cuxhaven port and emphasised the importance of neutrality to Hanover. Prussian troops took possession of Cuxhaven on 23 November 1800.[29]

Britain challenged Prussia's claim that the line of demarcation extended into the Ems. Grenville demanded that Prussia supply official documentation of Dutch recognition of Prussian authority. For Britain, access to the Ems allowed them to attack French shipping at the port of Delfzijl. Grenville argued that France attacked British commerce from Delfzijl and George III intended to persist in countering French aggression. Prussia's application of territorial neutrality to coasts proved a reoccurring frustration for the British. Disagreements regarding the boundaries of the neutrality line, as it related to British efforts to fight France and control the seas, demonstrates a key conflict between Britain and North German neutrality.[30] Although British foreign policy opposed Prussian management of the neutrality lines, British commerce also profited from access to markets that neutrality protected.

The convergence of British and Hanoverian policy, regardless of the emphasis on separation, prompted the diplomats to apprise one another of intelligence indicating a recognition that communication aided their shared interests. Hanover, the secondary power in

27 Carysfort to Grenville, 15 November 1800, *Dropmore Papers*, Vol. VI, p.381; TNA: FO 64/59, pp.91–92, Carysfort to Grenville, 16 November 1800; Dwyer, 'Second Armed Neutrality', pp.103–104.

28 TNA: FO 64/59, pp.95–97, Note to Haugwitz, 16 November 1800.

29 TNA: FO 64/59, pp.116–118, Haugwitz to Carysfort, 20 November 1800; Horst Carl, 'Restricted Violence? Military Occupation during the Eighteenth Century', in Erica Charters, Eve Rosenhaft and Hannah Smith (eds.), *Civilians and War in Europe, 1618–1815* (Liverpool: Liverpool University Press, 2012), pp.118–128; 'Unter fremder Herrschaft: Invasion und Okkupation im Siebenjährigen Krieg', in Bernhard R. Kroener and Ralf Pröve (eds.), *Krieg und Frieden. Militär und Gesellschaft in der Frühen Neuzeit* (Paderborn: Schöningh, 1996), pp.331–348; *Okkupation und Regionalismus. Die Preußischen Westprovinzen im Seibenjährigen Krieg* (Mainz: Philipp von Zabem, 1993).

30 TNA: FO 64/59, pp.99–103, Grenville to Carysfort, 18 November 1800; FO 64/59, pp.213–214, Grenville to Carysfort, 2 December 1800.

North Germany, feared Prussian expansion at the expense of the Electorate. Prussia's stance on Cuxhaven, to protect the demarcation line, meant a petition for Hanoverian troops for defence. Reden relayed to Carysfort the Regency's receipt of an appeal for soldiers to assist in protecting neutrality. Reden's news only furthered Carysfort's distrust of Prussian ambitions. He suspected the advancement of Prussia's domination of North Germany as an incentive for their actions. Furthermore, he faulted Russian influence and pressure for Prussia's decision while simultaneously citing Prussian envy regarding Russian efforts to revive the Armed Neutrality.[31]

Consistent rumours substantiating the founding of a league against British naval policy strained the Anglo-Prussian relationship and prioritised determining Prussian involvement. Carysfort met with Haugwitz who admitted to conversations with Baron Krüdener, denied providing an official response regarding the Armed Neutrality, and noted that Frederick William and his ministers aimed to find a solution to secure neutral commerce.[32] On 3 December, Grenville warned of the likelihood that an official agreement had occurred and validated Carysfort's suspicions that the Cuxhaven incident related to the Armed Neutrality. He lambasted the falsity of Haugwitz's 'shallow and frivolous pretences' and cited evidence that proved the existence of a link between Prussia, Russia, and Cuxhaven. Grenville directed Carysfort to maintain the 'apparent good understanding between the two courts' and be judicious in discourse to prevent any advancement in hostilities with Prussia.[33] British policy toward Prussia prioritised flexibility since they depended on Prussia to aid their own continental policy.

As Anglo-Russian animosity intensified, Grenville's frustration with Prussian circumspection and reluctance to align with Britain increased. On 25 November, Lewis de Drusina, the British envoy for Memel and Königsberg reported that Paul I issued a second embargo on British ships in Russian ports until Britain recognised Russian rights to territory on Malta.[34] Thomas Grenville informed his brother that Prussian fear of Russia dictated their choices and they preferred to 'employ the arms of Russia in a dispute with us than to take any step to divert that storm.'[35] While Prussia persisted in their assurances to act as an intermediary to resolve British hostilities with Russia, British policy viewed mediation with Russia as unfeasible. Grenville determined that the embargo represented an act of war and Prussia's position of maintaining a 'community of interest' with Russia conveyed an unfriendly message towards Britain.[36] Grenville's stance claimed that any action against British maritime rights, as they understood them, threatened their greatest strength, naval supremacy. He promised the destruction of 'foreign commerce & consequently the domestic industry' of any country who joined the Armed Neutrality. Grenville directed Carysfort to persuade Prussia that British resistance to any formation of a maritime league proved detrimental to Prussia. He,

31 TNA: FO 64/59, pp.112–114, Carysfort to Grenville, 20 November 1800; Carysfort to Grenville, 20 November 1800, *Dropmore Papers*, Vol. VI, p.390.
32 TNA: FO 64/59, p.104, Carysfort to Grenville, 19 November 1800.
33 TNA: FO 64/59, pp.216–219, Grenville to Carysfort, 3 December 1800.
34 TNA: FO 64/59, p.179, Lewis de Drusina to Carysfort, 25 November 1800.
35 Thomas Grenville to Lord Grenville, 28 November 1800, *Dropmore Papers*, Vol. VI, p.394.
36 TNA: FO 64/59, pp.220–222, Grenville to Carysfort, 3 December 1800; Grenville to Carysfort, 2 December 1800, *Dropmore Papers*, Vol. VI, p.400.

again, framed the Armed Neutrality as harmful to Britain's war against France and any weakening of British naval supremacy presented an opportunity for France to dominate.[37] Grenville's argument captured the British ministry's attitude toward the Armed Neutrality and insistence on centring the conflict with France.

Hanover emerged as a British policy concern during conflict due to Prussian efforts to strengthen itself in North Germany at the expense of other powers. At the end of November, Carysfort shared reports that demonstrated Prussia's conflict of interest in relation to Hanover. Although he expected Prussian inaction toward Hanover, he noted that Prussian acquisition of 'the property or privileges of the Elector of Hanover, the military authority, and the possession of ports' meant Prussian hegemony in North Germany and 'must be objects of jealousy and uneasiness.'[38] Britain monitored Prussian actions in North Germany, which intertwined with Russian and French affairs. Prussian control of Hanover prevented British access to commerce, an importance that Britain, Russia, and France recognised. Despite misgivings about Prussia in North Germany, the priority for Britain remained the discovery of Prussia's designs regarding the Armed Neutrality. In early December, Grenville's intelligence revealed the intentions of Prussia and Denmark to grant their ministers the power to negotiate an agreement to secure neutral shipping. He told Carysfort to inform Haugwitz of Britain's confirmation of Prussian engagement. Grenville urged Carysfort to leverage the Anglo-Prussian relationship and convey George III's disappointment in Prussia's inability to alert him to the machinations against Britain. Still, fear of French control persisted in Britain's message that the Royal Navy prevented French control in hope of influencing Prussian decisions.[39]

Distrust of Prussia furthered Britain's insistence on linking the Cuxhaven affair to the efforts of the northern powers to weaken Britain's maritime strength. Grenville accused Prussia of possessing Cuxhaven to provoke George III's suspicions of Prussian intentions to join the Baltic powers. Grenville viewed the Prussian position as antagonistic to Britain and wished for Carysfort to stress George III's exasperation with Prussia's reticence regarding the maritime league, and again, demand proof of Prussian authority respecting the Ems.[40] Regardless, Haugwitz remained steadfast in resisting Carysfort's requests for official documentation that Prussian jurisdiction extended to the middle of the Ems and affirmed the validity of the Prussian stance.[41] Grenville explicitly stated that the security of North German neutrality dominated British policy regarding Prussia, North Germany, and the Armed Neutrality. Once protected, Britain intended to dispute the boundaries of the demarcation line in relation to important rivers but endorsed disregarding any demand that hindered attacks on French shipping.[42]

Prussian control of Cuxhaven interfered with British attacks on enemy shipping and motivated Britain to consider Hanover in their reaction to Prussian aggression. Grenville

37 TNA: FO 64/59, pp.223–224, Grenville to Carysfort, 3 December 1800.
38 Carysfort to Grenville, 29 November 1800, *Dropmore Papers*, Vol. VI, p.395.
39 TNA: FO 64/59, pp.260–261, Grenville to Carysfort, 9 December 1800.
40 TNA: FO 64/59, pp.262–263, Grenville to Carysfort, 9 December 1800.
41 TNA: FO 64/59, pp.307–310, Carysfort to Grenville, 20 December 1800; TNA: FO 64/59, pp.311–317, Carysfort to Grenville, 23 December 1800.
42 Grenville to Carysfort, 16 January 1801, *Dropmore Papers*, Vol. VI, pp.425–426.

speculated on a possible British response and disclosed the option of withdrawing the British packet boats to Bremerlee, Hanover, to maintain access to the continent. Next, he suggested using Hanover to alarm Prussia and ensured the communication of any British actions to the Regency. Grenville ascertained that Prussia's current behaviour provided an image of a Prussian dominated North Germany and expressed his determination of not 'making ourselves the pandars of their inordinate ambition.'[43] He emphasised Britain's inability to overlook Prussian actions at Cuxhaven and notified Carysfort that maintaining the Anglo-Prussian relationship depended on Prussia's withdrawal from Cuxhaven.[44] Despite Grenville's scepticism, Carysfort believed that Prussian concerns about North German neutrality drove their conduct toward Cuxhaven, a decision disconnected from the designs of the Armed Neutrality. Nonetheless, he requested an official statement from Berlin to disavow any correlation between Cuxhaven and Russia and asked that Prussia denounce Russia's embargo against British ships.[45]

British anxiety over Prussian participation in the Armed Neutrality demonstrated the value of North German commerce and entry to the continent. Carysfort tried and failed to confirm Prussian assent to the league.[46] While Grenville avowed Britain's stance on defending their maritime interests against Russia and the Armed Neutrality, he also advised Carysfort to accentuate the effects of Britain attacking Prussian commerce.[47] Grenville directed him to pressure Haugwitz to:

> ... consider what they will do with the whole foreign commerce blocked up, and the sea at least as effectually shut against them as they can shut the land against us; with the difference that our sea has other shores, and their land has no sea, so that they must go around to Venice or Trieste for all the articles which they now purchase from us, not certainly in order to encourage our manufactures, but in order to supply their own consumption.[48]

British policy in North Germany required Britain maintaining influence at the Prussian court since they lacked direct access to the continent. As such, they employed their naval advantage, and Hanover when opportunistic, as leverage to force Prussia to acquiesce based on the desire for British goods, while simultaneously engaging the same position to sustain their own commerce.[49]

Britain directed criticism towards Prussia's antagonistic policy and remained insistent on the necessity of British naval power to counter French supremacy. Since 1795, Grenville contended, Prussia had behaved in a manner that reinforced Britain's adversaries to the

43 Grenville to Carysfort, 9 December 1800, *Dropmore Papers*, Vol VI, p.404.
44 TNA: FO 64/59, pp.297–303, Grenville to Carysfort, 16 December 1800.
45 TNA: FO 64/59, p.314, Carysfort to Grenville, 23 December 1800; TNA: FO 64/59, p.329, Carysfort to Grenville, 24 December 1800.
46 TNA: FO 64/59, pp.237–240, Carysfort to Grenville, 6 December 1800; TNA: FO 64/59, p.251, Carysfort to Grenville, 9 December 1800.
47 TNA: FO 64/59, pp.297–303, Grenville to Carysfort, 16 December 1800.
48 Grenville to Carysfort, 16 December 1800, *Dropmore Papers*, Vol. VI, p.408.
49 Grenville to Carysfort, 16 December 1800, *Dropmore Papers*, Vol. VI, p.408; TNA: FO 64/59, pp.297–303, Grenville to Carysfort, 16 December 1800.

detriment of Britain and in conflict with Prussian interests. In particular, he focused on Prussian relations with France who had also assumed the right to confiscate any neutral ship carrying British goods. His complaint rested on Prussia and the Baltic powers' failure to exhibit the same frustration with French seizures of neutral vessels as with Britain. Prussian responses adopted an adversarial attitude towards Britain. Although Grenville dictated the points he wanted Carysfort to impart to Haugwitz, he did not expect to alter Prussian policy. He believed nothing could persuade Prussia if the current state of European affairs and the increasing likelihood of French success at achieving domination failed to work.[50]

In January 1801, Anglo-Russian tensions escalated. Carysfort informed the ministry that Russia aimed to sustain 'the embargo with the utmost rigour,' and suggested the inevitability of 'open rupture.'[51] Grenville confirmed the official agreement of Armed Neutrality between Denmark, Sweden, and Russia and the commencement of plans to act 'against the Commerce and Colonies of Denmark and Sweden.' British intelligence also verified Prussian assent to the league. Grenville hoped that the Prussian ministry might provide details related to the conditions of their engagement. He further directed Carysfort to conceal this knowledge until told otherwise, and to promote Britain's intentions to remain on good terms with Prussia.[52] While he doubted its success, he wanted to convince Prussia that their policy of neutrality and inaction against Britain meant a more prosperous Prussia.[53] Grenville offered a spectrum of possible Prussian counters, the most extreme of which would be the occupation of Hamburg, a neutral city, and an embargo on British commerce. He wanted Carysfort prepared to inform the British ministers in Hamburg to counteract the move in the event it occurred.[54]

Prussian involvement in the Armed Neutrality prompted Britain to retaliate against the Baltic powers while attempting to prevent conflict with Prussia. Britain placed an embargo on Russian, Swedish, and Danish vessels and informed the Prussian ministry of Britain's decision as a deterrent.[55] Carysfort's mission remained the discovery of the promises Prussia made to the league. Grenville insisted that any terms that required Prussia 'to use force ... or to support the other Confederates in using force' against Britain proved intolerable.[56] In early January, confirmation, independent of Britain, of the Armed Neutrality and Prussia's participation reached Carysfort, which elevated British commercial unease and elicited worry from Hanover. He reported on the league's assessment of Britain's vulnerabilities and emphasised Britain's dependence on Baltic and North German exports. He relayed the argument that:

50 TNA: FO 64/60, pp.55–56, pp.59–61, Grenville to Carysfort, 9 January 1801.
51 TNA: FO 64/60, p.4, Carysfort to Grenville, 1 January 1801.
52 TNA: FO 64/60, pp.76, pp.78–80, Grenville to Carysfort, 13 January 1801.
53 Grenville to Carysfort, 13 January 1801, *Dropmore Papers*, Vol. VI, p.424.
54 TNA: FO 64/60, p.81, Grenville to Carysfort, 13 January 1801.
55 TNA: FO 64/60, pp.90, 92, Grenville to Carysfort, 15 January 1801; TNA: FO 64/60, pp.98–99, Grenville to Carysfort, 16 January 1801; Dwyer, 'Armed Neutrality,' pp.669–670.
56 TNA: FO 64/60, pp.102, 104–106, Grenville to Carysfort, 16 January 1801.

> ... the commerce of the Baltic is absolutely necessary to Great Britain;—if the King's yards have sufficient supplies to last even two or three years, the merchants are not in the same case; and deprived of the usual supply from the Baltic and from Norway, the whole mercantile Fleet of the British Dominions must be soon annihilated. In addition to this Great Britain depends upon the corn furnished by Poland and Prussia for subsistence.[57]

Carysfort denounced the effects as insignificant in comparison to Britain's destruction of their own commerce. Baron Reden, in conversation with Carysfort, reaffirmed Prussian involvement and expressed concern about a break between Prussia and Britain, which placed Hanover in a precarious position. Prussia assured Britain of their lack of hostility, but Carysfort remained sceptical. For him, Prussia's intentions mattered little once Russia or France commanded Prussia to employ force.[58]

Knowledge of Prussian commitment to the maritime league and the obscurity of Prussian promises signified an impending break with Britain. Haugwitz refrained from supplying Carysfort with the conditions of the treaty and eschewed authenticating rumours that Prussian terms included a stipulation that prevented conflict with Britain. He delayed disclosing Prussian policy, but noted that the Armed Neutrality would disintegrate if tensions between Russia and Britain erupted in war.[59] Grenville instructed Carysfort to inform Haugwitz of his correspondence with Fyodor Rostopchin, Russia's foreign minister and reinforced Britain's resolution to defend its maritime rights. Moreover, he wanted to convey the gravity of Russian actions, which consisted of the Russian confiscation of British merchant ships in Russian ports and facilitating the Armed Neutrality to impose new maritime rules on Britain. These offenses, Grenville argued, violated any Russian claim of neutrality, and instead, resulted in a declaration of war.[60]

Demands from each side that the other abandon entrenched positions on vital issues doomed the negotiations to failure from the start. On 21 January 1801, the envoy for Mecklenburg Schwerin, M. de Lutzow, approached Carysfort about deescalating Anglo-Russian hostilities. He requested that Carysfort forward the terms acceptable to Russia to the British ministry. Resolving the Anglo-Russian conflict centred on Malta. Lutzow divulged Paul I's inclination to concede the port of Malta and its defences to British control and that a reconciliation meant the dissolution of the Armed Neutrality. Carysfort stressed Britain's refusal to enter negotiations related to Malta until Russia removed the embargo.[61] Grenville upheld Carysfort's response to Lutzow and included the demand that Russia return the British merchant's confiscated goods and complained that Russia challenged British rights 'essential to the Maritime Power of the British Empire.'[62] Grenville ordered Carysfort to

57 TNA: FO 64/60, pp.14–15, Carysfort to Grenville, 4 January 1801.

58 NHstA: Cal. Br. 24/1003, pp.21–27, Reden to the Geheimräte, 10 February 1801; TNA: FO 64/60, p.15, Carysfort to Grenville, 4 January 1801; Carysfort to Grenville, 6 January 1801, *Dropmore Papers*, Vol. VI, p.423.

59 TNA: FO 64/60, pp.62, 64–65, Carysfort to Grenville, 10 January 1801; Carysfort to Grenville, 13 January 1801, *Dropmore Papers*, Vol. VI, p.425.

60 TNA: FO 64/60, pp.170–174, Grenville to Carysfort, 24 January 1801.

61 TNA: FO 64/60, pp.125, 128, Carysfort to Grenville, 21 January 1801.

62 TNA: FO 64/60, pp.313–317, Grenville to Carysfort, 17 February 1801.

notify Lutzow that discussions pertaining to Malta depended on Russia's cessation of the embargo and the disbandment of the Armed Neutrality.

Carysfort, regardless of Prussian motivations, centred Prussian policy in relation to Russia. He claimed that Prussia's current politics ignored Prussian interests and the only incentive for them 'is fear, and the fear of Russia,' which rumours affirmed noting Prussian distance and lack of communication with Britain.[63] At the end of January and early February, Carysfort's meetings with Haugwitz resulted in the Prussian minister's full dismissal of the creation of the Armed Neutrality and the accusation that Britain had acted with hostility. For Carysfort, this proved that Prussia had committed itself to implementing the plan it had agreed to with Russia. Despite Haugwitz's disregard for overtures, he maintained the diplomatic language emphasising Britain's preferential treatment to Prussia in hope of securing reciprocity in competition with the Baltic powers.[64]

With the likelihood of a rupture between Britain and Prussia, Hamburg and Hanover emerged as suspected targets to secure major rivers and markets in North Germany. Carysfort discussed his concerns with Haugwitz about the neutrality of the Elbe, which Haugwitz now avoided giving any assurances.[65] On 31 January, Carysfort relayed that Baron Jacobi-Kloest, the Prussian envoy at London, received orders to remind Britain of Hanover's vulnerability, and in early February, that retaliation against Britain meant an attack on Hanover. Fears of France only strengthened Prussian resolve to act against Hanover as the Duke of Brunswick urged an immediate occupation of the Electorate to prevent a French invasion. Although unsubstantiated, Carysfort speculated that Russia had agreed to provide Hanover as an indemnity to Prussia for any damage to Prussian trade.[66]

As hostilities with the Baltic powers and Prussia developed, Britain endeavoured to uncover Prussia's real ambitions.[67] Carysfort's efforts to acquire information proved difficult and Haugwitz insisted on blaming Britain for current hostilities. On 13 February, in response to Carysfort's notes of 27 January and 1 February, Haugwitz confirmed Prussia's assent to the league of neutrality and concluded that a return to stable relations required Britain removing the embargo against Denmark and Sweden. He contended that Denmark's actions remained defensive, while Britain's were offensive.[68] Carysfort forwarded Haugwitz's proclamation to Grenville with commentary, describing Haugwitz's behaviour as 'a display

63 TNA: FO 64/60, p.130, Carysfort to Grenville, 21 January 1801; Carysfort to Grenville, 17 January 1801, *Dropmore Papers*, Vol. VI, pp.428–429.

64 TNA: FO 64/60, pp.189–190, 193, Carysfort to Grenville, 27 January 1801; TNA: FO 64/60, p.224, Carysfort to Grenville, 1 February 1801.

65 TNA: FO 64/60, pp.248–249, Carysfort to Grenville, 3 February 1801; TNA: FO 64/60, p.257, Carysfort to Grenville, 7 February 1801; TNA: FO 64/60, p.265, Carysfort to Grenville, 10 February 1801; TNA: FO 64/60, p.278, Carysfort to Grenville, 13 February 1801.

66 TNA: FO 64/60, p.222, Carysfort to Grenville, 31 January 1801; TNA: FO 64/60, pp.258–259, Carysfort to Grenville, 7 February 1801; TNA: FO 64/60, pp.265, 269–270, Carysfort to Grenville, 10 February 1801; Dwyer, 'Second Armed Neutrality', p.116.

67 TNA: FO 64/60, pp.188–193, Carysfort to Grenville, 27 January 1801; TNA: FO 64/60, pp.224–227, Carysfort to Grenville, 1 February 1801.

68 TNA: FO 64/60, pp.195–206, Carysfort to Haugwitz, 27 January 1801; TNA: FO 64/60, pp.229–238, Carysfort to Haugwitz, 1 February 1801; TNA, FO/64.60, pp.294, 296, Note from Haugwitz, 13 February 1801; NHstA: Cal. Br. 24/1003, Reden to Geheimräte, 10 February 1801; NHstA: Cal. Br. 24/1003, Reden to the King, 12, 14 February 1801; Dwyer, 'Armed Neutrality', pp.672–673.

of ignorance, impudent lying, and gross insolence, without a parallel' and purposefully exaggerated Frederick William's dishonesty in comparing him to Paul I.[69] Carysfort's intelligence attributed the change in Prussia's demeanour to Russian pressure, although Prussia issued orders to advance on Hanover prior to Russian demands but after renewed French threats.[70] Prussia expected a negative response from Britain and once received they intended to invade and occupy Hanover.[71] While Carysfort believed Prussia's warnings, he simultaneously stressed the unreliability of Prussian action determining 'the longing they have for Hanover gave them a momentary appearance of resolution.'[72]

In late February 1801, the official communication of Grenville's resignation and the appointment of his replacement, Robert Jenkinson, Lord Hawkesbury (the future 2nd Earl of Liverpool) reached Carysfort in Berlin.[73] On 1 March, he reported to Hawkesbury that Adolphus Frederick, Duke of Cambridge, arrived in Berlin from Hanover. Carysfort expressed worry and optimism about Adolphus's visit. He speculated that Adolphus's stay could prompt Prussia to act or, perhaps, Hanover and Britain would profit from the prince's personal relationship with Frederick William. Carysfort hoped that Adolphus succeeded in convincing the king that a rupture with Britain was injurious to both parties, and that George III intended to 'maintain the most important rights of His Empire,' connecting British maritime rights to North Germany and the Baltic.[74] Adolphus, in an effort to distinguish Hanover from Britain, continued Reden's previous attempt to negotiate a unified North German coalition to maintain neutrality and protect neutral maritime rights. The prince noted the difference between the wishes of Frederick William and the complexity of Prussian circumstances. He remained uncertain about the ramifications for Hanover, but the Regency attempted to ally with Prussia in its own self-interests to protect neutrality.[75] While that might appear to run counter to British policy, any success it achieved potentially aided Britain's ability to negotiate access to the continent without a Prussian occupation.

Adolphus, along with Johann Frederick von der Decken, a Hanoverian general, who accompanied him, intervened in North German politics in defence of Hanover. Adolphus's and Decken's involvement benefited Carysfort's understanding of the shifting dynamics. Decken held the confidence of Frederick William and obtained a private meeting with the king, which he relayed to Carysfort. The king confessed to Decken that he felt incapable of resisting French and Russian pressure to engage, although he disagreed with his government's actions, and planned to defer participation as long as possible. He instructed

69 Carysfort to Grenville, 13 February 1801, *Dropmore Papers*, Vol. VI, p.446.

70 Dwyer, 'Armed Neutrality', pp.673–674.

71 TNA: FO 64/60, pp.331–332, Carysfort to Grenville, 21 February 1801; TNA: FO 64/60, p.338, Carysfort to Grenville, 24 February 1801; TNA: FO 64/60, p.350, Carysfort to Hawkesbury, 4 March 1801.

72 Carysfort to Grenville, 28 February 1801, *Dropmore Papers,* Vol. VI, p.457.

73 TNA: FO 64/60, p.340, Carysfort to Hawkesbury, 28 February 1801.

74 TNA: FO 64/60, pp.343–344, Carysfort to Hawkesbury, 1 March 1801.

75 NHstA: Cal. Br. 24/1003, pp.113–116, Adolphus to the Geheimräte, 10 March 1801; NHstA: Hann. 92/1635, Reden to Haugwitz, 12 February 1801; NHstA: Cal. Br. 24/1003, Reden to the King, 14 February 1801; NHstA: Hann. 92/1635, Decken to Lenthe, 2 March 1801; Riotte, *Hannover*, pp.99–100, 103–104; Dwyer, 'Second Armed Neutrality', pp.155–156; Ford, *Hanover and Prussia*, pp.215–216.

Decken to inform Carysfort that reconciliation with Paul I remained an option and that Prussian threats to Hanover related to British hostilities with Russia. Decken's intelligence provoked Carysfort to disclose his conversations with Lutzow regarding efforts to restore relations with Russia.[76] Decken's unofficial role as intermediary between Carysfort and Frederick William benefited all parties by allowing Carysfort to communicate directly with the Prussian king bypassing Haugwitz. Hawkesbury supported Carysfort's handling of Prussian affairs, work to promote the benefits of an Anglo-Prussian friendship, and agreed that employing Decken as a liaison proved advantageous to British interests.[77]

Russian frustrations with Prussian delays coupled with French threats to Hanover amplified Prussian pressure to occupy the Electorate and prevent British access to the Elbe, Weser, and Ems. Possessing knowledge of Prussian orders to assemble troops, Carysfort conveyed his anticipation with the British fleet headed to the Sound, arriving on 21 March, to disengage Denmark could prevent the advance of Prussia into Hanover.[78] On 14 March, Carysfort reported to Hawkesbury that Haugwitz opened a confidential channel of communication with him to avoid a rift with Britain. Haugwitz claimed that the danger of a French invasion of Hanover forced Prussia to adhere to the terms of the maritime neutrality agreement, and that Frederick William regretted that the situation meant the seizure of Hanover. Although Haugwitz emphasised Russia and France as the forces compelling Prussia to possess Hanover, he determined that it would be a temporary military occupation with no alterations to the government. Hopes of Frederick William's intervention also proved disappointing. Carysfort believed Frederick William's 'Intentions ... to be honourable, but his weakness is extreme.' He doubted the king's promise to Adolphus to postpone advancement of Prussian troops because of his inability to sustain a prolonged resistance.[79]

Carysfort recognised and promoted the opportunity to employ Hanover to counter Prussian occupation. He proposed to Hawkesbury 'that a British Army may be formed in that part of His Majesty's dominions which is North of the Elbe' and 'An Army so placed would cover Hamburgh & Lubeck, make the advance of a Prussian Army to the Weser very hazardous.' His scenario depended on Britain's ability to deescalate conflict with Denmark granting the Royal Navy control of the Baltic and the Elbe protecting communications and endangering Prussia on land and at sea. British engagements against Denmark corresponded with Prussian actions against Hanover. They endeavoured to disconnect Denmark from its allies, and on 2 April, defeated Denmark at the Battle of Copenhagen, but not in time to employ their naval presence against Prussian aggression. Carysfort acknowledged his lack of military acumen and the likelihood that his suggestions proved distasteful, but

76 TNA: FO 64/60, pp.352–354, Carysfort to Hawkesbury, 4 March 1801; Carysfort to Grenville, 4 March 1801, *Dropmore Papers*, Vol. VI, p.459.

77 TNA: FO 64/60, pp.364–365, Decken to Carysfort, 3 March 1801; Carysfort to Grenville, 4 March 1801, *Dropmore Papers*, Vol. VI, p.460; TNA: FO 64/60, p.412, Hawkesbury to Carysfort, 17 March 1801; Dwyer, 'Armed Neutrality', pp.675–676; Riotte, *Hannover*, pp.103–104

78 TNA: FO 64/60, pp.374–376, Carysfort to Hawkesbury, 7 March 1801; TNA: FO 64/60, p.392, Carysfort to Hawkesbury, 10 March 1801.

79 TNA: FO 64/60, pp.393–394, Carysfort to Hawkesbury, 14 March 1801; TNA: FO 64/60, p.410, Carysfort to Hawkesbury, 15 March 1801; TNA: FO 64/60, p.420, Carysfort to Hawkesbury, 17 March 1801; NHstA: Hann. 92/1638, Adolphus to the Geheimräte, 21 March 1801.

his assessment demonstrated Hanover's value to Britain's commercial policy and the maintenance of communications to the continent.[80]

As the Prussian invasion loomed, Carysfort adjusted, and his suggestions about defence shifted. Towards the end of March, intelligence indicated that Prussian troops had received marching orders. Directions emphasised the possession of the Elbe, Weser, and Ems to close the major ports to British commerce. Frederick William blamed foreign pressure for actions taken against Britain, and Carysfort believed it a component while remaining suspicious of Prussia's ulterior motive towards Hanover.[81] Carysfort waivered in his opinion on Britain's defence of Hanover. He addressed the infeasibility of Britain organising a military defence to stop the impending Prussian occupation. Instead, he recommended feigning belief of Prussian promises of friendship to prevent immediate conflict and avoid a change in Prussian discourse.[82] Carysfort altered his earlier plan that Britain adopt an aggressive stance and offered an alternative. He proposed, with Prussian approval, the placement of a Hanoverian army under Adolphus's command 'behind the Elbe in the Duchy of Lauenbourg,' to restrain Prussia's ambitions and secure British access to the continent.[83]

Haugwitz's façade transformed as Prussia's invasion of Hanover approached. On 26 March, he shocked Carysfort with his accusatory tone toward Britain since Carysfort had assumed that Britain and Prussia had reached an understanding about the political circumstances. Haugwitz notified him that Prussian troops advanced toward Hanover to block British access to the North German ports due to Britain's failure to respond to accusations of British aggression against Denmark and Sweden. Haugwitz's attitude, although unexpected, confirmed for Carysfort that the maritime neutrality of the Baltic powers was not Prussia's primary motivation for occupying the Electorate.[84] Within a few days, Carysfort updated Hawkesbury on the troops intended for Hanover. He expected the Hanoverian army to surrender honourably to Prussia and have the time to decide whether to remain under Prussian authority or leave Hanover to enter British service.[85] Carysfort's determination to discover a solution to prevent Prussian action against Britain and Hanover failed, and on 1 April, he reported that Frederick William von der Schulenburg departed Berlin to organise Hanover's submission.[86] On 3 April 1801, Hanover capitulated to Prussia. In the proclamation, Prussia declared its reasons for action. First, it named Britain's consistent hostility toward neutral commerce as the primary factor for Prussian involvement in the maritime league. In addition, the declaration revealed that the terms to which Prussia agreed concerned the closure of major rivers to British access and the occupation of George III's German dominions.[87]

---

80 TNA: FO 64/60, pp.404–407, Carysfort to Hawkesbury, 14 March 1801; Dwyer, 'Second Armed Neutrality', pp.176–178.

81 TNA: FO 64/60, p.423, Carysfort to Hawkesbury, 22 March 1801; Dwyer, 'Armed Neutrality', pp.677–679.

82 TNA: FO 64/60, pp.436–437, Carysfort to Hawkesbury, 24 March 1801.

83 TNA: FO 64/60, p.439, Carysfort to Hawkesbury, 24 March 1801.

84 TNA: FO 64/60, pp.442–443, Carysfort to Hawkesbury, 26 March 1801.

85 TNA: FO 64/60, pp.455–456, Carysfort to Hawkesbury, 29 March 1801.

86 TNA: FO 64/61, p.9, Carysfort to Hawkesbury, 1 April 1801.

87 TNA: FO 64/61, pp.42–47, Declaration from Haugwitz, 8 April 1801; Dwyer, 'Armed Neutrality', p.684.

On 4 April Carysfort received news of Paul's assassination, which he suspected might affect Prussia's possession of Hanover.[88] The death of Paul meant the accession of his son Alexander I, and as expected, Russia and Britain entered a phase of reconciliation with the removal of the embargo against British ships. Rumours circulated that an agreement existed with Paul I to divide territory in North Germany among Prussia, Denmark, Sweden, and the Elector of Bavaria in which Prussia planned to gain most of Hanover. Carysfort commented, and Hawkesbury agreed, that 'whatever share the intrigues of the Cabinet of Berlin may have had in suggesting these ideas to the Emperor, the death of that Prince will have made it appear very improbable that any of them should be realised.' In the aftermath, Hawkesbury ordered Carysfort to inform the Prussian ministry that rapprochement proved difficult while Prussia continued its occupation of Hanover.[89] Britain's decision to send Lord St. Helen's to Russia for negotiations, Paul I's death, and the dissolution of the Armed Neutrality marked a shift in Prussia's occupation of Hanover that altered Russian policy, and thus, Prussian policy. Anglo-Russian reconciliation also prompted Britain to officially demand Prussian withdrawal from Hanover and any hope Prussia had of keeping the Electorate depended on France and the Anglo-French relationship. Resolving Anglo-Prussian relations revolved around Hanover, and the announcement of Anglo-French peace preliminaries in October, no longer allowed Prussia to justify occupation and they withdrew on 6 November 1801.[90]

Britain's continental enemies targeted Hanover as a British province and focused on occupying the Electorate to block British commercial access to North Germany. Hanover's commercial importance demonstrates that Hanover and British policy were not always contradictory, and in some circumstances, Hanover fit into a larger threat to imperial strategy. French, Russian, or Prussian threats to Hanover did not automatically imply the expectation that Britain planned to militarily rush to the Electorates defence. An occupation of Hanover detached Britain from continental communications, commercial access and attacked the component of British policy that mattered most, trade. Britain, instead of acting militarily, employed diplomatic efforts via Prussia to solve the non-naval crises in North Germany and manage the North Germany system that proved crucial to Britain's Empire. In 1801, the Baltic powers challenge to Britain's naval supremacy held priority over the defence of Hanover.

88 TNA: FO 64/61, pp.26–29, Carysfort to Hawkesbury, 4 April 1801.

89 TNA: FO 64/61, pp.32–35, Carysfort to Hawkesbury, 8 April 1801; TNA: FO 64/61, pp.79–80, Hawkesbury to Carysfort, 17 April 1801; TNA: FO 64/61, pp.131–133, Hawkesbury to Carysfort, 8 May 1801.

90 Riotte, *Hannover*, pp.106–108, pp.114–115; Dwyer, 'Armed Neutrality', pp.683–686; Simms, *Impact of Napoleon*, p.85

Select Bibliography

Manuscript Sources
The National Archives (TNA), Kew
FO 64/58–61
Niedersächsisches Hauptstaatsarchiv (NHstA), Hannover
Cal. Br. 24, Nr. 1003
Hann. 92, Nr. 1635
Hann. 92, Nr. 1638

Published Primary Sources
Aspinall, A., *The Later Correspondence of George III* (Cambridge: Cambridge University Press, 1967)
Bailleu, Paul (ed.), *Preussen und Frankreich von 1795 bis 1807: Diplomatische Correspondenzen* (Leipzig: S. Hirzel, 1881)
Fortescue, J. B. (ed.), *Report on the Manuscripts of J. B. Fortescue, Esq., Preserved at Dropmore* (London: Historical Manuscripts Commission, 1892-1927)

Secondary Sources
Dwyer, Philip G., 'Prussia and the Armed Neutrality: The Invasion of Hanover in 1801', *The International History Review*, Vol. 15, No. 4 (November 1993), pp.661–687
Feldbaek, *Denmark and the Armed Neutrality, 1800–1801: Small Power Policy in a World War* (Copenhagen: Akademisk Forlag, 1980)
Ford, Guy Stanton, *Hanover and Prussia, 1795–1803: A Study in Neutrality* (New York: Columbia University Press, 1903)
Harding, Nick, *Hanover and the British Empire, 1700–1837* (Woodbridge: The Boydell Press, 2007)
Müller, Leos, *Neutrality in World History* (London: Routledge, 2019)
Ragsdale, Hugh, 'A Continental System in 1801: Paul and Bonaparte', *The Journal of Modern History*, Vol. 42, No. 1 (March 1970), pp.70–89
Riotte, Torsten, *Hannover in der Britischen Politik (1792–1815): Dynastische Verbindung als Element Außenpolitischer Entscheidungsprozesse* (Münster: Lit Verlag, 2005)
Rosenhaft, Eve and Smith, Hannah (eds.), *Civilians and War in Europe, 1618–1815* (Liverpool: Liverpool University Press, 2012)
Simms, Brendan, *The Impact of Napoleon: Prussian High Politics, Foreign Policy and the Crisis of the Executive, 1797–1806* (Cambridge: Cambridge University Press, 1997)
Simms, Brendan and Torsten Riotte (eds.), *The Hanoverian Dimension in British History, 1714–1837* (Cambridge: Cambridge University Press, 2007)

8

A Timid Staff Officer? Reassessing Carl von Clausewitz's Role in the Battles of Ligny and Wavre (16–20 June 1815)

Vanya Eftimova Bellinger

In the days following Carl von Clausewitz's death in November of 1831 his wife, Marie, composed a grief-stricken letter to her close friends informing them of her sudden loss. Marie also recounted the milestones of the general's career and from that early moment onward, began shaping his public image and promoting his legacy. Recalling the 1815 campaign, Marie crafted some of the most memorable lines, quoted ever since by biographers: 'The night of June of 18th to 19th [after Waterloo] that the Field Marshal [von Gneisenau][1] spent pursuing Napoleon and cared to call the greatest of his life, was for [Clausewitz] after the Battle of Wavre the most horrible.'[2] Marie had always felt that that her beloved husband never received the recognition he deserved for his performance as an officer in the Napoleonic Wars. She wished, therefore, to draw the public's attention to Clausewitz's heroic efforts in the Battle in Wavre.[3] Although fought simultaneously and contributing to the glorious victory at Waterloo, in Clausewitz's lifetime, just as today, the events in Wavre were largely overlooked and often misconstrued. Despite Marie's wishes and the wide proliferation of her comment in biographies and studies, Clausewitz's experience in 1815 campaign remains a subject of dispute and misinterpretations.

Although his lifework *On War* dominates modern strategic thought, Clausewitz's actual performance as an officer on the battlefield is less well-known. This chapter reassesses Clausewitz's role during two of the 1815 campaign's engagements – at Ligny (16 June 1815) and Waterloo's twin battle at Wavre (18–19 June 1815). In the two centuries following the final destruction of Napoleon, the performance of the III Prussian Corps, where Clausewitz

---

1 In 1815, August Neidhardt von Gneisenau had not yet obtained the rank of *Generalfeldmarschall*, of course.

2 The letter is cited in Vanya Eftimova Bellinger, *Marie von Clausewitz: The Woman Behind the Making of ON WAR* (New York: Oxford University Press, 2016), p.221.

3 Bellinger, *Marie von Clausewitz*, pp.221–222.

served as chief of staff under *Generalleutnant* Johann von Thielmann, had repeatedly come under scrutiny and authors often blamed Clausewitz for much of the perceived timidity and indecisiveness. Peter Paret's biography *Clausewitz and the State* cites the accusations but suggests that, in order to accurately judge Clausewitz's performance, further examination is required.[4] Donald Stoker's recent work *Clausewitz: His Life and Work* offers more, but far from conclusive, analysis. Briefly recounting the accusations, Stoker asserts that concerning Ligny, the Prussian headquarters carried the overall responsibility for the conduct. He argues further that, due to lack of comprehensive sources and analysis, Wavre could not be considered a clear example of Clausewitz's abilities on the battlefield.[5]

In his lifework, the philosopher of war devoted considerable space and energy on the need for commanders to display initiative and grasp opportunities when they arise. Therefore, the criticism of Clausewitz's performance in 1815 has raised genuine questions about his legacy – after all, most of the readers of *On War* are fellow officers and practitioners of international security who seek to apply these concepts to real-world challenges. This chapter argues that Clausewitz's role in the 1815 has been a subject of much misunderstanding as he acted primarily as a chief of staff and not a commander in his own right. Furthermore, there is little evidence for his alleged timidity in Ligny. The extended retreat after Wavre was a brazen risk, which, unfortunately for Clausewitz and Thielmann, failed to pan out. Much of the criticism was either due to partisan attacks, lack of understanding about the realities on the ground, or – as a result of his unexpected posthumous fame – desire to dispute Clausewitz's actual battlefield experience. The military theorist partially enabled the confusion, for he never openly reflected on his personal experience in Ligny and Wavre, despite discussing the 1815 campaign in various writings. A careful study of Clausewitz's performance reveals the difficulties of coalition warfare, the pitfalls of the warfare in the midst of military transformation, and the complexities of campaigning.

In the spring of 1815, Clausewitz received the news that he was finally readmitted back into the Prussian army, after resigning his commission to fight for Russia in 1812. As France's reluctant ally, the Prussian King Friedrich Wilhelm III was forced to provide an ancillary corps of 20,000 troops and thirty Prussian officers made the radical decision to switch sides. The *Grande Armée's* retreat from Moscow proved these rebels right in their belief that Napoleon could be defeated. Nonetheless, as Clausewitz discovered after returning to Central Europe as a victor in a Russian uniform, many in the homeland resented the act of open disobedience. Despite his preference to return to the ranks of Prussian army and win immortal glory on the battlefield, Clausewitz instead spent the remainder of 1813 and early 1814 in a Russian uniform as part of the Russo-German Legion and Wallmoden Corps, and was to serve in the less active northern theater. Clausewitz had fought in the legendary battles of 1812 – Smolensk, Borodino and Borissov – could boast a significant role in the inception of the Convention of Tauroggen (December 1812) which preceded the War of the Sixth Coalition; and he proved his mettle once more in the 1813 spring campaign's crucial engagement at Grossgörschen/Lützen. His absence from the great battles of Leipzig and

4 Peter Paret, *Clausewitz and the State: The Man, His Theories, and His Times* (Princeton, NJ: Princeton University Press, 1985), pp.248–250.

5 Donald Stoker, *Clausewitz: His Life and Work* (New York: Oxford University Press, 2014), pp.235, 247–249.

Dresden, however, forever darkened his memories of 1813–1814 period. Although allowed to keep his rank as an *oberst*, it was only after the 1814 campaign was over that the long-delayed process of Clausewitz's reentering in the Prussian army began. Napoleon's unfortunate return, it seemed, provided him with another opportunity to gain the military glory he so desired.

In April, the Prussian army was still undergoing reorganization and was spread throughout Rhineland. Like many other members of the Prussian military, Carl von Clausewitz was staying in Aachen, near the Belgian border, where Marie joined him. The couple were also enjoying the city's famous spas and hoped that the wellness procedures might bring relief to Clausewitz's many ailments.[6] When aged less than twelve years old, he joined the Prussian army as a young boy-soldier. The irregular lifestyle and the strain of frequent campaigning, especially the exertions of the Russian campaign, had taken a significant toll on his health. At the age of thirty-five, he suffered from gout, arthritis and endured migraine headaches, leading to insomnia and exhaustion that resulted in a surly mood and occasional outburst of rage. During the Russian campaign Clausewitz's hair thinned, and the extreme temperatures damaged blood vessels in his face and left a permanent redness that later made many suspect he was a secret drinker.[7] Nevertheless, when the call from the Prussian headquarters came, he did not hesitate.

Facing Napoleon Again

When the news of the emperor's return from Elba reached Carl and Marie von Clausewitz, the couple were far from surprised by this turn of events. Clausewitz had already judged the situation in Europe unstable and the conditions of the exile too generous for Napoleon not to be tempted to reclaim his throne.[8] Clausewitz still estimated that the emperor's efforts would remain unsuccessful – hence he reassured Marie that their separation would not last too long.[9] In his later monograph on the 1815 campaign, the military theorist echoed this sentiment writing that neither the Allies would accept Napoleon's return to the French throne, nor could the emperor gather a significant enough force to be able to prolong the war. Therefore, Clausewitz concluded, sooner rather than later, all of Napoleon's efforts were bound to fail.[10]

In preparation for the upcoming campaign, Clausewitz was expecting to work with his fellow reformers on the Prussian general staff, with Prince von Blücher's current chief of-staff, *Generalleutnant* August Neidhardt von Gneisenau, and his deputy *Oberst* Karl

6 Bellinger, *Marie von Clausewitz*, p.154.

7 Bellinger, *Marie von Clausewitz*, pp.134,149.

8 Clausewitz to Marie, 11 April 1814, Karl und Marie von Clausewitz, *Ein Lebensbild in Briefen und Tagebuchblätter (Correspondence)*, ed. by Karl Linnebach (Berlin: M. Warneck, 1925), p.317.

9 Unpublished part of Clausewitz's letter to Marie, 12 May 1815, Prussian Privy State Archives (GStA PK): VI. HA Familienarchive und Nachlässe, Nl Buttlar-Venedien, Nr.561.

10 Clausewitz's monograph 'The Campaign of 1815' is published in English as Carl von Clausewitz and Arthur Wellesley, 1st Duke of Wellington, *On Waterloo: Clausewitz, Wellington, and the Campaign of 1815*. ed./trans. Christopher Bassford, Daniel Moran, and Gregory W. Pedlow, (Washington: Clausewitz.com, 2010), p.81.

von Grolman.[11] Yet shortly after, he was named chief of staff for the III Corps, one of the four Prussian corps designated for the campaign against Napoleon. The corps was led by *Generalleutnant* von Thielmann, an officer Clausewitz had not previously worked for. Full of anticipation, he travelled to the III Corps' temporary headquarters at Ciney and soon enough wrote to Marie that he was getting to know Thielmann as a gregarious character who was open to his new chief of staff's advice.[12] Despite the correspondence's optimistic tone, Clausewitz's relationship with Thielmann came with complications. A veteran hussar, Thielmann was originally born in the Electorate of Saxony. In 1812, as part of the *Grande Armée*, the Saxon brigade Thielmann commanded fought with distinction in the Battle of Borodino. Disillusioned with Saxony's alliance with Napoleon, however, in May 1813 Thielmann resigned his command and transferred to Russian service. After the Treaty of Paris in 1814, he was tasked with commanding and reorganizing the 14,000 strong Saxon contingent within the Allied forces. Seen as a traitor by many of his countrymen, in early 1815, Thielmann officially entered Prussian service and a few days later was appointed as the commander of the III Corps.[13] In addition to Thielmann's fame as a bold and experienced battlefield commander, his transfer was a political coup for Berlin, as his example led other talented Saxon officers to seek positions in the Prussian army.[14] At the Congress of Vienna, in the hands of the Great Powers, Saxony lost one-third of its territory to Prussia and the latter was seeking to absorb a significant number of former Saxon troops within its ranks. Although Clausewitz and Thielmann met in Aachen before the campaign, the decision of the War Minister, Hermann von Boyen, to appoint Clausewitz as the III Corps's chief of staff a few weeks later must have come as something of a surprise to Thielmann.[15] An affable character, the general warmly welcomed Clausewitz at his headquarters, but his demeanor made Clausewitz suspect that he had expected someone else.[16] Both men considered themselves as outsiders in the Prussian army – Clausewitz had yet to overcome the stigma of his transfer to the Russian army in 1812 – and Thielmann most likely wished to have one of his fellow Saxons as his deputy.

Clausewitz arrived in Ciney on 9 May. He had to rapidly reorganize the troops and ensure continuity and constancy with the overall Prussian war efforts. After all, Clausewitz was among the most devoted students of Gerhard von Scharnhorst, the military reformer who championed the idea of a general staff and capable staff officers supporting battlefield commanders. In the autumn campaign of 1813 and then in 1814, Clausewitz had successfully assisted *Generalleutnant* Ludwig von Wallmoden-Gimborn. He helped get Wallmoden's

11 Peter Paret writes about Gneisenau's and Hermann von Boyen's plans to eventually move Clausewitz to Blücher's headquarters. According to a cited but now presumably lost document, on 1 May, Clausewitz also asked to be transferred to the line, but this request was denied, Paret, *Clausewitz and the State*, pp.245–246.

12 Clausewitz to Marie, 14 May 1815, *Correspondence*, p.375.

13 Herman von Petersdorff, *General Johann Adolph Freiherr von Thielmann: Ein Charakterbild aus der napoleonischen Zeit* (Leipzig: S.Hirzel, 1894), pp.63, 109–110, 112–117, 124, 265–266, 282.

14 Petersdorff, *von Thielmann*, pp.286–287

15 Petersdorff, *von Thielmann*, pp.284–285

16 Petersdorff, *von Thielmann*, p.288; Unpublished part of Clausewitz's letter to Marie, 12. May 1815, Prussian Privy State Archives ((GStA PK), VI. HA Familienarchive und Nachlässe, Nl Buttlar-Venedien, Nr.561.

22,000-men strong corps battle ready, a colourful bunch of German, Swedish, British and Russian troops, and coordinated the corps' actions with the overall Allied efforts.[17] It might have been Clausewitz's expertise in overseeing diverse troops that led Boyen to appoint him as a chief of staff for the III Corps. Nevertheless, to Thielmann, Clausewitz's appointment must have also signalled the Prussian leadership's obvious desire for strengthened control over the corps.[18] Although Clausewitz and Thielmann had much in common, most notably their love for Friedrich Schiller's poetry, trust and cognition of each other's strengths and weaknesses had yet to develop.

The Prussian military reform movement's tireless leader Gerhard von Scharnhorst had advanced the concept of the general staff as an indispensable structure in the modern warfare. With the exponential growth of armies, the need for command and control and effective administration and logistics, became paramount. Napoleon's principal staff officer, Louis Alexandre Berthier, was an experienced and hard-working subordinate able to translate the emperor's wishes into stellar orders. Nonetheless, Napoleon's general staff remained an organization built around his personal needs, without continuity and authority of its own. In the 1815 campaign, Napoleon could no longer rely on Berthier and historians judge the lack of a capable chief of staff able to compose clear orders and coordinate the different corps as detrimental for the overall performance of the French army.[19] Scharnhorst believed that carefully selected and superbly prepared staff officers – especially when the Prussian army lacked a leader to rival Napoleon's operational genius and charisma – could provide invaluable advice to their commanders, keep them from committing grave mistakes, and enhance and coordinate the conduct of armies on the battlefield. The chief of staff ought to serve not as a mere translator and executor of his commander's wishes – as was the case for Napoleon and Berthier – but as the commander's closest partner and adviser.[20] After Scharnhorst's unexpected death in June 1813, the fellow reformer and famed war hero Gneisenau took control of Blücher's headquarters and the overall Prussian war effort. In 1815, Blücher and Gneisenau functioned as coequal partners: Blücher was the charismatic and daring commander, while his chief of staff Gneisenau shaped the Prussian strategy and operations.[21] As this chapter reveals, throughout the campaign, Clausewitz effectively advised Thielmann and played an important role in shaping III Corps' performance. Nonetheless, there is no evidence that he enjoyed Gneisenau's wide prerogatives.

In many of its features, the Prussian general staff of 1813–1815 resembled its modern version. Nonetheless, it was yet to become the army's nerve centre which, while close to the battlefield and in constant contact with it, focuses on overseeing the engagements and informing the commander, evaluating reports and intelligence, communicating with the

17 Paret, *Clausewitz and the State*, p.243; Stoker, *Clausewitz: His Life and Work*, pp.174–175.

18 On the role of corps' chief of staff in 1815, see Peter Hofschröer, *1815 The Waterloo Campaign: Wellington, his German Allies and the Battles of Ligny and Quatre Bras* (London: Greenhill Books, 1998), pp.62–63.

19 Gunther E. Rothenberg, *The Art of Warfare in the Age of Napoleon* (Bloomington: Indiana University Press, 1980), pp.208–210.

20 On the general staff's emergence in Prussia, see Paret, *Clausewitz and the State*, p.68. On Scharnhorst's concept, see Charles Edward White, *The Enlightened Soldier: Scharnhorst and the Militärische Gesellschaft in Berlin, 1801–1805* (Westport, CT: Praeger, 1989), pp.103–105.

21 F.C.F von Müffling, Philip Yorke (ed.), *Passages From My Life* (London: Richard Bentley, 1853), p.150.

various components, and keeping the strategic goals in mind. Albeit being the chief of staff of Prussia's Army of Silesia, at the Battle of Großgörschen/Lützen, Scharnhorst, for instance, still led the last cavalry attack and suffered a wound to the leg resulting in his untimely death.[22] Maintaining the informational flow and keeping the decision-making process intact remains a challenge in the best of battlefield circumstances. Scharnhorst's acolytes Gneisenau and Grolman began devoting most of their time and energy to supporting the commander and coordinating the action, but the limitations of slow communication and rudimental intelligence hampered their efficiency and concentration. Just like in Blücher's headquarters, the corps' chiefs of staff and their staff officers had to frequently ride between extended positions, gather and evaluate their own intelligence, deliver orders or oversee engagements in person, physically meet and inform their commanders or gallop to the army's headquarters for consultations, and lead troops in action when required. Overall, the Prussian general staff officers in 1813–1815 performed an outstanding job; nonetheless, they also displayed quite a few lapses in judgement when strategic issues were at play or delayed reactions to pressing matters. Without this context, modern practitioners of war – accustomed to a well-developed general staff – could hardly understand seemingly inexplicable errors and communication blunders displayed by otherwise outstanding officers.

Aside from building a close working relationship, III Corps' command team also faced monumental challenges preparing their troops for the impending war. In total for the campaign against Napoleon, Prussia relied on about 113,000 troops and 288 artillery pieces.[23] It was an army that, for the most part, mobilized and mustered between April and May and contained all the shortcomings and inadequacies inherent with such short planning. Prussia's economy still needed to recover from the earlier devastation suffered between 1806–1813, and its agents could not pay the prices local suppliers demanded. Soldiers' letters offered abundant and concurrent complaints about hunger and deprivations.[24]

Designated as a reserve, compared to the other Prussian corps, III Corps was among the least equipped with artillery, with only six heavy pieces. Furthermore, it had only 30 infantry battalions, while the other corps relied on 36 each. As compensation, it received six veteran *Landwehr* regiments. Altogether III Corps amounted to about 23,900 troops, while the other three corps had approximately 30,000 men each.[25] Buried in paperwork, working long hours, and constantly worrying about his corps' readiness, Clausewitz slept little. In the few hours downtime that he could steal, his many ailments tormented him again. In the turbulent months of May and June 1815, Clausewitz relied on opium to ease his pains, often

22 Klaus Hornung, *Scharnhorst: Soldat, Reformer, Staatsmann* (Munich: Bechtle Verlag, 2001), pp.274–278.

23 Rudolf Friedrich, *Die Befreiungskriege: Der Feldzug 1815* (Berlin: Mittler und Sohn, 1913), Vol. IV, p.96.

24 See for instance Clausewitz to Marie, 21 [23] Juni and 3 July 1815, *Correspondence*, p.382 and p.386. The long report about the campaign Major Wilhelm von Grolman sent to his wife contains many details about the scant provisioning. He was the brother of Karl von Grolman and served in the III Corps, Wilhelm von Grolman, 12 July 1815, Landesarchiv Thüringen: Staatsarchiv Altenburg, Familien Nachlass Grolman.

25 Karl Rudolf von Ollech, *Geschichte des Feldzuges von 1815 nach archivalischen Quellen* (Berlin: Mittler und Sohn, 1876), pp.16–17, 62. Friedrich, *Der Feldzug 1815*, IV, pp.95–96.

worrying about developing an addiction; but he still decided to take the drug, for without sleep his work would suffer more.[26]

Napoleon's Last Victory

Napoleon's strategy relied on rapid campaigning and a decisive victory before the allies could mobilize their full military might. On 12 June, Napoleon secretly left Paris and moved northeast to the Belgium border. He organized the Army of The North into three great columns marching along the roads leading to the Belgian town of Charleroi. Aware that the allies had distinctively separate camps and headquarters, and that their forces were spread throughout the Low Countries, Napoleon planned to fight his enemies one by one, first the Prussians and then Wellington's Anglo-Dutch forces. On the 14th, I Prussian Corps's advanced guard under *Generalleutnant* von Ziethen observed the enemy's movement, and the news prompted Blücher to order his army to concentrate around Sombreffe. On the next day, the French offensive began with the first clashes at Thuin, while I Corps slowly retreated, as ordered, to give time for the rest of the Prussian army and Wellington's forces to gather for a united counteroffensive. On the night of 15th, Zeithen's troops finally retired past Fleurus, in the vicinity of the Ligny brook, mainly between the villages of Ligny and Saint-Amand.[27]

While Wellington was slow to respond to the news of Napoleon's advance and immediately order his troops to concentrate, Blücher's energetic actions set his army in motion. As ordered, on the 15th, II Corps under the command of *Generalleutnant* von Pirch reached Onoz and Mazy, while III Corps moved on Namur. The orders sent to IV Corps, led by *General der Infanterie* von Bülow, however, were less assertive, as Bülow was senior to Gneisenau, who composed the orders. Therefore, IV Corps's headquarters failed to recognize the situation's urgency and was yet to march, as required, from Liege to Hannut. On the night of 15th, Blücher's headquarters realized that Bülow's troops would arrive late.[28]

The position at Ligny appeared a sensible choice, and with hindsight, in his monograph on 1815, Clausewitz still judged it as 'the most natural point' for Blücher and Wellington to join their armies. It was situated on the Brussels-Namur Road, which connected the two forces, and in the vicinity of Brussels-Charleroi highway where Wellington intended to concentrate his left-wing. While not particularly deep or steep, the Ligny brook and its side streams offered protection for the Prussian forces, especially on the position's higher left side. As Clausewitz concluded, the location could be held by one to two corps for a long time, while with the other two corps, and with support from Wellington, Blücher could confidently attempt a counterattack.[29] Yet this plan's success depended on two variables – first that Bülow's IV Corps would hurry up and arrive on the afternoon of 16 June, and

26 Clausewitz to Marie, 20 May 1815, *Correspondence*, p.377.
27 Peter Hofschröer, *1815 The Waterloo Campaign*, pp.186–187.
28 Hofschröer, *1815 The Waterloo Campaign*, p.188. In *On War*, Clausewitz also named the unclear orders as the reason for Bülow's delay, Carl von Clausewitz, *On War*, ed. and trans. by Michael Howard and Peter Paret (Princeton: Princeton University Press, 1989), p.329.
29 Clausewitz, 'The Campaign of 1815', pp.82–83.

second, that Wellington would be able to support the Prussians. The assumption, then, was that for the first part of the battle, the Prussian centre had to bide its time and hold firm until the reinforcements came, but by the end of the day, Blücher could crush Napoleon with attacks in the flanks.

On 16 June, despite also experiencing a delay in receiving its orders, as Clausewitz wrote with a barely hidden sense of pride, III Corps rushed to Ligny and arrived at around 10:00 a.m. Blücher's headquarters counted on the IV Corps appearing around 4:00 p.m.[30] Therefore, I Corps concentrated between the villages Brye, St. Amand, St. Amand La Haye, and Ligny, and II Corps stood behind it as a reserve. Considering its smaller size and insufficient equipment, III Corps received the better protected higher grounds behind Ligny brook near the villages of Sombreffe, Le Point du Jour, Tongrinne, Boignee, and Balatre. This was both the original Prussian line of retreat on the road to Namur and the direction from where IV Corps was expected to arrive. The Prussian position, therefore, consisted of two fronts, for the Ligny brook separated III Corps from the centre and although not critically, still obstructed the communications between the two forces. The Prussian right, where Blücher's headquarters expected Wellington's support, was exposed. However, since Anglo-Dutch forces were not too far away, the headquarters correctly judged that Napoleon would not, initially, take the risk attacking it and possibly being crushed between the two armies.[31]

At 1:00 p.m. Blücher and Wellington met at the windmill at Brye. In the German historiography, to this day, the meeting is surrounded by a passionate debate whether the Duke firmly promised that his forces would support the Prussians, no matter what. Facing *Maréchal* Ney's troops by Quatre Bras, Wellington, however, meant he would do so, if he was not attacked himself.[32] In his late nineteenth century study of the campaign and examining various accounts, the prominent military historian Karl Rudolf von Ollech placed the blame on the shoulders of the Prussian liaison officer in Wellington's headquarters, Karl von Müffling. No matter what had been said or not said at the windmill, according to Ollech, Müffling should have informed the Prussian leadership about the actual conditions of Wellington's forces. Despite the Duke's hopes, his army was still concentrating while engaging Ney, and thus unable to directly support the Prussians.[33] Blücher and Gneisenau went into battle adamantly believing that Wellington would arrive soon, just as Napoleon waited for Ney to defeat Wellington in Quatre Bras and then attack the Prussians from the rear.

The Battle of Ligny began around 3:00 p.m. Napoleon relied on 61,000 troops, while Blücher had about 83,000 men, although a significant number of them were new recruits and there was uncertainty over how well they would perform in combat. Napoleon planned to fiercely attack the centre and wait for Ney to assault the rear, thus destroying two-thirds of the Prussian army and pushing it back to the east and away from Wellington. Napoleon

30 Clausewitz, 'The Campaign of 1815', p.99.

31 As Clausewitz wrote, this analysis applied only to the initial positioning of forces. Nothing could prevent Napoleon from attacking once he knew that the Anglo-Dutch forces were neutralized. Clausewitz, 'The Campaign of 1815', pp.99–100.

32 Hofschöer offers an exhaustive analysis and eyewitness accounts on the matter, Hofschöer, *1815 The Waterloo Campaign*, pp.233–242.

33 Ollech, *Geschichte des Feldzuges von 1815*, p.127.

ordered an attack straight from the south, a shrewd decision which forced the Prussians to hold their extended front in its entirety. Pinned down by the French artillery on the left and unable to leave the line of retreat unprotected, III Corps could not effectively support the centre. Throughout the afternoon, in the centre, the adversaries bitterly fought for St. Amand, Ligny, and St.Amand La Haye, and the villages changed hands several times. In the evening, a severe storm and lightning temporarily diminished the visibility on the battlefield. For the first part of the action, III Corps observed the events, but around 6:00 p.m. the fight engulfed the villages of Balatre and Tongrinne, as well.[34] *Major* Wilhelm von Grolman, commander of the 4th Kurmärkisches Landwehr Regiment, wrote a lengthy letter to his wife describing the heavy bombardment from the French artillery in Tongrinne that prevented him and his troops from ever moving.[35]

The public controversy concerning III Corps' performance in Ligny began just a few months after the war, in the autumn of 1815, and originally stemmed from Prussian anger and mistrust against the British. Namely, in his *Rheinisches Merkur* the fiery publicist Joseph Görres commented angrily on reports about the Foreign Secretary Viscount Castlereagh's remarks in the British parliament. Castlereagh claimed that at Waterloo, the age's two greatest commanders met, namely Napoleon and Wellington; therefore, Blücher and the Prussian army's crucial contributions in the campaign were left out. Görres's ire brought about the debate on how and why Ligny was lost: Had the battle been won, so the logic went, the victory over Napoleon would have been seen as mainly Prussian. Was it because Bülow was late, or Thielmann reticent?[36] The questions within the Prussian army, then, swirled around whether III Corps, which saw less action, should have moved to the centre and perhaps decided the battle's outcome. Should Blücher's headquarters have given Thielmann such orders – or should Thielmann, realizing the new developments, have abandoned the line of retreat to Namur on his own accord?[37] Later German historians also pondered if Thielmann and Clausewitz, from their positions, could have clearly observed the engagements in the villages Ligny, St. Amand, and St. Amand La Haye.[38] Thielmann's biographer, Herman von Petersdorff, claimed that the general was ill-served by the timidity of his chief of staff, Clausewitz – as a cavalry officer, Thielmann's instincts surely would have been to move and support the Prussian centre.[39] Petersdorff's statement, however, remains a pure speculation, a biographer's partisan desire to defend his protagonist and find an easy explanation for the events on 16 June. Thielmann, in fact, never raised such claim, nor is there any record suggesting that he found it necessary to publicly defend his decisions in Ligny.

In his study of the 1815 Campaign, Clausewitz also named the failure to effectively use III Corps as one of the mistakes in the battle. From Clausewitz's perspective there were

34 Hofschöer, *1815 The Waterloo Campaign*, p.318

35 Wilhelm von Grolman, 12 July 1815, LandesArchiv Thüringen: Staatsarchiv Altenburg, Familien Nachlass Grolman.

36 Joseph Görres, 'Aus Chartes, 15 August,' *Rheinisches Merkur*, Nr. 291, 30 August 1815. Additional details in Hans Joachim Schoeps, (ed.), *Aus den Jahren Preussischer Not und Erneuerung. Tagebücher und Briefe der Gebrüder Gerlach und ihres Kreises 1805–1820* (Berlin: Haude und Spenersche Verlagsbuchhandlung, 1963), p.162.

37 Schoeps, *Gebrüder Gerlach*, p.167.

38 Oscar von Lettow-Vorbeck, *Napoleons Untergang 1815* (Berlin: Mittler und Sohn, 1904), p.339.

39 Petersdorff, *von Thielmann*, p.294.

two options. The first was that III Corps could have been ordered to abandon the line of retreat toward Namur; but that required rethinking the Prussian plan for the battle and a much earlier reshuffling of positions.[40] Throughout the battle, Blücher's headquarters drew on parts of III Corps to bolster the centre, but the extended Prussian position prevented its quick concentration later. Therefore, the crucial mistake the Prussian leadership committed in the course of the battle, when the initial assumptions failed to pan out (i.e., Wellington and IV Corps not coming through), was not rapidly readjusting to the changing realities. Ultimately, as Donald Stoker writes, this error should be assigned to Blücher and Gneisenau, who oversaw the whole battlefield.[41]

The other option was to send the corps to attack in full strength against the French right. Between 7:00 and 8:00 p.m., in fact, III Corps staged a flanking attack, with its cavalry and some of the reserve artillery moving forward. The manner Clausewitz specifically wrote about this manoeuvre, implies that the bold move may have been his idea. The flanking movement, however, was unsuccessful, and the French captured several artillery pieces. In his monograph on 1815, Clausewitz argued that the manoeuvre should have been staged much earlier, around 4:00 and 5:00 p.m., and at full strength. Such action would have forced the French to either withdraw or be supported by the Imperial Guard, inevitably requiring Napoleon to use his reserves much earlier. In the end, the Battle of Ligny was decided by Napoleon's masterful use of his reserves, while the tattered Prussian force was unable to hold their positions any further.[42] Yet the passage was written in the 1820s and reveals Clausewitz's contemplations afterwards about what could have been done differently. There is no evidence and no claim by Clausewitz that he had actually proposed this bold action at an earlier moment on 16 June. Gneisenau's orders for III Corps had been to cover the road to Namur and Thielmann and Clausewitz fulfilled them. Furthermore, examining the chances for an effective and independent flanking attack, the historian Ollech judged it as unrealistic – the corps simply did not have enough artillery and cavalry to achieve anything substantial on its own. An assault from the left could have only succeed, in Ollech's view, with a massive support from the rest of the Prussian army, but that required for the centre to have already routed the French troops.[43] These circumstances explain why in the early hours of the battle, neither Gneisenau requested, nor Thielmann and Clausewitz considered, attempting an attack on the left. The flanking manoeuvre between 7:00 and 8:00 p.m. came, in fact, as a result of an error. Misreading movements and believing that the French were retreating, III Corps' leadership took its chances and ordered the bold attack, only to be repulsed. The attempted assault, in fact, did echo Clausewitz's belief that commanders should aggressively exploit every opportunity they see. Unfortunately, in this case, it failed.

The unsuccessful flanking attack in the evening had one consequence – feeling weakened and under assault, at around 8:30 p.m., III Corps' leadership denied Gneisenau's demands for two brigades as additional reinforcements for the centre.[44] It was this decision that most likely gave rise to the claims concerning Thielmann and Clausewitz's alleged timidity. In the

40 Clausewitz, 'The Campaign of 1815', p.119.
41 Stoker, *Clausewitz: His Life and Work*, p.235.
42 Clausewitz, 'The Campaign of 1815', p.117.
43 Ollech, *Geschichte des Feldzuges von 1815*, pp.145–146.
44 Ollech, *Geschichte des Feldzuges von 1815*, p.152.

end, the combat inexperience of Blücher's troops ultimately tipped the scale in Napoleon's favour. Afraid that their new recruits and replacements from the new provinces would falter – and as many as 8,000 soldiers mostly from Rhineland and Westphalia deserted after the battle[45] – Prussian commanders rushed to commit more and more troops to the fight in the centre until I and II Corps ran out of fresh reserves.[46] Albeit far from consisting only of veterans, the seasoned backbone of the French army and Napoleon's trust in their steadfastness finally broke the enemy's centre.[47] In his later study, Clausewitz suggested that deploying III Corps in the centre at the end of Ligny still would not have mattered, as by that point the Prussian losses were too great.[48] What Blücher and Gneisenau needed was a whole fresh corps, but it was nowhere to be found. As darkness fell, in order to fight another day, the Prussian army had to disengage and retreat, before Napoleon utterly destroyed it.

At Ligny, the Prussians suffered about 3,600 dead.[49] During the evening, they withdrew to the north, towards the small town of Wavre. Throughout the night, III Corps heroically covered the retreat of the rest of the Prussian army, and considering the circumstances, the withdrawal turned out to be remarkably orderly. 'The village of Brye remained in our possession during the night, as well as Sombreffe, where General Thielmann had fought with the III Corps, and whence he, at day-break, slowly began to retreat towards Gembloux, where the IV Corps, under General Bülow, had at length arrived during the night,' Gneisenau wrote in his after-action report.[50] III Corps' extended position caused Clausewitz great pains, as he personally rode between locations and oversaw the troops' retreat. Clausewitz recalled the events in a letter to Marie a few weeks later: 'In that night, I believe my hair turned grey and beside a brief moment when I wrote the report to the Field Marshal [von Blücher], never left the saddle.'[51]

The Aftermath of Wavre or Who Let Grouchy Escape

Throughout 17 June, the Prussian army gathered around the town of Wavre. This new position did not lie on its original line of retreat, but as Napoleon attacked straight from the south and the Prussian centre fell back, the troops began naturally to move up to the north. Realising its strategic advantages for the preservation of the communications with Wellington, Gneisenau and Grolman seized on the new direction. Wellington had also withdrawn north towards Brussels. As III Corps' troops had fought all night, its leadership insisted on letting them rest until 2:00 p.m. in Gembloux, and only after that reunited with the rest of the Prussian army. While not under the direct threat of combat, the soldiers were

45 Hofschröer, *1815 The Waterloo Campaign*, p.327.
46 Friedrich, *Der Feldzug 1815*, Vol. IV, p.149.
47 Clausewitz, 'The Campaign of 1815,' p.123.
48 Clausewitz, 'Campaign of 1815,' p.119.
49 Hofschöer, *1815 The Waterloo Campaign*, p.348.
50 August Neidhardt von Gneisenau, 'Marshal Blücher's Official Report of the Organization of the Prussian Army of the Lower Rhine, transcribed by General Gneisenau,' in F.C.F von Müffling, *History of the Campaign of 1815*, trans.by Sir John Sinclair (Wakefield, UK: S.R.Publishers Limited, 1970), p.121.
51 Carl to Marie, 3. July 1815, *Correspondence*, p.385.

exhausted and the route to Wavre proved another test of perseverance. The troops endured the forced march in the middle of a storm and torrential rain, on terrible and muddy roads.[52]

After his victory at Ligny, throughout the morning of June 17, Napoleon received reports that the mass of Prussian troops had withdrawn to the east– a development favourable for the French, but obviously based on faulty reconnaissance. Napoleon sent in the afternoon *Maréchal* Grouchy, leading Gerard's and Vandamme's Corps, or one-third of the Army of the North, after Blücher.

As Clausewitz wrote in his campaign study, III Corps' perseverance proved a blessing in disguise two days later.[53] Since his troops were relatively intact and had suffered fewer casualties, Blücher ordered Thielmann to hold back a possible French rear assault and secure the Prussian line of retreat, while the rest of the Prussian army (together with the newly arrived IV Corps) rushed to support Wellington at Waterloo. On the morning of 18th, confused reports by local inhabitants – who spotted IV Corps marching in two and III Corps in one column – led Grouchy to believe that three Prussian corps were moving further north towards Leuven, using the east bank of the Dyle river as protection, and seeking to reunite with Wellington near Brussels. Grouchy calculated that by quickly moving on Wavre, he could thrust himself between the two armies – and fulfil Napoleon's orders never to lose the Prussians from his sight and to keep them away from Wellington.[54]

Leaving behind a few battalions to protect the Dyle bridges, III Corps, as ordered, departed Wavre in the early afternoon and was about to march to Waterloo when its leadership suddenly realized that Grouchy was on their heels. Therefore, III Corps' leadership judged that by turning around and re-occupying Wavre, they would enjoy a stronger defensive position.[55] Acting on the old orders, the 9th Brigade, the corps' strongest, followed the main force's march, thereby leaving only 15,000 Prussians to engage Grouchy's 30,000 men.[56] 9th Brigade had been situated further south from Wavre, while III Corps' attention concentrated on the action at the Dyle. Clausewitz and Thielmann assumed that they could always call upon the brigade when reinforcements were needed, hence its disappearance remained unknown to the headquarters for a long time.[57] This error certainly speaks to the rapid pace with which III Corps had to perform its turnaround movement and face the enemy. Under heavy fire and losing ground, III Corps sent reports to headquarters requesting reinforcements, but Gneisenau let them know that Waterloo was the place where 'the affair was to be decided.'[58] Later historians found it inexplicable that neither III Corps' leadership, nor Grouchy considered it necessary to regularly send couriers inquiring about the course Waterloo was taking – such intelligence would have been useful when deciding on whether to escalate the combat.[59] Although clearly supporting the main battle, the adversaries still concentrated on winning the contest at hand.

52 Friedrich, *Der Feldzug 1815*, Vol. IV, p.160.
53 Clausewitz, 'Campaign of 1815,' p.119.
54 Friedrich, *Der Feldzug 1815*, Vol. IV, p.179–180.
55 Friedrich, *Der Feldzug 1815*, Vol. IV, p.203.
56 Clausewitz to Marie, 3 July 1815, *Correspondence*, p.387.
57 Ollech, *Geschichte des Feldzuges von 1815*, pp.209–211.
58 Gneisenau, 'Official Report,' p.124.
59 Ollech, *Geschichte des Feldzuges von 1815*, p.213.

Another calamity revealing weakened communications and hasty staff work occurred around 10:00 p.m. Battalions from II Corps charged with protecting the Dyle southwest from Wavre, by the village of Limal, had followed the main army too, without, as Clausewitz lamented, informing III Corps's headquarters about their movement. Ollech squarely placed the fault on Thielmann's and Clausewitz's shoulders for failing to confirm that the crucial bridges were defended, and the Prussian right flank protected.[60] The French assault surprised the Prussians, and despite a rapid counterattack, in which Clausewitz participated, III Corps allowed Grouchy to cross the Dyle. 'The enemy held firm, and we turned in disarray; we had great difficulty in restoring order,' Clausewitz wrote to Marie.[61] Finally receiving uncertain reports about the victory at Waterloo, Thielmann let his troops loudly cheer the success, hoping to discourage Grouchy; but it was in vain.[62]

With uncertain news about Napoleon's defeat, the Prussians endured more French assaults on the 19th, long before daybreak. 'At 10:00 a.m., we received a note from General von Pirch [commander of II Corps], which informed us about the glorious victory, and that he was about to cut off the corps facing us. However, the points where he wanted to do so were so far away that they were of no help for us. Again separated from the main army, due to the enemy's flanking maneuver, we were left on our own,' Clausewitz recounted.[63] In another case of faulty intelligence, Clausewitz and the rest of the corps' leadership falsely believed that they were now facing 45,000 Frenchmen.[64] III Corps held on to Wavre for another hour, but were eventually forced to withdraw.

Although the battle was lost, III Corps had ultimately fulfilled its objective of holding off Grouchy and preventing him from interfering with the main Prussian army's advance on Waterloo. Nonetheless, the retreat on 19 June led to another controversy about Clausewitz's role in the 1815 campaign. Namely, whether he was responsible for letting Grouchy slip away and make his way through Belgium and back to France – something which ultimately prolonged the war.

Around noon, III Corps began its retreat in the direction of Leuven. The famous conservative politician Friedrich Ludwig August von der Marwitz, serving as the commander for III Corps' 1st Cavalry Brigade, named Clausewitz as the author of the plan to withdraw toward Leuven.[65] Years later, when asked about the events, Thielmann also asserted that his chief of staff had insisted on finding an advantageous position to engage Grouchy again.[66] Marwitz summarized Clausewitz's proposal in the following terms: 'The further the enemy follows us, the likelier his destruction, and when he makes a halt, we will turn around.'[67] Drawing Grouchy north to Leuven – and away from his natural line of retreat – would undoubtedly have been a shrewd move and an opportunity to destroy the French, especially

60 Ollech, *Geschichte des Feldzuges von 1815*, p.212.
61 Clausewitz to Marie, 3 July 1815, *Correspondence*, p.387.
62 Clausewitz, 'Campaign of 1815,' p.155.
63 Clausewitz to Marie, 3 July 1815, *Correspondence*, p.387.
64 Clausewitz to Marie, 3 July 1815, *Correspondence*, p.387.
65 Marwitz was also Marie von Clausewitz's former brother-in-law, but he and Carl von Clausewitz were not close. Friedrich August Ludwig von der Marwitz, *Aus dem Nachlasse Friedrich August Ludwig von der Marwitz*, (Berlin: Mittler und Sohn, 1852), Vol. II, p.121
66 Petersdorff, *von Thielmann*, p.300.
67 Marwitz, *Aus dem Nachlasse*, Vol. II, p.121.

if II Corps attacked them from the rear. Far from being timid, Clausewitz's actions suggest that he was still planning to facilitate a decisive blow against Bonaparte's last remaining cohesive force in Belgium.[68]

Nonetheless, it is rather implausible that a perceptive officer like Clausewitz would have overlooked the possibility of the enemy seeing through the plan. The decision to move north, therefore, held another advantage – if Grouchy did not take the bait but retreated, this provided the exhausted Prussian troops the chance to rest for a night. In any case, in its current state, III Corps could hardly carry out an assault. This was exactly what occurred. In a feint designed to confuse the Prussians of his intentions, Grouchy successfully deployed skirmishers to hold the bridges across the Sambre River and harassed the Prussian rearguard until nightfall, while his main force withdrew south.[69] At daybreak, III Corps resumed its advance, with the whole of its cavalry boldly moving forward supported by an artillery battery. III Corps was gearing up for a big battle.[70] However the French were long gone.

Again, it is difficult to imagine that an experienced staff officer like Clausewitz, who chided commanders for losing sight of the enemy, was so careless himself.[71] What is more likely is that Clausewitz and Thielmann took a risk – but could never admit it publicly when it was later considered a crucial mistake. Asked about the error years afterwards, Thielmann, for instance, carefully deflected the question about what had actually happened.[72] In his campaign study, Clausewitz also wrote that Thielmann 'had decided that under no circumstances would he send his utterly exhausted troops to purse the enemy that day, as they were greatly in need of rest and it could be foreseen that the enemy's rear guard would not withdraw before nightfall, making it impossible for an advance to be decisive.'[73] In his memoir, Marwitz also complained that once the engagement came to a standstill by the village of Sint-Agatha-Rode, nobody at the headquarters answered his requests for additional infantry support for the rear-guard. The location was a defile unsuitable for cavalry outposts, and since his men were exhausted, hungry, and sleep-deprived, he ordered them to dismount and rest.[74] Marwitz, too, appeared unconcerned about losing contact with the enemy. These statements support the suspicion that III Corp's leadership took a deliberate risk in order to rest their troops from the previous day's exertions.[75]

Moreover, they were expecting that II Corps could also intercept Grouchy, but this overreliance proved misguided. In fact, when the controversy about Grouchy's escape was raised in the Berlin newspapers in 1816, Clausewitz admitted in a confidential correspondence to Gneisenau no other mistake but failing to appropriately inform Blücher's headquarters and

68 This is also the assessment of Ollech, *Geschichte des Feldzuges von 1815*, p.261.
69 Marwitz, *Aus dem Nachlasse*, Vol. II, pp.121–122.
70 Marwitz, *Aus dem Nachlasse*, Vol. II, pp.123–124.
71 On Clausewitz criticizing Bernadotte for losing contact with the enemy after the Battle of Sehestedt, see Stoker, *Clausewitz: His Life and Work*, p.248.
72 Petersdorff, *von Thielmann*, p.300.
73 Clausewitz, 'Campaign of 1815,' p.156.
74 Marwitz, *Aus dem Nachlasse*, p.123.
75 Without citing sources but based on his own analysis, the German General Staff chief historian Rudolf Friedrich concluded, too, that Thielmann must have learned already in the night of 19th that Grouchy was retreating, but decided grant a few more hours of rests to the exhausted troops. Friedrich, *Der Feldzug 1815*, Vol. IV, p.221

Pirch about the situation. Earlier on 18 June, before the tide turned against the Prussians at Wavre, Clausewitz wrote told Gneisenau, he had reported back to Blücher's headquarters that Grouchy had only 10–12,000 men.[76] This initially created the false impression to headquarters that intercepting Grouchy was not such a crucial task, and at that moment Blücher and Gneisenau lacked other sources of intelligence. On the evening of 19th, however, the new but erroneous reports that Grouchy had 45,000 men came into play – surprised by this new number and thinking that his 16,000 men would be badly outnumbered, and with no clear knowledge of where III Corps was, Pirch decided to remain in the town of Mellery.[77] Among other factors, this explains Clausewitz's harsh assessment in *On War* concerning intelligence's usefulness, which so perplexes modern readers. He famously wrote that 'many intelligence reports in war are contradictory; even more are false, and most are uncertain... As a rule most men would rather believe bad news than good, and rather tend to exaggerate the bad news.'[78] In 1815, headquarters and commanders on all sides often dealt with incomplete facts and made bad calls based on faulty perceptions, anxieties, and overestimations.

Grouchy was able to regroup unmolested in Namur, and the subsequent assault on the town cost the Prussian forces some 1,650 men. Grouchy escaped once more, without significant casualties, and slipped into France.[79] For two more weeks, the allies had to fight their way to Paris.

When, in 1816, the inflammatory article openly accused the commander of II Corps *Generalleutnant* von Pirch of letting Grouchy escape via Namur – and indirectly exonerated III Corps' performance – Clausewitz still defended Pirch. What angered Clausewitz the most was the fact that II Corps' delayed actions were not analysed as mistakes committed in the midst of a difficult situation, and instead Pirch's character and qualities were questioned.[80] Peter Paret summarizes Clausewitz's sentiment: 'As always in war, everyone had made mistakes, and in the end victory had gone to the side that was stronger and erred less.'[81] In his letter to Clausewitz, Gneisenau admitted that on the afternoon of 19 June, he should have sent one more corps straight to Namur, the most natural French point of retreat, to intercept Grouchy – but the move was opposed by Blücher.[82] German historians, however, asserted that Gneisenau, too, advocated that the main body of the Prussian army should march directly on Paris, in order to beat Wellington there; something that obviously contradicts Gneisenau's later claims to Clausewitz.[83] Accepting Gneisenau's account, Clausewitz criticized Blücher's decision not to send troops to intercept Grouchy on 19 June in the few paragraphs in *On War* devoted to the Waterloo Campaign: 'Part of the victor's force must follow the retreating army on the road it has taken, mopping up everything it

76 Clausewitz to Gneisenau, 27 December 1817, Carl von Clausewitz, *Schriften-Aufsätze-Studien-Briefe, Dokumente aus dem Clausewitz-, Scharnhorst- und Gneisenau-Nachlaß sowie aus öffentlichen und privaten Sammlungen*, ed. Werner Hahlweg (Göttingen: Vandenhoeck und Ruprecht, 1990), Vol. II, pp.241–242.

77 Friedrich, *Der Feldzug 1815*, Vol. IV, p.221.

78 Clausewitz, *On War*, p.117.

79 Friedrich, *Der Feldzug 1815*, Vol. IV, p.222.

80 Clausewitz to Gneisenau, 27 December 1817, Clausewitz, *Schriften*, Vol. II, pp.241–242

81 Paret, *Clausewitz and the State*, p.250

82 Gneisenau to Clausewitz, 5 February 1817, Clausewitz, *Schriften*, Vol. II, p.241, n.5.

83 Ollech, *Geschichte des Feldzuges von 1815*, p.265.

leaves behind, and to impress the pursued force with its presence. Blücher, whose pursuit after [Waterloo] was a model in all other respects, missed this point.'[84]

Understanding Clausewitz's Experience

Published posthumously and in instalments between 1832–1834 by Marie von Clausewitz, *On War* was welcomed by enlightened officers and civilians alike, but was far from an instant bestseller. Also released as a part of *Posthumous Works*, Clausewitz's 1815 campaign study made its way to Great Britain, where prompted by it, Duke of Wellington wrote his own account of the events.[85] With the passing of time, Clausewitz's and *On War*'s fame grew, especially after the astounding victories in the Wars of German Unification drew the international public's attention to the Prusso-German strategic thought.[86] Clausewitz's first biography, written by Karl Schwarz in 1878, was a hagiographic work that offered scant critical analysis of his intricate career.[87] In the second part of the nineteenth century, void of comprehensive knowledge about Clausewitz's actual role, thinking, or the specific circumstances he operated under – but enamoured by his growing fame – military writers seized on accusations and insider claims, without examining them in-depth. No other corps chief of staff's actions in 1815 received such scrutiny, but the errors made were directly ascribed to the commanders, as the concept of general staff and chief of staff were still taking hold in the Prussian army. Only Gneisenau's actions were criticized, but he was also a well-known war hero. Thielmann's position as an outsider and Clausewitz's good connections to Gneisenau might have given the latter a sway at III Corps' headquarters. Nonetheless, it remains implausible that a competent and confident commander like Thielmann would have accepted Clausewitz's advice if he did not largely agree with it. In accounts published in the years immediately after Waterloo, Clausewitz's name was never mentioned. Furthermore, in his monograph on 1815, Clausewitz, too, ascribed all the decisions solely on Thielmann as the commanding general. The accounts criticizing Clausewitz directly and cited throughout this chapter were all published in the late nineteenth century. The perception of Clausewitz's influence over the 1815 Campaign, it appears, grew with the time and proportionately to his later fame.

Although an insightful analysis, Clausewitz's own study of the events did not help students of war understand his experience nor was it intended for publication.[88] Prepared as a series of lectures for the crown prince and his entourage in the late 1820s, *The Campaign of 1815* focused on the strategic lessons learned. In the polarized atmosphere after 1815, moderate reformers like Gneisenau and Clausewitz were politically attacked and marginalized,

84 Clausewitz, *On War*, p.269.

85 Christopher Bassford, 'Introduction,' in Clausewitz, 'Campaign of 1815,' p.6–10.

86 Michael Howard, *Clausewitz* (New York: Oxford University Press, 1983), p.60.

87 Karl Schwarz, *Leben des Generals von Clausewitz und der Frau Marie von Clausewitz, geb. Gräfin von Brühl*. 2 Bde. (Berlin: Dümmler Verlag, 1878).

88 See Werner Hahlweg's introduction to the campaign study in Clausewitz, *Schriften*, Vol. II, pp.337–338.

in order for the reactionary faction to reaffirm its grip on the Prussian government.[89] Gneisenau, often the target of public criticism concerning the actions of the Prussian army's headquarters in 1815,[90] also discussed his actions mostly in private, as the admission in his letter to Clausewitz concerning the events on 19 June suggested.[91] No surprise, then, that the publicly reticent Clausewitz avoided forthrightly speaking, especially in front of the crown prince, about his experience in 1815. Thus, the military theorist never offered a clear and comprehensive narrative about his encounters, motivations, and possible mistakes. In such an informational vacuum, a negative analysis could easily take hold.

Commenting on III Corps' extended retreat after Wavre, the eminent historian Hans Delbrück concluded that Clausewitz's calculating mind had been less suited for the Napoleonic warfare's daring and improvising nature; he could have been the right type of senior officer for the Wars of German Unification with their coordinated actions.[92] Even so, as the analysis in this chapter suggests, Clausewitz's performance and the Prussia's then-nascent general staff system were rather a mix of old and new military approach, less improvisational but not quite fully coordinated. In this regard, Clausewitz remained a transformational figure: he anticipated the complex operational level which signifies modern war, without yet having adequate structures and procedures with which to do so while campaigning.

The campaign of 1815 demonstrated both the strengths of coalition warfare with the glorious allied victory in Waterloo, but also its pitfalls with the infamous meeting between Wellington's and Blücher's headquarters by the windmill at Brye before Ligny. Perhaps inspired by the lessons learned, in the late 1820s, Clausewitz, in fact, envisioned devoting a whole chapter in *On War* to supreme command in coalition warfare.[93] Unfortunately for modern practitioners of war – for to this day, coalitions warfare remains of the most complex forms of planning and waging a campaign – Clausewitz's untimely death prevented him from sharing his insight.

The most consequential echo of the 1815 experience is the role of chance in war, in general, and in the soldier's career, in particular. Some of *On War*'s most memorable and insightful lines are devoted, too, to this phenomenon: 'From the very start there is an interplay of possibilities, probabilities, good luck and bad that weaves its way throughout the length and breadth of the tapestry. In the whole range of human activities, war most closely resembles a game of cards.'[94] In retrospect, the 1815 campaign provides numerous examples of chance's role in warfare – had Bülow understood his orders correctly and arrived in Ligny on 16 June; had the Prussian army retreated towards Namur, instead of Wavre; had Grouchy realized

89 Paret, *Clausewitz and the State,* pp.266–267, 271, 320-323.

90 See for instance the discussion about the criticism Gneisenau experienced in the correspondence of Savigny to Niebuhr, 5 December 1816, Adolf Stoll, (ed.), *Friedrich Karl von Savigny: Professoren Jahren in Berlin* (Berlin: Carl Heymanns Verlag, 1929), pp.215.

91 In the letter, as a sign of his desire to remain discreet, Gneisenau did not even call Blücher by his name but wrote 'I was dissuaded – can you guess by whom – and the troops' weariness was used as the argument," Gneisenau to Clausewitz, 5 February 1817, Clausewitz, *Schriften,* 2:1: 241, n.5.

92 Hans Delbrück, 'General von Clausewitz,' in *Politische und Historische Aufsätze,* (ed.) by Hans Delbrück, 2nd Edn (Berlin: Georg Stilke, 1907), p.222.

93 Clausewitz, *On War,* p.633.

94 Clausewitz, *On War,* p.86.

the actual direction of the Prussian retreat and acted accordingly; had III Corps, instead of being left at Wavre, marched to Waterloo, the campaign's course might have been different. In his monograph on 1815, Clausewitz concluded that Napoleon's real chances for success were slim to none — the Allies would have never accepted his return to the French throne, and even if they had lost at Waterloo, they would have continued the war.[95] Nonetheless, any of these scenarios might have changed Clausewitz's life and perhaps, granted him the military glory he deserved.

Bibliography

Archival Sources

Unpublished part of Clausewitz's letter to Marie, May 12, 1815. Prussian Privy State Archives (GStA PK), VI. HA Familienarchive und Nachlässe, Nl Buttlar-Venedien, Nr.561

Wilhelm von Grolman, Letter from July 12, 1815. LandesArchiv Thüringen, Staatsarchiv Altenburg, Familien Nachlass Grolman

Printed Primary Sources

Clausewitz, Karl und Marie von. *Ein Lebensbild in Briefen und Tagebuchblätter (Correspondence).* Ed. by Karl Linnebach (Berlin: M. Warneck, 1925)

Clausewitz, Carl von and Arthur Wellesley, 1st Duke of Wellington, *On Waterloo: Clausewitz, Wellington, and the Campaign of 1815.* Ed./trans. Christopher Bassford, Daniel Moran, and Gregory W. Pedlow. (Washington: Clausewitz.com, 2010)

Clausewitz, Carl von. *On War.* Ed./trans. by Michael Howard and Peter Paret (Princeton: Princeton University Press, 1989)

Clausewitz, Carl von, *Schriften-Aufsätze-Studien-Briefe, Dokumente aus dem Clausewitz-, Scharnhorst- und Gneisenau-Nachlaß sowie aus öffentlichen und privaten Sammlungen*, ed. Werner Hahlweg (Göttingen: Vandenhoeck und Ruprecht, 1990)

Görres, Joseph. 'Aus Chartes, 15 August,' *Rheinisches Merkur,* Nr. 291, 30 August 1815

Marwitz, Friedrich August Ludwig von der. *Aus dem Nachlasse Friedrich August Ludwig von der Marwitz,* 2.Band (Berlin: Mittler und Sohn, 1852)

Müffling, F.C.F von, Philip Yorke (ed.), *Passages From My Life* (London: Richard Bentley, 1853)

Schoeps, Hans Joachim, (ed.), *Aus den Jahren Preussischer Not und Erneuerung. Tagebücher und Briefe der Gebrüder Gerlach und ihres Kreises 1805–1820* (Berlin: Haude und Spenersche Verlagsbuchhandlung, 1963)

Stoll, Adolf (ed.), *Friedrich Karl von Savigny: Professoren Jahren in Berlin* (Berlin: Carl Heymanns Verlag, 1929)

Secondary Sources

Bellinger, Vanya Eftimova. *Marie von Clausewitz: The Woman Behind the Making of ON WAR* (New York: Oxford University Press, 2016)

Delbrück, Hans. *Politische und Historische Aufsätze,* 2nd Edn (Berlin: Georg Stilke, 1907)

Friedrich, Rudolf. *Die Befreiungskriege: Der Feldzug 1815* (Berlin: Mittler und Sohn, 1913)

Hofschröer, Peter. *1815 The Waterloo Campaign: Wellington, his German Allies and the Battles of Ligny and Quatre Bras* (London: Greenhill Books, 1998)

Hornung, Klaus. *Scharnhorst: Soldat, Reformer, Staatsmann* (Munich: Bechtle Verlag, 2001)

Howard, Michael. *Clausewitz* (New York: Oxford University Press, 1983)

Lettow-Vorbeck, Oscar von. *Napoleons Untergang 1815* (Berlin: Mittler und Sohn, 1904)

Müffling, F.C.F von. *History of the Campaign of 1815,* trans. by Sir John Sinclair (Wakefield, UK: S.R.Publishers Limited, 1970)

95 Clausewitz, 'Campaign of 1815,' p.81.

Ollech, Karl Rudolf von. *Geschichte des Feldzuges von 1815 nach archivalischen Quellen* (Berlin: Mittler und Sohn, 1876)

Paret, Peter. *Clausewitz and the State: The Man, His Theories, and His Time* (Princeton, NJ: Princeton University Press, 1985)

Petersdorff, Herman von. *General Johann Adolph Freiherr von Thielmann: Ein Charakterbild aus der napoleonischen Zeit* (Leipzig: S.Hirzel, 1894)

Rothenberg, Gunther E. *The Art of Warfare in the Age of Napoleon* (Bloomington: Indiana University Press, 1980)

Schwarz, Karl. *Leben des Generals von Clausewitz und der Frau Marie von Clausewitz, geb. Gräfin von Brühl* (Berlin: Dümmler Verlag, 1878)

Stoker, Donald. *Clausewitz: His Life and Work* (New York: Oxford University Press, 2014)

White, Charles Edward. *The Enlightened Soldier: Scharnhorst and the Militärische Gesellschaft in Berlin, 1801–1805* (Westport: CT: Praeger, 1989)

Index

From Reason to Revolution – Warfare 1721-1815

http://www.helion.co.uk/series/from-reason-to-revolution-1721-1815.php

The 'From Reason to Revolution' series covers the period of military history 1721–1815, an era in which fortress-based strategy and linear battles gave way to the nation-in-arms and the beginnings of total war.

This era saw the evolution and growth of light troops of all arms, and of increasingly flexible command systems to cope with the growing armies fielded by nations able to mobilise far greater proportions of their manpower than ever before. Many of these developments were fired by the great political upheavals of the era, with revolutions in America and France bringing about social change which in turn fed back into the military sphere as whole nations readied themselves for war. Only in the closing years of the period, as the reactionary powers began to regain the upper hand, did a military synthesis of the best of the old and the new become possible.

The series will examine the military and naval history of the period in a greater degree of detail than has hitherto been attempted, and has a very wide brief, with the intention of covering all aspects from the battles, campaigns, logistics, and tactics, to the personalities, armies, uniforms, and equipment.

Submissions

The publishers would be pleased to receive submissions for this series. Please contact series editor Andrew Bamford via email (andrewbamford@helion.co.uk), or in writing to Helion & Company Limited, Unit 8 Amherst Business Centre, Budbrooke Road, Warwick, CV34 5WE

Titles

No 1 *Lobositz to Leuthen: Horace St Paul and the Campaigns of the Austrian Army in the Seven Years War 1756-57* (Neil Cogswell)

No 2 *Glories to Useless Heroism: The Seven Years War in North America from the French journals of Comte Maurés de Malartic, 1755-1760* (William Raffle (ed.))

No 3 *Reminiscences 1808-1815 Under Wellington: The Peninsular and Waterloo Memoirs of William Hay* (Andrew Bamford (ed.))

No 4 *Far Distant Ships: The Royal Navy and the Blockade of Brest 1793-1815* (Quintin Barry)

No 5 *Godoy's Army: Spanish Regiments and Uniforms from the Estado Militar of 1800* (Charles Esdaile and Alan Perry)

No 6 *On Gladsmuir Shall the Battle Be! The Battle of Prestonpans 1745* (Arran Johnston)

No 7 *The French Army of the Orient 1798-1801: Napoleon's Beloved 'Egyptians'* (Yves Martin)

No 8 *The Autobiography, or Narrative of a Soldier: The Peninsular War Memoirs of William Brown of the 45th Foot* (Steve Brown (ed.))

No 9 *Recollections from the Ranks: Three Russian Soldiers' Autobiographies from the Napoleonic Wars* (Darrin Boland)

No 10 *By Fire and Bayonet: Grey's West Indies Campaign of 1794* (Steve Brown)

No 11 *Olmütz to Torgau: Horace St Paul and the Campaigns of the Austrian Army in the Seven Years War 1758-60* (Neil Cogswell)

No 12 *Murat's Army: The Army of the Kingdom of Naples 1806-1815* (Digby Smith)

No 13 *The Veteran or 40 Years' Service in the British Army: The Scurrilous Recollections of Paymaster John Harley 47th Foot – 1798-1838* (Gareth Glover (ed.))

- No 14 *Narrative of the Eventful Life of Thomas Jackson: Militiaman and Coldstream Sergeant, 1803-15* (Eamonn O'Keeffe (ed.))
- No.15 *For Orange and the States: The Army of the Dutch Republic 1713-1772 Part I: Infantry* (Marc Geerdinck-Schaftenaar)
- No 16 *Men Who Are Determined to be Free: The American Assault on Stony Point, 15 July 1779* (David C. Bonk)
- No 17 *Next to Wellington: General Sir George Murray: The Story of a Scottish Soldier and Statesman, Wellington's Quartermaster General* (John Harding-Edgar)
- No 18 *Between Scylla and Charybdis: The Army of Elector Friedrich August of Saxony 1733-1763 Part I: Staff and Cavalry* (Marco Pagan)
- No 19 *The Secret Expedition: The Anglo-Russian Invasion of Holland 1799* (Geert van Uythoven)
- No 20 *'We Are Accustomed to do our Duty': German Auxiliaries with the British Army 1793-95* (Paul Demet)
- No 21 *With the Guards in Flanders: The Diary of Captain Roger Morris 1793-95* (Peter Harington (ed.))
- No 22 *The British Army in Egypt 1801: An Underrated Army Comes of Age* (Carole Divall)
- No 23 *Better is the Proud Plaid: The Clothing, Weapons, and Accoutrements of the Jacobites in the '45* (Jenn Scott)
- No 24 *The Lilies and the Thistle: French Troops in the Jacobite '45* (Andrew Bamford)
- No 25 *A Light Infantryman With Wellington: The Letters of Captain George Ulrich Barlow 52nd and 69th Foot 1808-15* (Gareth Glover (ed.))
- No 26 *Swiss Regiments in the Service of France 1798-1815: Uniforms, Organisation, Campaigns* (Stephen Ede-Borrett)
- No 27 *For Orange and the States! The Army of the Dutch Republic 1713-1772: Part II: Cavalry and Specialist Troops* (Marc Geerdinck-Schaftenaar)
- No 28 *Fashioning Regulation, Regulating Fashion: Uniforms and Dress of the British Army 1800-1815 Volume I* (Ben Townsend)
- No 29 *Riflemen: The History of the 5th Battalion 60th (Royal American) Regiment, 1797-1818* (Robert Griffith)
- No 30 *The Key to Lisbon: The Third French Invasion of Portugal, 1810-11* (Kenton White)
- No 31 *Command and Leadership: Proceedings of the 2018 Helion & Company 'From Reason to Revolution' Conference* (Andrew Bamford (ed.))
- No 32 *Waterloo After the Glory: Hospital Sketches and Reports on the Wounded After the Battle* (Michael Crumplin and Gareth Glover)
- No 33 *Fluxes, Fevers, and Fighting Men: War and Disease in Ancien Regime Europe 1648-1789* (Pádraig Lenihan)
- No 34 *'They Were Good Soldiers': African-Americans Serving in the Continental Army, 1775-1783* (John U. Rees)
- No 35 *A Redcoat in America: The Diaries of Lieutenant William Bamford, 1757-1765 and 1776* (John B. Hattendorf (ed.))
- No 36 *Between Scylla and Charybdis: The Army of Friedrich August II of Saxony, 1733-1763: Part II: Infantry and Artillery* (Marco Pagan)
- No 37 *Québec Under Siege: French Eye-Witness Accounts from the Campaign of 1759* (Charles A. Mayhood (ed.))
- No 38 *King George's Hangman: Henry Hawley and the Battle of Falkirk 1746* (Jonathan D. Oates)
- No 39 *Zweybrücken in Command: The Reichsarmee in the Campaign of 1758* (Neil Cogswell)
- No 40 *So Bloody a Day: The 16th Light Dragoons in the Waterloo Campaign* (David J. Blackmore)
- No 41 *Northern Tars in Southern Waters: The Russian Fleet in the Mediterranean 1806-1810* (Vladimir Bogdanovich Bronevskiy / Darrin Boland)
- No 42 *Royal Navy Officers of the Seven Years War: A Biographical Dictionary of Commissioned Officers 1748-1763* (Cy Harrison)
- No 43 *All at Sea: Naval Support for the British Army During the American Revolutionary War* (John Dillon)
- No 44 *Glory is Fleeting: New Scholarship on the Napoleonic Wars* (Andrew Bamford (ed.))
- No 45 *Fashioning Regulation, Regulating Fashion: Uniforms and Dress of the British Army 1800-1815 Vol. II* (Ben Townsend)

No 46 *Revenge in the Name of Honour: The Royal Navy's Quest for Vengeance in the Single Ship Actions of the War of 1812* (Nicholas James Kaizer)

No 47 *They Fought With Extraordinary Bravery: The III German (Saxon) Army Corps in the Southern Netherlands 1814* (Geert van Uythoven)

No 48 *The Danish Army of the Napoleonic Wars 1801-1814, Organisation, Uniforms & Equipment: Volume 1: High Command, Line and Light Infantry* (David Wilson)

No 49 *Neither Up Nor Down: The British Army and the Flanders Campaign 1793-1895* (Phillip Ball)

No 50 *Guerra Fantástica: The Portuguese Army and the Seven Years War* (António Barrento)

No 51 *From Across the Sea: North Americans in Nelson's Navy* (Sean M. Heuvel and John A. Rodgaard)

No 52 *Rebellious Scots to Crush: The Military Response to the Jacobite '45* (Andrew Bamford (ed.))

No 53 *The Army of George II 1727-1760: The Soldiers who Forged an Empire* (Peter Brown)

No 54 *Wellington at Bay: The Battle of Villamuriel, 25 October 1812* (Garry David Wills)

No 55 *Life in the Red Coat: The British Soldier 1721-1815* (Andrew Bamford (ed.))

No 56 *Wellington's Favourite Engineer. John Burgoyne: Operations, Engineering, and the Making of a Field Marshal* (Mark S. Thompson)

No 57 *Scharnhorst: The Formative Years, 1755-1801* (Charles Edward White)

No 58 *At the Point of the Bayonet: The Peninsular War Battles of Arroyomolinos and Almaraz 1811-1812* (Robert Griffith)

No 59 *Sieges of the '45: Siege Warfare during the Jacobite Rebellion of 1745-1746* (Jonathan D. Oates)

No 60 *Austrian Cavalry of the Revolutionary and Napoleonic Wars, 1792–1815* (Enrico Acerbi, András K. Molnár)

No 61 *The Danish Army of the Napoleonic Wars 1801-1814, Organisation, Uniforms & Equipment: Volume 2: Cavalry and Artillery* (David Wilson)

No 62 *Napoleon's Stolen Army: How the Royal Navy Rescued a Spanish Army in the Baltic* (John Marsden)

No 63 *Crisis at the Chesapeake: The Royal Navy and the Struggle for America 1775-1783* (Quintin Barry)

No 64 *Bullocks, Grain, and Good Madeira: The Maratha and Jat Campaigns 1803-1806 and the emergence of the Indian Army* (Joshua Provan)

No 65 *Sir James McGrigor: The Adventurous Life of Wellington's Chief Medical Officer* (Tom Scotland)

No 66 *Fashioning Regulation, Regulating Fashion: Uniforms and Dress of the British Army 1800-1815 Volume I* (Ben Townsend) (paperback edition)

No 67 *Fashioning Regulation, Regulating Fashion: Uniforms and Dress of the British Army 1800-1815 Volume II* (Ben Townsend) (paperback edition)

No 68 *The Secret Expedition: The Anglo-Russian Invasion of Holland 1799* (Geert van Uythoven) (paperback edition)

No 69 *The Sea is my Element: The Eventful Life of Admiral Sir Pulteney Malcolm 1768-1838* (Paul Martinovich)

No 70 *The Sword and the Spirit: Proceedings of the first 'War & Peace in the Age of Napoleon' Conference* (Zack White (ed.))

No 71 *Lobositz to Leuthen: Horace St Paul and the Campaigns of the Austrian Army in the Seven Years War 1756-57* (Neil Cogswell) (paperback edition)